MONASTIC LIFE IN MEDIEVAL ENGLAND

1. FOUNTAINS ABBEY

MONASTIC LIFE
IN MEDIEVAL ENGLAND

BY

J. C. DICKINSON

WITH FIFTY-SEVEN PHOTOGRAPHS
AND SIX PLANS

GREENWOOD PRESS, PUBLISHERS
WESTPORT, CONNECTICUT

Library of Congress Cataloging in Publication Data

Dickinson, John Compton.
  Monastic life in medieval England.

  Reprint of the ed. published by A. & C. Black,
London.
  Bibliography: p.
  Includes index.
  1. Monasticism and religious orders--England.
2. Monasteries--England. 3. Monasticism and religious
orders--Middle Ages, 600-1500. I. Title.
BX2592.D48 1979   271'.00942   78-25804
ISBN 0-313-20774-7

First published 1961 by A. and C. Black Ltd., London

Reprinted with the permission of A & C Black Limited.

Reprinted in 1979 by Greenwood Press, Inc.
51 Riverside Avenue, Westport, CT 06880

Printed in the United States of America

10 9 8 7 6 5 4 3 2 1

TO

MY MOTHER

PREFACE

THIS book aims to give the general reader a detailed picture of the buildings which made up an English monastery in the later Middle Ages, and an account of those who lived therein. Much work on particular aspects of English monastic architecture has accumulated, but no modern attempt has been made to survey the whole scene. My effort to do so, is based on a course of lectures given for the Faculty of Fine Arts at Cambridge University, and owes a good deal to an extensive survey of the architectural remains of the English Austin canons which I am in the process of concluding. Despite the destruction of medieval monastic buildings at the Reformation and since, there are still several hundred sites with something to show the archaeologist. I have not visited all of them, but can claim to have seen monastic remains in every county of England including almost all the major ones and a good many of the lesser ones. The examples I quote are illustrative, not exhaustive.

The history of the monastic orders in medieval England has attracted a steady stream of students over a very long period, so that much of it is known as well and not infrequently better than that of the same orders on the continent. Professor M. D. Knowles' majestic and graceful volumes have recently given us a survey of English monastic life to which all writers on the subject must be heavily indebted for a very long while to come. My obligations to his books in the latter parts of this book will be apparent. Not the least valuable aspect of his work has been the manifestation that modern scholars have come very near to agreed solutions of a number of historical problems over which their Victorian predecessors expended much unwise emotion.

Because History is 'the study of man as a changing animal' it seemed reasonable to say little of the rather static epoch of monastic history which immediately preceded the Reformation, and to lay stress on the process whereby English monastic life was suppressed, the more so since modern research has shown that this process differed in notable respects from the partisan pictures of it too common in the last century and not yet extinct. The storms of the English Reformation form a complex story to which only partial reference is relevant.

In writing these pages I have been very conscious of the debt I owe to the late Professor Hamilton Thompson, whose immense kindnesses to me over many years included an imperturbable readiness to put at my disposal his deep knowledge and understanding of the subject with which I am here concerned.

The illustrations are mostly from my own largish collection, but I am much indebted to the following for filling various gaps: the British Museum for Pl. 27b, the Victoria and Albert Museum for Pls. 30a, 30b, 31a, 31b, the Department of Air

Photography at Cambridge University for Pls. 1, 2a, 2b, the University of Leeds (Riley Fortune collection) for Pls. 10b, 24a, the Master and Fellows of Corpus Christi College Cambridge for Pl. 27a, Messrs A. E. Coe and Sons and the Curator of the Norwich Museums for Pl. 23a, Mr. W. Kersting, F.R.P.S., for Pl. 8, Mr. N. C. B. H. Allen, A.R.P.S., for Pls. 19a and 25a, *Country Life* for Pl. 19b and the Dean and Chapter of Westminster Abbey for Pl. 28c. I must also record my thanks to Mr. Allen for help in preparing prints, Mr. A. M. P. Brookes for invaluable photographic aid and to Mrs. E. Eames, Mr. C. C. Oman and Mr. L. E. Tanner for help on archaeological points. Pl. 22a is taken from the Buck print of Bradenstoke priory and Pl. 22b from the illustration in R. Warner, *A History of the Abbey of Glaston . . .* (Bath,1827). The identification of the undercroft of Ixworth priory as part of the eastern cloister range is the work of Mr. P. G. M. Dickinson.

Whilst this book was in the press the Victoria and Albert Museum acquired a chalice which may have belonged to the priory of St. Thomas by Stafford; if this is so, my note on page 135 requires qualification.

J. C. D.

Feast of St. Dunstan, 1961

CONTENTS

ILLUSTRATIONS

PLANS

MONASTIC LIFE IN MEDIEVAL ENGLAND

PART ONE

THE HOME OF THE MONK

CHAPTER ONE

THE BACKGROUND

ALTHOUGH there are those who resemble that Elizabethan dean of Durham who 'could not abyde any anncyent monuments, nor nothing that apperteyned to any godlie religiousnes or monasticall liffe', there are also many who resemble that early antiquary of whom it was noted 'he will goe forty miles to see a Saint's well or ruin'd abbey'. Saints' wells are now thin on the ground and their popularity is not what it was, but few parts of England are very far from monastic remains which are still very visible and their popularity shows no sign of waning. It is the aim of the following pages to give the general reader the wherewithal to see such remains in their historical and architectural context and thereby gain a richer understanding of them and the life behind them.

First let us be clear of what, in point of fact, the monastic life consists. Its foundation is a triple vow—to remain unmarried, to own no private property and to promise lifelong obedience to the rule of the monastery. What this rule involves varies considerably today and has varied for centuries. Some monks spend their life in one place, but nowadays many move busily about the world. Monasticism has never been static and in the Western Church most particularly has shown a remarkable versatility, steadily revising old ideas and adding new ones. Here our concern is only with such developments of western monasticism as affected medieval England. These will be considered in detail at a later stage, but here we may note that the western monastic tree then developed three great branches—monks who, from an early date, followed the *Rule of St. Benedict*, regular canons who followed the *Rule of St. Augustine,* and friars who followed no one rule but had a highly distinctive common pattern of life.

'Buildings are documents' it has been claimed, and this is undeniable if by 'document' we mean something which records information for the future. Any piece of building, be it Roman fort, Tudor manor house or modern submarine tells the intelligent observer not a little about the age of which it is an integral part. If the evidence provided by the structure itself is reinforced by good written evidence, our knowledge of the age in question may be much increased. In the next few chapters we shall examine the light thrown on the monastic life of medieval

I

England by the buildings erected for the monks* of those days and our task is greatly aided by the considerable written evidence hereon still extant, as well as by the labours of an almost unbroken succession of English scholars who, from the seventeenth century onwards, have worked on this subject. In the interests of clarity and brevity, some use of technical architectural terms is essential; a glossary of these is given below (see page 149).

Medieval monastic life in this country lasted almost a thousand years, the Norman Conquest of 1066 dividing it into two almost equal parts. In the first of these, monasteries contributed very much to literary and missionary work, but the architectural standards of the time were generally low. Largely because of this, early English monastic buildings have left only scanty and unimpressive remains. The living quarters were often of the humblest description, being mere wooden huts of no great size with thatched roofs arranged on no special plan. The most impressive building was the church, which was normally of stone, though generally small in size and rough in workmanship. Many such buildings were first erected in the seventh and eighth centuries when monasticism first firmly established itself in England. They were often surrounded by nothing more substantial than ditches and walls mostly made of wood and earth.

Almost all of these religious houses fell into ruin in the course of Viking invasions which began in the last years of the eighth century and continued with great ferocity for two hundred years. In the mid-tenth century a process of rebuilding began, but it was still on a modest scale and the number of monasteries involved was not considerable. There were only about forty-eight houses of men and twelve of women in England at the time of the Norman Conquest of 1066. Though the buildings then existing were generally an improvement on the earlier ones, they mostly seemed small and inelegant to the vigorous and often wealthy rulers of English monasteries in the years after 1066, who had no hesitation in rebuilding their monasteries on a scale far more imposing than England had hitherto seen, using stone with a lavishness unparalleled here since the days of the Roman Empire.

The enormous increase in size and splendour of English monastic buildings in the period after the Norman Conquest is one of the most striking features of the age. It was due partly to the considerable religious fervour of the times, partly to the growth in economic prosperity and partly to the unhurried approach of those in authority, who were quite content for the sort of buildings they desired to take fifty or even a hundred years to complete. From now on for centuries the passion for rebuilding gripped men much as it gripped them at the time of the Renaissance, and it was rare indeed for ancient buildings to be regarded as so sacrosanct as to

---

* Although 'monk' in its technical sense does not include members of later monastic orders, such as regular canons and friars, it has so long been used in this general sense that it would seem pedantic to reject it.

be spared demolition in the interest of some larger and more modern structure. Thus at Durham soon after the Conquest the bishop pulled down his cathedral 'being not well content with the smallnesse and homelinesse of that buildinge'.

Henceforward rebuilding was a constant feature of the Middle Ages amongst monasteries who could afford it, or thought they would be able to do so in the end, and not a few from time to time involved themselves in serious debts through the lavish scale of their building campaigns. Not infrequently fires made rebuilding essential. An inevitable result of this is that very little remains of pre-Conquest monastic architecture. Crypts survive from seventh-century monasteries at Hexham and Ripon purely because they did not get in the way of later erections. A few fragments remain of a handful of ancient monasteries such as Jarrow, but generally little early building was spared; thus even the lordly abbey church which Edward the Confessor began at Westminster was almost completely rebuilt two centuries later.

In recent times the sites of several of the most venerable of English monasteries have been excavated. But the results, though full of interest to the archaeologist, showed little of architectural interest. Excavations still in progress at Glastonbury have emphasised the interest and antiquity of what was the richest and oldest of all the monastic houses of medieval England. At Whitby excavations before the last war produced a number of small finds which included a fragment of cloth and part of the tombstone of a princess Aethelflaed recording correctly (as we know from other sources) that she had lived in the abbey 'from infancy'. But the architectural remains were scanty and unprepossessing.

After the Norman Conquest of 1066 not only did the scale and style of monastic building improve enormously but the number of English monasteries, as we shall see, increased fantastically. There was quickly and firmly established a tradition of majestic and rational building which the following chapters will consider in detail. But before doing this, there are two preliminary points which must be stressed.

Firstly it is essential to realise that the monastic orders of medieval England did not all have the same sort of régime and because of this did not all have the same sort of buildings. For example, from the twelfth century onwards it was usual for almost all members of a monastery of men to be in priest's orders and to be accustomed to say mass if not daily at least very frequently. This necessitated the provision of a large number of side chapels, where these masses could be said. In houses of women these were not needed, since women could not be ordained to the priesthood. Again, some orders aimed to maintain an elaborate and splendid round of worship in which intercession was made for living and departed. For this a large and magnificent conventual church was increasingly found to be the obvious setting. But, as we shall see, the friars found this expense and elaboration undesirable and insisted on much simpler buildings, though their stress on sermons led them to build the first churches designed for preaching that England had seen.

Some monasteries inherited the site and endowment of a parish church for whose parishioners they were legally bound to provide facilities for public worship. For long, this they normally did in part of their own church. The Cistercians (a large Benedictine order) had no parishioners but, at first, a considerable number of lay brothers, and the provision of quarters for these, as we shall see, had an important influence on the layout of their buildings; whilst the small Carthusian order (a minor Benedictine order) did not live the intense communal life of most of the other orders, but had their own cells, thereby creating a very special monastic plan.

Secondly, the very considerable variety in size of English monasteries must be appreciated. At the time of the suppression of the monasteries by Henry VIII their annual income varied wildly from a few dozen pounds to several thousand. The richest houses had almost all been founded before the Norman Conquest, in days when a pious and minute population inhabited a country abounding in undrained and unwanted land. Some of these antique monasteries then acquired from royal and other benefactors enormous areas of land, and by the end of the Middle Ages had built up an income equal to many thousands of pounds in modern money. It was, indeed, said that if the abbot of Glastonbury (the richest English house) were to marry the abbess of Shaftesbury (the richest English nunnery) they would be wealthier than the king of England! However, such plutocratic institutions must not be taken as typical, for they numbered only two or three dozen out of a final total of over a thousand English monasteries. Below them ranged houses of every size down to not a few where a mere handful of brethren maintained a meagre existence, with the danger of bankruptcy never very distant. Poverty was especially marked in the case of houses of nuns and the orders of friars. Thus any precise generalisation about English monastic wealth needs considerable qualification.

This great disparity of financial resources clearly affected the number of brethren maintained and equally obviously had important architectural repercussions. The wealthiest English monasteries (mostly Benedictine abbeys founded before the Norman Conquest) in their heyday had between fifty and a hundred brethren. But at the other end of the scale we can find houses of Benedictines and Augustinians which had less than half a dozen members. The great majority of English houses lay between these two extremes, many houses reaching double figures, specially common being those founded for the 'full convent' of a head and twelve brethren, reminiscent of Christ and the twelve apostles. For the Cistercians this 'full convent' of thirteen was the minimum number permissible—a wise rule preventing the existence of communities too small to live an effective common life.

Clearly monasteries had normally to cut their coat according to their cloth, and since the size of the cloth varied so greatly, so also did that of the coat. Hence English monastic churches varied in length from mere chapels a bare hundred feet long to gigantic edifices five times that size, like Winchester or St. Albans. Other monastic buildings varied similarly in size and to some extent in building material, small houses continuing to use wood long after big ones scorned anything but stone.

Thus it is evident that there is no such thing as a typical English medieval monastery, only a great variety of monasteries, large, medium and small. However, it is true that, with a few important exceptions, there were no major differences between any of the numerous Augustinian and Benedictine monasteries; the great majority of these were neither very large nor very small and they had many similar features. Numerically such houses constitute nearly two-thirds of the monasteries of medieval England and it is with them that the next two chapters will be concerned.

In attempting to reconstruct the home of the medieval English monk, we are, of course, much handicapped by the partial or complete destruction of the vast proportion of English monastic buildings at and after the Reformation. But much of the buildings of certain old monasteries has survived, notably in those English cathedrals which were originally monasteries, whilst considerable remnants of hundreds of others are still visible.

This archaeological evidence is greatly illuminated and extended by the considerable documentary evidence. Thus the details of the monastic routine are very clearly set forth in what are known as 'custumals', or 'observances' and surveys of monastic property drawn up at the time of the Suppression give us invaluable pictures of the buildings and furnishings of some, though by no means all, of the monasteries. An unusual and particularly valuable source is the so-called *Rites of Durham*, a minute description of the life in the great Benedictine monastery of Durham, on the eve of the Dissolution written by a former inmate of the house. With the aid of such sources it is possible to reconstruct with complete confidence the main details of the home of the medieval English monk.

The Site

The age in which medieval monasteries flourished was one in which for the great mass of English people life was simple and agricultural, with most food and clothing produced locally. Because of this economic situation most monasteries, like the country houses of later days, found it desirable to associate with their living quarters ground and buildings to provide for various agricultural necessities. Hence we often find gardens, orchards and sometimes fields as well as stables, granaries, bakeries, breweries, mills, fish-ponds and dovecotes figuring within monastic precincts of the older orders, along with accommodation for travellers, lodgers and guests, and the monks' own living quarters and church. Privacy—one of the essentials for monastic life—led to the whole monastic establishment being strictly enclosed by a lofty wall.

All this meant that a prime necessity for founding a monastery was a largish piece of land, if possible fairly flat, on which these buildings could be laid out without overcrowding or difficulty. If a monastery was founded outside a town, a

convenient site was generally not difficult to obtain. Most Augustinian and Benedictine houses were able to procure such spacious and convenient areas on which
they erected their monasteries. But some of the oldest Benedictine houses were
established in the crowded towns of medieval days, where provision of space for
the large and elaborate buildings that became usual after the Norman Conquest
was often a serious problem. Smallish places like Rochester cathedral never quite
got over it, though wealthy houses like Christ Church, Canterbury, solved the
question after a good deal of trouble and expense.

The problem was made worse by the profound attachment of medieval man to
consecrated sites; 'Once a church, always a church' was the normal rule. Whatever
complications might ensue, it was almost unheard of for the site of an ancient
church to be used for any other purpose. From this came trouble. Old Benedictine
houses were generally built near a public road that was often to the south of the
church with a cemetery in between. When in post-Conquest days they were
rebuilt on a grand scale on the old site, the great new church frequently took up
most of the available room on the south side thus making it necessary to build the
cloister buildings on the rather inconvenient north side (see pages 14-15), as we find
at Christ Church and St. Augustine's Canterbury, Chester, and even at the comparatively new house at Waltham.

The Cistercian abbeys were set 'in places remote from human habitation' so
had few headaches over their layout, but some of the lesser Augustinian and Benedictine houses also had trouble through being established at churches in towns
where space was inadequate, and the monastery both cramped and noisy. In some
cases, as at St. Oswald's Gloucester, this had to be endured, but in other cases it
was found feasible to move away from original inconveniences. Thus Daventry
priory left its original site 'both because of the lack of water supply and of nearness
to the castle', and the monks of Thetford moved outside the town because their
original site was 'cramped and hemmed in by houses of the citizens'. The little
priory founded within the castle at Porchester moved to a much ampler and more
secluded site at Southwick and canons at St. Mary's church in Huntingdon, transferred to a site outside, it is said, 'because of the noise of the town'. One of the
reasons which led to the removal of the priory at St. Giles' church in Cambridge to
Barnwell, well clear of the city, was the fact that the original site 'was not adequate
for all the buildings needed by the canons'.

Some of the worst sufferers over this site problem were the friars. They mostly
settled in towns, and their strict poverty prevented them buying up land for
extension in the way the Benedictines could do. In the early days the Franciscans
and Dominicans especially started with small, unprepossessing sites in crowded
areas. Thus the first Franciscans in Cambridge lived in part of an old synagogue, the
rest of which served as a jail, and had a chapel so simple that it had been constructed by one carpenter in one day. To save expense several houses of friars used
a corner of the town wall as their boundary. When, later on, for good and sufficient

reasons rebuilding on a larger scale was often desired, it was frequently difficult to effect. Several houses of friars gave up the struggle and moved outside the town, some others rather tryingly petitioned for permission to remove a chunk of the town wall which hemmed them in.

For a monastic site a good water supply was as important as suitable space. Water was needed for drinking, for drainage and for the fish-ponds which, as we shall see, were an inevitable part of the monastic economy. It was not always possible to get all three from a single source. Drinking-water was the most difficult to obtain. A beck might provide for drainage and ponds but might not give pure enough water for drinking purposes. A spring or springs together with a beck provided the ideal combination, even though this might mean erecting the main monastic buildings on the slope in which the springs so often rose. This ideal combination existed at Fountains (near Ripon), the greatest Cistercian abbey of England. This took its name from the springs that formerly existed there, and the beck on which much of its sanitation depended is still to be seen [Pl. 1]. In some cases the spring was covered by a well-house to preserve the purity of the water supply. There is an early example of this at Canons Ashby, and a finer one at Haughmond [Pl. 4b], from which the water runs down to the site of the fish-ponds. At Rievaulx no use was made of the stream in the bottom of the valley, the abbey being built on a steep hillside with water supplied by springs. At Leeds (Kent) a spring high up on the hill seems to have been ingeniously dammed to provide a fish-pond or fish-ponds, then went under the buildings for drainage, finally emerging triumphantly to work the mill, which it still does.

Naturally, for monasteries in towns the supply of fresh water was often a particularly difficult problem. Some overcame this by moving, like the canons who left St. Giles' Cambridge for Barnwell partly because the former site 'had no supply of running water' and the latter had 'little springs active and pure enough'. But it was more usual to pipe it from an external source by means of conduits. A twelfth-century drawing now in Trinity College, Cambridge, shows the very complex conduit system then established at the great abbey of Christ Church, Canterbury, and another contemporary drawing shows the layout of the water supply for the cells of the brethren of the London Charterhouse (see page 51). Few conduits have left much trace, but part of one made by Sherborne abbey was found in 1937. The English Franciscans are known to have devoted much attention to this matter. At the Suppression it was reported that the Franciscan conduit at Coventry was 'much better than that of the town and has a better head', and that its retention was essential. At Bristol and Lincoln the Franciscan water systems were acquired by the town and used long after the Suppression. The great fountain of Trinity College, Cambridge still is fed by a conduit laid out by the Cambridge Franciscans.

There is no doubt that English medieval monasteries paid far more attention to drainage than was usual in their time. Medieval towns were incorrigibly slack in this matter, as a long trail of complaints and fruitless resolutions in their records bears witness. But monasteries often seem to have devoted considerable care to the layout and construction of their drains. These were often carefully lined with stone and were usually several feet high. Because of this they have the appearance of underground passages and, after their re-discovery in modern centuries, they were repeatedly taken to be 'secret passages', especially if they pointed vaguely in the direction of a distant monastery of the opposite sex.

The main water supply was, of course, normally provided by a stream, the principal buildings being sited in careful relation to its course. Over the stream would be normally some or all of the monastic lavatories and one or more kitchens as at Furness. At Fountains the series of five parallel watercourses under the infirmary, is perhaps the largest of its kind in the country.

Fish-ponds played a large part in providing the medieval monastic diet. This was partly because meat was expensive, but principally because of the Church's rule of abstaining from fresh meat on the numerous fast days. Transport being so difficult, it was obviously convenient to have home-grown supplies of fish. Carp was a popular fish (it has recently been claimed that an acre of water stocked with carp produces more food than an acre of land sown with wheat) but Worcester accounts show ponds were also stocked with tench, roach, perch, breams, eels and pike. There is generally more than one pond and sometimes we find several created by the simple expedient of damming a stream at various levels as at Kirklees and Chipley; other series of ponds can be seen at Little Dunmow and the tiny priory of Stonely. Though there can be no doubt that the water supply was a major consideration in siting a monastery, which generally explains much of the layout, it is rare for much of the original system to have remained and the whole subject is in need of systematic study.

These exigencies of ample space and water supply were not easily supplied. Other reasons sometimes led to changing the site. Sawley was founded because experience showed that the first site was in too inhospitable an area to provide the necessary support. As a contemporary character curiously puts it, it was 'a foggy, rainy country side', where corn 'already white unto harvest . . . went rotten on the stalk', and because of bad weather and scarcity of all necessities, the size of the convent was diminished and its poverty 'a cause of shame'. Sawley was a Cistercian house, and several others of this order seem to have accepted sites too uncritically and had to move in consequence. Kirkstall abbey left its original site not far from where the first Sawley monks had settled, because of the rain which 'almost every year drowned their crops', and Jervaulx moved from its original site in Wensley-dale because of 'the poorness of the place and the intemperance of the weather'.

It is easy to forget how enormous was the monastic need for firewood at this time. The monks of Kingswood had early moved because they lacked water and firewood, and it is said that Pipewell almost moved house in the fourteenth century because the local folk were helping themselves so liberally to their firewood! Monks moved to Thame from Otley (Oxfordshire) because, it is recorded, their first site was 'fitter for an ark than a monastery', whilst the Cistercians of Stoneleigh are said to have transferred because of lack of food and the burdensomeness of the local foresters! Generally a single change of site proved enough, but the community which finally came to rest at Byland abbey had the odd record of having had no less than four sites in fifty years.

Though many monasteries were built on a quite new site, others replaced houses of clergy or hermits. In such cases the existing church would be allowed to remain *pro tem.* and temporary domestic buildings erected alongside it; otherwise a chapel would be built at an early stage. All these would be on a much smaller scale than the permanent stone ones which replaced them as soon as circumstances allowed. The first part of the latter to be built was generally the south wall of the church and the west wall of its south transept* (if, as was usual, the cloister was on this side); but these might not be carried to their full height at this stage, as we can see at Lanercost, where an unusual change of stone during the process of construction betrays the early work. The rest of the outer wall of the cloister would be completed and its adjacent buildings gradually erected. The monks' living quarters in the eastern range had a high priority, though in Cistercian houses understandable precedence might be given to the quarters of the lay brethren (as at Furness and Byland) who probably did much of the rough work required whilst the monastery was a-building. The south transept and east end of the church were generally the first parts of it to achieve permanent form. The north transept and western limb might only be completed half a century or so after work had begun. In the meantime temporary partition walls were put up to guard the privacy of the cloister. Monasteries founded in the twelfth century frequently took a full hundred years to erect all their buildings in the elaborate form contemporary opinion now expected.

The size of the monastic precinct varied considerably. Those of the friars were generally small, because of their strict ideas about poverty and their habit of living in towns, where space was limited and expensive. Thus a number of English Franciscan sites covered less than ten acres; the important London house had only four and that at York a mere one. But in districts where local alms were unlikely to be adequate for the simple needs of the friars, there were larger areas to allow some agriculture. Thus the Franciscans of Llanfaes in Anglesey had thirty acres and those of Babwell forty-three—but these were exceptional. Amongst the older orders there was the great variation one would expect from their great variation in wealth. The precinct of Glastonbury is said to have covered sixty acres; many houses would be content with something near half that area.

In all but the smallest sites, the great part of the precinct area would be taken up by fields, orchards, fish-ponds, gardens and the like. As we shall see, the chief buildings were generally concentrated in several courts, one just inside the main gate, the main one centring on the church and cloister. The whole area was strictly

* For a glossary of architectural terms see page 149.

enclosed, generally by a massive and lofty wall of stone, but in a few cases as at Michelham, Shulbrede, Chacombe and Little Wymondley by a moat.

Stretches of this boundary wall have frequently survived the spoliation of centuries, especially in country districts where stone is plentiful, as at Maxstoke. The wall was too lofty to be easily scaled and, like the Oxford and Cambridge college grounds, was entered by a main gatehouse, with sometimes one or two side gates. The latter might not be open to the public, the former was carefully guarded by a porter, who had the not-too-easy job of separating welcome from unwelcome visitors.

The monastery required peace and quiet, so necessary for that full recollection of God to which its members were called, but also had to show a friendly face to the outside world. The *Rule of St. Benedict* ordered that a guest be received 'as if he were Christ' and this expressed the monastic attitude of all houses except the very small minority whose vocation lay in almost complete seclusion.

Many people had perfectly legitimate reasons for seeking entrance to the monastery. Such might be visiting ecclesiastics, domestic staff, local tradesmen and farmers and travellers (great, medium and small). Automatic welcome was not accorded to members of the opposite sex or to bishops or dogs. Medieval dogs seem often to have been anything but genteel, and not to have required the presence of conventual cats to exert a distinctly untranquil effect. There were many occasions when bishops came and went unchecked. But medieval monasteries guarded their privileges with the same intense passion as modern trades unions, and from time to time found themselves involved in the same head-on collisions with those in authority. Several major monastic orders and a select few of the great houses of other orders had privileges exempting them from visitation by local ecclesiastical officials, deriving thereby some social kudos and minor financial advantages. From time to time various dignitaries, notably archbishops, bishops and archdeacons tried to put into effect controversial claims of visitation; in such cases they might well find the great door of the gatehouse firmly closed. Exceptional as were such incidents, the porter had to be a man of sense and charity, and monastic regulations stress the need for choosing suitable men for this responsible post.

Having thus seen the factors that governed the choice of a site of a monastery and the nature of its precinct, let us now examine the buildings to be found within.

CHAPTER TWO

THE OUTER COURT AND CONVENTUAL CHURCH
OF THE BENEDICTINES AND REGULAR CANONS

The Gatehouse

THE Gatehouse by which the visitor entered was a large building, often rectangular, and was set in the boundary wall. Through it ran a wide passage leading from the outer world to the monastic precinct. This was guarded by a massive door usually set at the outer face of the passage. But at Walsingham it was set back to allow a peephole to the street through which the porter could observe the many visitors to that house. At Worksop, by a merciful dispensation, the door was set half-way down the long passage, thus providing a useful shelter for the outsiders attending the market held outside the gates. The gatehouse passage was usually vaulted or groined, as at Whalley and Cartmel, but it is occasionally ceiled, as at Worksop. The original door of the gatehouse has nearly always disappeared but that of the London Charterhouse is still in position, and has in it a minute grating, to enable preliminary inspection of the caller before opening the door: doors at Maxstoke and Thornton also retain original work. In some cases gatehouses were entered by a single large door that covered the whole entrance, as at Cleeve, Cartmel, Burnham Norton [Pl. 24b] and Bromefield, but it is not uncommon to find larger monasteries having a small side door as well, as at Ely [Pl. 5a], Bridlington, Torre, Thornton and the little priory of Polesworth; the lordly gatehouse of St. Osyth had two side doors [Pl. 5b]. Whether a small door was inserted in a single main door, as with some Oxford and Cambridge college gates, is not certain, but seems likely enough.

Over the entrance was a room generally reached by a stair from the passage. This room is sometimes quite small, as in friars' gatehouses, such as the exquisite Carmelite gatehouse at Burnham Norton, but more usually is of substantial size. Where the monastery was lord of the manor the room might be used as a court-room and in some cases was evidently used as a school, for both of which public purposes it was well suited and situated. Some of the larger gatehouses, such as those at St. Osyth and Pentney, have side rooms which were probably used for guest accommodation. This may well have been the case also at Worksop, where the handsome main chamber with its great fireplace has small rooms leading off it.

At Walsingham the porter's accommodation adjoined the gatehouse but it was more often part of the same building. The roof of the gatehouse was generally covered by lead or tiles, and had battlements, which were reached by a continuation of the stair that led up to the main room from below. In some cases a separate stair led from the precinct to the main room, as at Worksop. The gatehouse had a some-what military look. This was generally bogus, but in a few cases in the disturbed Border districts we do find properly fortified buildings, of which the best-known example is Ewenny. Certain of the larger gatehouses, such as those at Ely and Bridlington, included a prisoner's cell.

A large number of gatehouses, have survived, including ones at Thornton, Butley, Bury St. Edmunds, St. Albans, Colchester (St. John's) Worcester, Battle and the façade of a fine ruined one at Kirkham (Yorks.). The noble one at Pentney was evidently kept to provide accommodation when the rest of the priory was destroyed, and the same seems to have been the case with the equally handsome gatehouses of Butley and St. Osyth. In other cases the outer wall of the gatehouse was preserved, but the rest allowed to go to ruin as at Llanthony by Gloucester, Waltham, Hexham, Lanercost and Guisborough. In a few of the largest monas-teries, where the claims of hospitality were heavy, there was more than one large gatehouse, as at St. Augustine's Canterbury where two remain, the second having a magnificent guest chamber. But in general there was only one major entrance, other entrances being mere side gates. In a few Cistercian abbeys we find an inner and an outer gate.

In general all the main buildings were within the precinct. But in the case of the Cistercians there was normally to be found, just outside, a *Gatehouse Chapel* (*capella ad portas*). This was a small place of worship mainly for the use of depen-dants of the monastery (Cistercian abbeys generally being some distance from any parish altar) and for women, who were not usually admitted to the conventual church. It was normally rectangular and unaisled. A fine early example of a gate-house chapel remains at Coggeshall [Pl. 3a]. It looks very like a Nonconformist chapel outside and is one of the earliest examples of medieval English brick work. Other good ones are at Kirkstead and Merevale (an unusually elaborate example). At Rievaulx the old chapel has been restored for use as a place of worship. In non-Cistercian houses the need for this chapel did not normally exist, as most houses either had parish churches near by or were quite prepared to allot part of their church to the use of the parishioners. But we get a similar chapel at Barnwell (Cambs.) perhaps built on the site of an old hermitage and still in use, and possibly at Llanthony Prima (Mon.).

In the case of a fair number of Augustinian or Benedictine houses the parish-ioners had rights in the church at which the monastery was founded. Often convent and people continued to share the church throughout the Middle Ages, but it was obviously better for both if the people's place of worship could be moved outside. This generally came to pass in the case of wealthy monasteries, as Glastonbury, Abingdon, Westminster, Cirencester, Merton and Bodmin where we find parish churches just outside the precinct and the same is the case with some smaller houses like Bruton and Kenilworth. But there were plenty of cases where this was not done, and even some plutocratic houses like Waltham still had two churches under one roof at the time of the Dissolution, perhaps because the parishioners, who were legally responsible for the fabric of their place of worship, could not afford to move.

Immediately within the Gatehouse was to be seen an *Outer Court*. This was not necessarily, or indeed normally, arranged on any very stereotyped plan, but was merely an open space, round which were ranged various buildings concerned with the administrative side of the monastic estate and not with the maintenance of divine worship.

Obviously necessary was stabling and living accommodation for the travellers and their steeds, who so steadily poured in and out of monastic gateways at these times. Then there was sometimes need for accommodation for poor people maintained at the monastery either in return for bequests or, later on, as a result of individual settlements known as corrodies—a very primitive form of insurance. Buildings for these purposes were not of major importance, and in smaller monasteries were sometimes constructed of wood or similar material, but wealthy monasteries would build in stone, as witness the great ranges at Ely. There are comparatively few instances of much of this outer court remaining, though occasionally odd buildings still exist. An extremely fine range of buildings of this type represents almost all that is to be seen above ground of the once mighty abbey of Abingdon. It includes a tower with a fine fireplace, a long upper floor with a corridor on one side and signs of partitions which probably divided it into sleeping and living rooms; below is a similar long floor of uncertain purpose, perhaps for stores and stabling. A few remains of outer buildings adjoin the gatehouse of Kirkham priory. At Fountains a group of three guest houses, simple rectangular structures, stand some way from the now vanished main gatehouse [Pl. 3b]. Stabling accommodation was generally of simple construction and seldom survives. A number of monasteries are known to have maintained poor people within their precincts and in some cases their quarters may have been in this outer court, though later on, in some houses at least, accommodation was found in or near the main cloister buildings.

In the case of small monasteries agricultural buildings may have lain in or near this outer court, but the larger ones were able to arrange for these to be laid out separately in another part of the precinct, with a minor gateway. This clearly convenient plan existed at Ely and probably prevailed at Cartmel, where the 'Barngarth' lay across the beck from the church and cloister. It was certainly the case at Bridlington at the time of Dissolution. Here we have an invaluable description of what must have been a particularly grand set of farm buildings.

The Barne Yarde—Item There is a great Barne Yarde on the Northside of the seid Priorie containing by estimacion foure Acres.

The Barne Item, there is on the Northside of the same Barne Yarde a very faire Barne, conteyning in length Est and West CXVII paces and in breddith XXVII paces, well covered with lede to the value of five hundred markes. . . .

The *Garnerd*—Item on the South side of the same Barne standith a Garnerd to lay Corne in, conteyning in length North and South XXVI yards, and in breddith X yards covered with lede.

The *Malthouse*—Item on the Est side of the same Garnerd standith the Malthouse containing in length North and South XLIIII yerds and in breddith XVII yards well covered with lede; and on the North side of the same Malthouse standith a prety House with a Chamber where the Hervest men did alwayes dine, covered with slatt.

The *Kilne House*—Item on the Est side of the same Malthouse standith a Kilne House covered with slatt.

Olde Stables and Oxestalles—Item on the Est and West side of the Barne Yerde standith olde Stables, Oxestalles, with other old houses builded with stone, covered with slatt, greatly in decay.

Much the most useful building was the barn which housed an invaluable part of the convent's food supply, and was strongly built of stone doubtless as a precaution against fire and thieves. In these barns monasteries not only kept the produce of their own estates, but frequently tithes or tenth parts of produce from lands in parishes they owned. Thus a very large amount of accommodation for this was required, and barns might be of very considerable size. At Selby abbey the great barn was originally 313 feet long, evidently about the same length as that at Bridlington. The great barn of Abbotsbury survives little damaged; it is 272 feet long by 31 feet broad, and had two porches. A good set has survived at Westacre. These barns are built well away from the main buildings, partly so as to respect monastic privacy and partly, perhaps, as an additional precaution against that dreaded and over-frequent medieval visitor—fire. After the Dissolution the new owners of the monastic lands seldom farmed on anything like the same scale as the old monastery had done. Thus they generally found these sort of buildings much too big for their needs and demolished some or let them fall into decay.

The Cloister Court

Beyond the outer court and gatehouse and frequently to the east of it lay the focus of all monastic life, the church and cloister. Originally a 'cloister' merely denoted some enclosed space, but gradually in monastic parlance the word was specially applied to a square or rectangular court, having an open area in the middle which was edged by a broad covered passage, around which were grouped the major monastic buildings, notably the church.

The Conventual Church

In lands like England, common sense directed that the church should normally stand on the north side of the cloister. It was much the loftiest building in the area, so that in any other position it would be likely to blot out the all-too-infrequent sunlight, whilst a northern position made it also an admirable screen against the chilly winds to be expected from that quarter. But there were a considerable minority of houses where, for one reason or another, this was not possible, and the church was on the south side. As we have seen, in some cases this occurred because an old church had been turned into a monastery and by the time of the conversion the land which lay to the south was cramped and noisy or had long been given over to a cemetery. In other cases the fall of the land (as at Bricett) or the key position of the water supply (as at Stavordale) dictated a change in position. At Maxstoke the southern side of the church seems to have been too boggy for building.

It was an almost uniform rule that the church ran east and west. The old idea that this was done for some semi-pagan reason has no evidence to support it and in this, as in most other points of medieval monastic planning, a severely practical explanation is much more likely, namely the need of cheap lighting in a rather sombre country. In Italy where the light is strong, medieval folk put few windows in their churches and paid little attention to orientation. But in England the light was poor for much of the year. If artificial light could have been obtained cheaply this would not have mattered. But the reverse was the case, medieval artificial lighting coming mainly from oil and tallow* at a time when both were expensive things. Hence the maximum use had to be made of natural light. This was one reason why medieval windows get bigger and bigger as time goes on, and also why, as we shall see, the monastic daily routine varied in length according to the time between sunrise and sunset. It is true that the English passion for stained glass cut across this tendency (see page 56) but its disadvantages were minimised, partly by the development of larger windows, partly by increasingly transparent glass. As the major part of the monastic services came before midday, and all masses were said at this time, it was most desirable to make the best possible use of daylight by having the monks' choir and as many as possible of the side chapels at the east end so as to take advantage of the morning sunlight. There are very few cases in England where the church did not run, at least roughly, east and west with the choir at the east end. At Rievaulx abbey the normal orientation was quite impossible, as the site of the monastery was a very steep hillside running north and south; it is significant that in this case the choir faced the sunny south, not the north as would have been architecturally equally feasible.

The plan of English monastic churches varied somewhat. In some very small houses of the Augustinian and Benedictine orders and in a number of houses of nuns it was a simple rectangular building with or without an aisle or aisles as at Worspring and Stavordale. But in England from the early twelfth century the most popular shape amongst houses able to afford it was the cruciform or cross-shaped

* Lighting might be in the form of candles or tapers, but monasteries made much use of *cressets*, blocks of stone with holes scooped out, in which wicks floated in oil. These cressets varied in size and shape, many being square, but more attractive ones survive from Furness abbey and Blackmore priory [Pl. 28a, 28b].

church, the western arm normally being much the longest, the northern and southern being shallow transepts of about equal size [see pp. 143, 144, 146; Pls. 2a, 2b, 20a]. The eastern limbs were often originally short and dark, especially in the Cistercian order, and because of this were frequently later rebuilt on a much grander scale, as we shall see. An apsidal or semicircular end to a transeptal chapel or to the eastern limb was common on the Continent in the eleventh and twelfth centuries, and spread somewhat in England after the Norman Conquest, but it never caught on, the rectangular east end becoming increasingly popular here in the later Middle Ages. The eastern limb in France frequently had a large aisled apse with chapels arranged neatly within. Beaulieu and its daughter house of Hailes are amongst the very few English monastic churches where this occurs. Rather more common was a simpler apse with side chapels projecting from it, as at St. Bartholomew's Smithfield and Norwich.

As we have seen, the gatehouse generally lay to the west of the church, and it was perhaps to give a fine impression along the main line to the approach that the west end of the church was frequently treated in a very elaborate fashion, with an imposing main door, set in an often complex façade of windows and blind arcading. This elaboration is very notable in the Cluniac order, and its house at Castle Acre (Norfolk) has bequeathed to us one of the loveliest and most elaborate façades of any smallish English monastery [Pl. 6b]. A simpler façade of similar type is at St. Botolph's Colchester. The Benedictine abbey of Peterborough added a very grand one in the thirteenth century and to the same period belong the smaller Augustinian one at Newstead in Sherwood [Pl. 6a] and the simpler but attractive one at Lanercost (Cumb.). (These last two have a curious bogus feature: though they have only a single side aisle, in the interests of symmetry the façade gives the appearance of having two.) Very frequently after the twelfth century the west front had twin towers as at Durham, Llanthony (Mon.), Dunstable, St. German's and Bourne. Cistercian west fronts were of the simplest, in accordance with the regulations of the order. But occasionally they show traces of a curious feature which the Cistercians brought with them from Burgundy. This is a narthex or portico of one storey supported on a low arcade, attached to the west front. Part of this can be seen at Fountains (reconstructed) and less substantial signs at Byland and Rievaulx. But for a complete one we must cross the Channel, that at Pontigny (Yonne) being the prize example. However, this narthex does not seem to have been universally used and is seldom found after the twelfth century.

As time went on the west front was sometimes altered by the addition of a great belfry tower. Bell ringing had been popular in England long before the Conquest, and by the fifteenth century the construction of elaborate belfries became widespread. Often they were provided by heightening the walls of the central lantern of the church as at Durham, Gloucester, Worcester, Christ Church Canterbury, Carlisle and Kirkstall, though Cartmel had the unique idea of a square tower set diagonally on the lantern [Pl. 20a]. But use of the lantern was apt to be dangerous, as its foundations might not prove to be as strong as was desirable. This was found to be the case at both Fountains and Furness, where attempts to add a new belfry in this position had to be abandoned after serious signs of collapse appeared in the piers of the crossing. A much safer plan was to build a tower at the west end of the church and this is where we find late Gothic towers at Furness, Shap and Bolton. At Fountains a very late tower was built at the end of the north transept [Pl. 1], a most odd and not very attractive position. Spires are comparatively rare in English monasteries, Norwich being the most glorious exception.

The Nave

On passing through the great west door, which was usually large and complex, as at Castle Acre, the visitor would find the nave of the church stretching out before him. In smaller houses, such as Beeston Regis and Lilleshall, and especially in houses of nuns, e.g. Nun Monkton, the nave would have no aisles. Some other houses had a single aisle, on the opposite side of the church to the cloister. This we find at Newstead in Sherwood, Lanercost and Bolton and it formerly existed at Launde. But the naves of all the larger houses and even some of the smaller ones like Creake, had north and south aisles, divided from the main body of the church by arcades above which was a triforium (or series of arches opening into the space immediately beneath the lean-to aisle roof) and clerestory (a range of windows at the top of the side walls, immediately below the roof). Some houses omitted the triforium, the Cistercians and friars mostly through austerity others probably through lack of funds. The nave arcade was always more prominent than the triforium or clerestory and tended to become more so. The length of the naves varied greatly. There were only three or four bays in small houses but up to a dozen in large ones: the majestic naves of Norwich and Peterborough have twelve bays and the wealthy Cistercian house of Fountains eleven.

Contrary to modern taste, a medieval monastic church had its interior split up by a series of partitions, some dividing off sections of the aisles from the main body of the church, others cutting up the aisles or transepts. The main partition, which was a very substantial and complex one, ran right across the eastern end of the nave dividing it into two distinct parts. It consisted of the rood screen and the *pulpitum* and varied somewhat in plan.

The part first visible to the visitor coming up the western limb of the church was the rood screen, which was built of stone, and probably generally wainscotted. It cut the church in two and against its western face stood altars, one in the middle of the main aisle and one in the side aisle or aisles. On either side of the main altar were two small doors, leading to the monks' choir and used in procession; these remain in various places such as St. Albans, Dunstable, Boxgrove, Tynemouth, Wymondham [Pl. 12a] and Crowland [Pl. 7]. At the Dissolution, in certain cases where the western part of the church belonged to the parishioners, this stone screen

3

was retained to serve as the base of the eastern wall of the dismembered church as at Wymondham, Waltham and Dunstable.

The rood screen itself had a broad top with a line of panelling on either side, thus creating a passage which was known as the rood loft. On the top of the loft were lights. The loft was generally entered by a spiral stair, often in the adjoining north wall. High above the rood loft was the rood itself, a representation of Christ on the Cross, with Our Lady and St. John on either side, each often accompanied by an angel. In some parish churches this was painted, but in monasteries the rood was normally carved in wood, the cross and figures standing on a lofty beam that ran from wall to wall high above the screen. A fine modern rood in its ancient position may be seen in Wymondham church [Pl. 12a], but all medieval examples were lost in the fury of the Reformation.

East of the rood screen was the retro-choir, and beyond it the *pulpitum* and choir stalls.

The *pulpitum* was an elaborate screen, normally of stone which formed the western end of the choir stalls and had a large central door giving access to them. Its western face was elaborately decorated. A favourite design here, as in secular churches such as Ripon and York, was a series of niches filled with statues of English kings. A magnificent example of this remains at Canterbury cathedral. That formerly at Durham had 'most excellent pictures, all gilted verye beautifull to behould, of all the Kinges and Queenes, as well of Scotland as England, as weere devout and godly Founders and Benefactors of this famous Church, and sacred monument of St. Cuthbert, to incite and provoke theire posteritie to the like religious endeavours'. Christchurch (Hants.) has a less elaborate example. A fine wooden *pulpitum* remains at Hexham [Pl. 10a] and a less attractive one at Carlisle.

In most cases there was a single bay separating the rood screen and *pulpitum*. This was ceiled over and might have the main organ on top. Sometimes there were two bays with a screen between; in such cases the western bay was a retro-choir with a small altar on either side of the eastern screen and the eastern bay was ceiled over. In a third type there was a single bay between rood screen and choir stalls which was not ceiled.

The *Rites of Durham* gives a useful description of the cathedral organs, of which there were three. One of the three 'did stand over the Quire dore, only opened and played uppon at principall Feasts, the pipes being all of most fine wood and work-manshipp, very faire, partly gilded uppon the inside and the outside of the leaves and covers up to the topp, with branches and flowers finely gilted, with the name of Jesus'. The second stood on the side of the choir 'beinge never playd uppon but when the four Doctors of the church was read, viz. Augustine, Ambrose, Gregorye and Jerome. . . .' 'The third paire was daily used at ordinary service.' Doubtless most monasteries had to make do without a special doctoral organ.

The position of the rood screen and *pulpitum* in relation to the nave varied. At first the area between the two was generally opposite to or easily accessible from the eastern alley of the cloister, which, as we shall see, was in line with the eastern-most bay of the nave [pp. 144, 146]. This was clearly a convenient plan in view of the constant movement of brethren between cloister and choir. It also meant that the choir stalls would be directly under the lantern, which at first, at least, must have been one of the lightest parts of the church. In later times the eastern limb of a monastic church was often rebuilt on a much larger scale and in such cases the *pulpitum* and rood screen were often moved further east.

As we have noted (see page 4), in a number of Augustinian and Benedictine monastic churches the area west of the rood screen housed the parishioners and the main altar against it was for their use. This arose from the fact that nearly all such houses had been founded at an already existing parish church, and thereby acquired not only its site and endowment, but also its legal responsibilities to provide a place of public worship for the parishioners. In most cases the nave was found to be the most convenient part of the church to allot for this purpose; it lay near the monastery's main entrance and left the precious east end free for the monks, with their greater need for its advantages.

At the Dissolution this western part containing the parish altar was usually kept when the rest of the church was ruined, for Henry VIII found it good to maintain the existing rights of the parishioners. Hence such half-ruined churches as Old Malton, Bolton, Lanercost, Binham, Bourne, Dunstable, St. German's and Worksop, to mention but a few. In a handful of cases a transept was used for popular worship, including Chester and probably Hexham, and at Crowland the north aisle of the great nave was used for this purpose probably before as well as after the Reformation. In a few other instances the south chancel aisle was evidently used, as at Cartmel, Little Dunmow and Swavesey; and the north chancel aisle was used in the same way in the non-parochial, ruined churches of Beeston Regis and North Creake. In all, or almost all such cases the aisle used was that on the opposite side of the church to the cloister.

As we have already noted, this habit of having two different rounds of worship established under the same roof had obvious inconveniences, and in a number of cases, notably among the wealthy houses, the situation was remedied by special parish churches being constructed outside the gates of the monasteries (see page 12). This had the melancholy result that at the Reformation the parishioners had no right to retain any part of the great conventual church and no major incentive to buy it. As a result some of the most magnificent of English monastic churches have disappeared without trace or almost without trace. A few were saved by being already cathedrals, five more (Oxford, Bristol, Gloucester, Chester and Peter-borough) by being converted into cathedrals, but most of the greatest conventual churches were completely wrecked. Such was the fate of Glastonbury, St. Augustine's Canterbury, Reading, Abingdon, Bury St. Edmunds, Cirencester, Holy Trinity Aldgate, Leicester and Merton. In some cases the parishioners acquired the whole church at the time of the Dissolution as at Tewkesbury, Christchurch (Hants.) and Cartmel, but these cases are most rare.

Normally the part of the nave west of the rood screen was far larger than the needs of parochial worship required, and it is doubtful if the great naves of some English monasteries were ever filled with people, except perhaps on rare occasions in the few cathedral monasteries. The naves would, of course, offer a magnificent setting for monastic processions. For most of the time much of the western limb must have been empty, except for a few individuals at private prayer.

The nave aisles gradually acquired a series of side altars, though these do not normally seem to have been numerous. Such side chapels were often closed in with wainscotting. They had a small altar on their eastern side. By medieval times this was normally rectangular and made of stone as at Jervaulx [Pl. 9b]. On top was a single altar stone marked with five crosses, one in each corner and one in the middle. Beneath it by this time it had become usual to enclose relics. Some of these were found still in position when altars at Rievaulx were uncovered between the wars. Behind the altar might be a retable or reredos. This was often a painting or wooden or alabaster carving showing Scriptural scenes or figures of saints (see page 53). On a pedestal or in a niche close to the altar might be a statue of the saint to whom the altar was dedicated, and near it, sometimes, were specially endowed lights. Close by the altar was a piscina, a shallow bowl through which water could drain away. This was used at mass for the washing of the priest's hands and, after the communion, for washing the sacred vessels. The piscina was often set in the wall under an elaborate niche, but sometimes was detached on a small, short pillar, or was merely set in the floor. Close to the piscina might be an aumbry or small recess in the wall, generally rectangular in shape with a shelf and a door inset, for holding the vessels used at the altar. The pavement of the altar platform was frequently tiled.

We have seen that Cistercians did not have parish altars in their churches. The area west of the screen in their churches was principally used by their lay brethren (see page 74), people who lived under monastic vows but devoted most of their time to manual labour. They were very numerous in the twelfth and thirteenth centuries but few thereafter, so that in Cistercian naves, also, there must have been an enormous amount of free space west of the screen, at least in latter days. The naves of the greater English churches were often extremely long by continental standards; the reason for this has not been established.

As we have noted, many Augustinian and Benedictine churches were cruciform. The area which separated the north from the south transept, and the nave from the eastern limb, was known as the *Crossing* [pp. 144, 146]. It was generally square in plan with very lofty arches supporting a central tower. Some of the great Benedictine monasteries early built very imposing towers here, such as those of St. Albans and Tewkesbury. Later Norwich added a magnificent spire here and Malmesbury one, now lost. The early Cistercians, however, with their very austere ideas, insisted that their towers should only be a single storey high; this seems to have been the case with many early Augustinian towers as at Brinkburn and Cartmel, probably largely for financial reasons. However, as we have seen (pages 16–17), a passion for belfry towers later ensued, and many early lanterns were raised.

Adjoining the east side of the *pulpitum* were the choir stalls. These were reached through the great door in the centre of the *pulpitum* and were divided by it into two L-shaped blocks, their main axis running east and west with the stalls returned across the western end—a layout still preserved in our cathedrals. Like much English woodwork of the Middle Ages the stalls were elaborately carved and, for protection from damp, often stood on stone bases. There were generally one or two rows of stalls either side. The outer seats would have lofty wooden backs and canopies with desks in front, inner ones being merely benches and desks set at a lower level against the outer stalls. The stalls with their lofty pinnacled backs in effect closed in most of the choir, a necessary thing to do in days when heating was difficult. Not infrequently the outer faces of the choir stalls were painted, as at Carlisle where we find an elaborate series of pictures of the lives of St. Cuthbert, the favourite Northern saint, and St. Augustine of Hippo, whose Rule the brethren followed. The panels at the back of the seats and even the front of the desks are painted at Hexham, but may not be in their original position.

From an early date the seats of the stalls were constructed to swing up against the back of the stall. At least from the thirteenth century such seats had boldly projecting undersides with a highly carved bracket known as a *misericord*, generally flanked by two small carvings. These brackets were made to give some little physical support to those saying the very long offices of the medieval church, and were not a monopoly of monastic churches.

The designs carved on them were very varied and make a most interesting field of study. Some were simple floral patterns or grotesques but a big proportion illustrated well-known medieval stories. Some of these were from secular literature such as the story of Reynard the Fox but a great many more were medieval 'cautionary tales'. Notable were those designs taken from the Bestiary, a sort of 'Good Boy's Book of Beasts', where animals of fact and fiction were described with varying degrees of accuracy and pious morals drawn from their behaviour. Thus an elephant was sometimes shown with a tree trunk appearing beneath it. This had reference to an unfounded belief that the elephant had no joints to its legs and could therefore ultimately be captured by sawing partially through the tree trunk against which it customarily leant to slumber; the moral of which was that the elephant is a type of Adam who also 'fell through a tree'! In front of the seats ran sloping desks, broad and solid and terminating in elaborately carved bench ends.

The head of the house, whether abbot or prior, had usually the first stall on the south side, i.e. the one at the western end, which faced east and adjoined the central entrance. His second in command occupied the corresponding one on the north side, the rest of the brethren being seated from west to east in order of seniority. The number of stalls often greatly exceeded the number of brethren. Thus Hexham had thirty-six stalls but is not known to have had more than twenty-six canons, and at Carlisle forty-six stalls survive for a house with about twenty-six brethren. The spare seats were presumably for friends and visitors. Although hundreds of these stalls perished at the Reformation a fair number survive. Big monastic collections exist, notably at the cathedrals of Ely (a very fine set), Carlisle, Winchester, Norwich, Gloucester, Chester and Westminster abbey.

Between the choir stalls and towards their western end stood a large book-desk or lectern. This supported the books used during the singing of the offices. The *Rites of Durham* notes 'Also ther was lowe downe in the Quere another Lettorn of brasse, not so curiously wroughte, standinge in the midst against the Stalls, a marveilous faire one, with an Eagle on the height of it, and hir winges spread abroad, whereon the Monks did lay theire bookes when they sung theire legends at mattens or at other times of service.' Because of bad lighting and lack of spectacles (which only appear here about the fifteenth century*) these music books were frequently made with very large letters and musical notation.

By a most unusual arrangement, a number of English medieval monasteries were also cathedrals. This meant that there was need of a bishop's chair or *cathedra*, the word from which a cathedral takes its name. The early ones were of stone like that at Norwich (now known to be of pre-Conquest date). If the church had an apse, the chair was placed in it behind the altar and facing west—a feature often to be seen on the Continent, but of which Norwich is the only surviving example in England. The chair at Canterbury [Pl. 26b] is of post-Conquest date but it acquired the name, of 'St. Augustine's Chair'. As the Middle Ages wore on, grander styles prevailed, and the bishop's throne in the choir at Durham is a most elaborate affair. The *Rites of Durham* records that bishops there were installed in a stone chair in the chapter house; it is not clear whether this was a usual practice.

East of the choir stalls was the presbytery, a large open area with the high altar at its far end, where was celebrated the convent's major act of worship, the High Mass. The altar was similar to those already mentioned (see page 2) but more elaborate. Behind it was a painted or sculptured reredos. The mightiest sculptured one remaining is that at Winchester cathedral, but very few can have been on this scale. A damaged, less elaborate one remains at Christchurch (Hants.). Much commoner were small alabaster screens carved in a series of panels, and painted and gilded. At either end of the altar were curtains to keep off some of the draught. On the altar might be a crucifix, normally of metal, sometimes very precious and intricately worked. From about the twelfth century candlesticks were also placed on the altar, but except on great feasts they were not numerous (probably because of the expense of candles). At the north end of the altar was often a special lectern. At first simple and of wood, by later times this was frequently of metal and crowned by a large figure of an eagle. One of this type, together with two candlesticks, was found in a lake at Newstead priory (Notts.) where it had apparently been deposited in Reformation times. It is now to be seen at Southwell cathedral; inside it were

* The statue of St. Matthew in the Henry VII chapel, Westminster, has spectacles.

preserved a number of deeds. The *Rites of Durham* describes one of this type: 'At the north end of the High Altar there was a goodly fine Letteron of brasse where they sunge the epistle and the gospell, with a gilt pellican on the height of it, finely gilded, pullinge hir bloud out hir breast to hir young ones and winges spread abroade, whereon did lye the book that they did singe the epistle and the gospel.'

Near the south side of the altar and at right angles to it ran the sedilia, a series of seats in the south wall of the sanctuary for those celebrating a sung mass. The people's altars at Cartmel, Beeston Regis and Creake have but two seats, presumably for the priest and his server. But for a high mass at the conventual altar three were required for priest, deacon and subdeacon and this is the usual number. Near the sedilia was the piscina, used for ablutions and a cupboard or aumbry. Amongst the finest surviving sedilia is that at Furness abbey [Pl. 25b], where there are four seats; included with them under an elaborate canopy is a niche holding the piscina bowl and two others for the towels used at the ablutions. Near by is the aumbry. Like the similar one at Durham this would be used for 'the chalices, the basons and the crewetts (cruets) that they did minister withall at the high masse'. The sedilia at Westminster is of wood with remains of fine painting.

In the smallest houses of the Augustinian and Benedictine orders, generally in houses of nuns and almost always in houses of friars, the east end of the church was a simple rectangle without aisles. But even houses of moderate size frequently added aisles to all or most of the eastern limb. The Augustinians developed a useful plan of having aisles to all but the easternmost bay, which allowed the insertion there of large windows in the north and south walls to throw light on the high altar, as at Lanercost, Cartmel and Brinkburn. The aisles would normally contain side altars. In the case of larger churches a series of side chapels might also be added east of the high altar, in which case the eastern limb would have a broad passage connecting its chapels, known as an ambulatory, as at Christ Church, Canterbury, Tewkesbury and Norwich. Durham preferred a rectangular east end in which were set nine altars, and so did Fountains where in the mid-thirteenth century was added an eastern transept that is one of the most graceful works of a graceful age. Rievaulx was less grandiose but rebuilt its eastern limb on an imposing scale at the same time, including five chapels along its eastern wall [Pl. 12b] and Abbey Dore had the same number. In these latter cases the side chapels themselves were rectangular in plan, in the former all or most had apsidal ends. However, these elaborate eastern limbs were rare, being largely confined to a few rich secular cathedrals and the biggest Benedictine and Cistercian houses. St. Bartholomew's Smithfield is one of the few Augustinian churches with an ambulatory and it is very unlikely that any friars' church had one.

In aisled chancels, the partition created by the lofty backs of the choir stalls was continued eastward on both north and south sides in the form of a screen, which was pierced by a door, and provided privacy and a little shelter from the cold. The floor of the presbytery was not infrequently richly tiled (see pages 53–4). In 1268 the presbytery of the great abbey of Westminster acquired an exceptionally magnificent pavement of Purbeck marble, inlaid in the finest Italian style with glass and coloured stone.

To the modern churchman it seems curious that, for much of the Middle Ages, a sacristy in which vestments and vessels could be stored and set out for use was not regarded as a necessity. But from about the early fourteenth century these were found useful. One was added at Selby about this time on the south side of the chancel, and rather later one was made in the south transept at Furness. Earlier, part of the south aisle of the chancel was sometimes used for this. But the vestments and vessels were often kept in cupboards in the chapel at which they were to be used.

The Transepts

Almost all major English churches and a good many moderate-sized ones, as we have noted, had a plan in the shape of a Latin cross. The southern and northern arms of the cross (known as transepts) were generally of equal length and were normally much shorter than the western limb [pp. 143, 144, 145]. Their only important, practical function was to provide additional side chapels, and it is because of this that they are rarely found in houses of nuns, where generally only a small number of masses were said.

Many transepts have an eastern aisle in which the altars (generally two or three in number) were set. The layout of these chapels, one of which survives at Jervaulx [Pl. 9b], was similar to those in the nave already noted. A second (western) aisle in a transept is most rare, but is sometimes found as at Byland, Ely and Winchester. Sometimes transepts are unaisled, as at Cartmel, Llanthony, Bayham and Great Malvern. Normally, the elevation of the transepts corresponded to that of the rest of the church, having triforium and clerestory and an arcade below opening into the aisle. In a few cases there was in or near one transept a sort of cabin for the night watchman. It is mentioned at Durham, and a small fireplace in the wall of the south transept at Peterborough may have belonged to one of these.

In the north wall of the north transept there was often a door leading to the community's cemetery, corresponding to a similar door at the west end of the north wall of the nave leading to the lay cemetery (see page 30). The monastic cemetery was usually to the east of the church and sometimes grave slabs and stone coffins can yet be seen there, as at Roche. The lay cemetery was often on the north side of the nave, but if the site was awkward or the church was older than the monastery, it might be on the south.

In the north-west angle of the north transept was frequently a circular stair leading up to the roof and triforium. The south transept differed little from the north, except for one clearly marked special feature. This was the dormitory door and steps known as the *Night Stair*. As we shall see, the cloister was generally on the south side and had at first-floor level the dormitory, which either adjoined the south transept or was separated from it by only the width of a passage. Since monastic worship began very early in the morning, it was clearly convenient to have direct access to the church from the dormitory, from where the monks went direct to the service and to which they returned when it was over; hence this night stair from the dormitory to the church was usually situated at the west end of the south wall of the transept. After the Dissolution the dormitory was generally demolished and the door blocked up. The staircase was normally henceforth useless and has therefore nearly always disappeared as well. But a few survive, of which much the finest example in England is at Hexham [Pl. 11a], where, by a curious device, it also connects with a passage inside the transept. Other night stairs of simple type can be seen at Sawley and Tintern. Blocked dormitory doors are very common.

There is also sometimes to be found a door at the north end of the west wall of the south transept. This opened into the adjoining cloister, from which, as we shall see, two other doors in the nave wall led to the western limb of the church. These doors were needed in the great procession of the brethren before the major Sunday mass. In the course of this the brethren went from the church round the cloister and back. In cases where the nave had no southern aisle and the *pulpitum* blocked the west side of the crossing there was no easy access to the easternmost cloister door. Hence for the Sunday procession to proceed from the church to the cloister would have been difficult without this door to the cloister in the west wall of the transept, of which we have good examples at Bolton [Pl. 13a] and Lanercost.

Two other features of some, though by no means all, medieval monastic churches remain to be noted—Lady chapels and shrines. From the eleventh century onwards popular devotion to Our Lady developed very rapidly in the west, and it became quite common to build elaborate chapels in her honour, generally on a much grander scale than the minor side chapels already noted. A frequent position for these was the east end of the church, to which generally a smallish building could often be attached without considerable difficulty, as at Sherborne, Southwark and Gloucester. The Lady chapel is often an eastern extension of the choir entered from the ambulatory behind the high altar; but occasionally it was built on to the north-east corner of the church as at Ely, perhaps the finest of its kind in England. Various of these were destroyed after the Reformation as at Peterborough, Great Malvern, Romsey, doubtless because of the cost of upkeep. It should be noted that a Lady chapel could only exist where the church was not dedicated to Our Lady, as in this case the high altar would be the Lady altar.

In some cases this cult of Our Lady showed itself in devotion to particular statues of Our Lady. Much the most celebrated of these in England was the statue of Our Lady of Walsingham which, from the late thirteenth century onwards, built up an enormous popularity. It was probably visited by every king of England from this time to the Reformation as well as by thousands of lesser folk. The statue was housed in a twelfth-century chapel built as an imitation of the Holy House of

Nazareth and which stood on the north side of the nave of the conventual church.* By the time of Henry VIII this little shrine and its treasury was stacked with gifts, many of gold and silver. Ultimately, Walsingham seems to have attracted more alms than any other shrine in England. Generally no separate building was needed for such statues but a chapel was added to the church. One or two pilgrimages in medieval England took place to specially venerated crucifixes. None of them were very important, that of the Holy Rood at St. Paul's being perhaps the best known, and another at Boxley having some following for a time.

England had no important collection of the relics of Our Lord to attract the faithful such as Paris claimed to house at the Sainte-Chapelle, though one or two reputed relics of the True Cross had a temporary popularity, notably the Holy Rood of Bromholm (Norfolk), as had the Holy Blood of Hailes abbey. But the great mass of English pilgrimages to relics were to venerate the bodies or relics of local saints, a number of which were preserved in monastic churches.

Much the best known of these was the body of St. Thomas Becket, preserved at Canterbury cathedral where he was murdered when archbishop in 1170. His shrine, like that of Walsingham, drew pilgrims from the Continent though its intense early popularity seems to have waned markedly as time went on. Less spectacular had been the career of St. Edward the Confessor who rested in the mighty abbey of Westminster, the rebuilding of which he had undertaken. Though his cult was never immensely popular, in some degree because he lay in a royal free chapel, his shrine survived intact, almost alone in England, at the Reformation.

To have a saint venerated within the conventual church appealed to the local pride that burnt so strongly in medieval England, and might prove a useful source of income through the pilgrims' offerings. Several dozen monasteries set up local shrines. Such were St. Werburgh of Chester, St. Guthlac at Crowland, St. Wulfad at Stone, St. Swithin at Winchester, St. Birinus of Dorchester. Much the most important saint in northern England was St. Cuthbert, whose body, after many vicissitudes, found rest in the cathedral of Durham where it still reposes near that of the Venerable Bede.

The remains of such illustrious people were placed in elaborate shrines, with the coffin set on a heavy stone base and having a rich canopy over. To accommodate worshippers at any popular shrine a fairly large space was required together with a convenient entrance and exit. For this an obvious place in a large church with an ambulatory was the area behind the high altar. This is what we find at St. Albans [Pl. 26a] where the fragments of the base of the shrine were found and restored a century ago. At Durham, St. Cuthbert was thought to be too anti-feminist to approve of lady pilgrims invading his church, so his bones were laid in a special narthex at the west end!† Sometimes an aisle chapel was used for the shrine as at

* It was in this same position at Glastonbury that a chapel of Our Lady of Loretto was erected, shortly before the Dissolution.

† They survived the Reformation. The tomb was opened a century ago, when a number of interesting objects of great antiquity were found in it.

the rather minor one of St. Frideswide Oxford. However, in general, these shrines did not attract more than local fame and their influence had steadily decreased in the two centuries before the Reformation. English shrines were almost completely destroyed at the Reformation. Portions of some have, however, survived, as at Dorchester (Oxfordshire), Chester and Ely. In such cases as these, the shrine enclosed all or most of the body of the saint in question. Much more commonly, monastic churches built up an enormous supply of what were believed to be minor relics of the saints. Some of these were enclosed in altars, others mounted in cases; they might be very small in size. These were vigorously destroyed at the Reformation and very few escaped. Some were found at Rievaulx abbey during excavations between the wars, but these are almost unique in England, as is the remarkable casket at Bodmin which formerly contained relics owned by the medieval priory there.

No consideration of a medieval church is complete without mention of the minor arts by which it was extensively and colourfully adorned. These are considered below (see pages 52-6).

CHAPTER THREE

THE CLOISTER AND INFIRMARY COURT
OF THE BENEDICTINES AND REGULAR CANONS

THE cloister was the heart of the monastery. As we have seen, for sound practical reasons it lay normally on the south side of the church, and the following descriptions will assume that this is so; but there are a very substantial minority of cases where it was built on the north, for reasons already noted. Almost without exception, the cloister lay in the angle between the nave wall and the transept. Any other arrangement would have been much less convenient, as the normal position was easy of access to both eastern and western parts of the church and also to the outer court of the monastery. Rochester is almost unique in having a cloister east of the transept: this was not the original arrangement and was due to lack of space there.

In post-Conquest days the cloister consisted of the cloister garth, an open plot of ground generally square in shape, surrounded by four broad covered alleys with lean-to roofs. The latter were supported on their outer side by the adjacent walls of major monastic buildings, and on their inner side by low walls having small arcades, or rows of arches. This plan of the cloister perhaps had a Mediterranean origin, in some ways resembling the courts of Roman villas. The early cloister arcades were merely of wood, and even if of stone might be unglazed, as can be seen at Rievaulx [Pl. 14b]. But the English climate and common sense suggested that the arcade be glazed, and this seems to have been usual from the late thirteenth century onwards.

Fragments of remaining Cistercian cloister arcades such as that at Rievaulx are of simple design in accordance with the tradition of the order, and contrast markedly with those of rich houses of other orders such as Bridlington, where very fine twelfth-century fragments remain. Cloister arcades of the greater houses seem often to have been rebuilt, in a grand manner. This was supremely the case at Norwich [Pl. 16] and Gloucester [Pl. 15], the two most magnificent examples which survive in England.

After the Dissolution the cloister arcade served no useful purpose and was frequently demolished (see pages 137-8). Hence very few survive intact. It is significant that most of the few surviving examples come from our cathedral monasteries —notably Norwich, Chester, Worcester, Gloucester, Canterbury, Durham and Oxford. They also survived in a few other places, such as the royal chapel of Westminster. At Newstead in Sherwood and Lacock they were incorporated in the mansion that replaced the monastery—a highly unusual device.

The cloister alley next to the church was, of course, normally the northern one.

It had a door at either end. The eastern one was greatly used, being the main means of communication between the church and the cloister—the two places where the major part of the monk's day was spent. Because of its importance this door was often an extremely elaborate one as at Norwich [Pl. 17a] and Lilleshall [Pl. 13b]. The western door gave access to the church from the western alley of the cloister. It also was in frequent daily use and every Sunday was used by the convent in the ceremonial procession which passed along the three sides of the cloister away from the church. Ely has a richly carved door here, known as the Prior's Door (as we shall see, the prior's lodging was often in this area).

This cloister alley next to the church normally faced south and so enjoyed the maximum sunlight. Partially because of this, the alley served as a place of study; it was also used as a means of communication between the various parts of the monastery. On the southern side of this north alley were set small desks known as carrels, at which the monks could work. There are many documentary references to these, but none have remained, though at Gloucester we can see the alcoves in which they were set [Pl. 15]. At Durham there were three to each window of the cloister, each monk having his own; here they 'studied books on a desk all after noune unto evensong tyme. This was their exercise every daie.' There were strict regulations about the carrels being always left unlocked, so that any breach of the rule which forbade the monks to have private property could be easily detected. In some cases at least, the northern cloister alley was reserved for older monks, their juniors being in an adjacent alley. As the walk was so wide there was ample space for movement between the carrels and the outer wall. There was wainscotting in the cloister and sometimes the alleys were decorated with the coats of arms of benefactors.

The eastern walk of the cloister gave access to the major monastic buildings which lay on the eastern and southern sides of the cloister garth. At its northern end we sometimes find niches (perhaps intended for a statue and lights) as at Norwich and Hickling. Very frequently there are still to be seen remains of a recess for the cupboard which held some of the monastery's books including those being used in the cloister. At Lilleshall the cupboard was small and set completely in the wall [Pl. 13b]. Much more often it was a quite large wooden one set back in a stone recess, which is the only remaining sign of it, as at Fountains [Pl. 18b].

The south wall of the south transept normally formed one side of a narrow passage across the eastern side of the cloister buildings, as at Sherborne, Hexham, Kirkstall and Llanthony. This passage was commonly known as the *Slype*. At Durham we are told that it was 'a place for marchannts to utter ther waires', but the tolerance of laity on this side of the cloister was highly unusual, and was due to the old road to the church being on this side at Durham. Much more usually, as we shall see, the place in which the brethren could meet members of the outside world was in the western not the eastern range. But a place on the eastern side was useful when brethren had occasion to speak together, as they spent much time in this part of the cloister and in all of it conversation was forbidden. In smaller houses the slype could easily be used for this, though others might have a separate parlour elsewhere in the eastern range. In Cistercian houses the slype did not usually adjoin the transept but was lower down the eastern range, a book store and sacristy taking its place, as at Fountains [p. 145] and Tintern. This sacristy could communicate directly within the church by means of a door in the south transept.

A slype was principally used to give access to the area beyond the cloister range, notably to the monk's Cemetery which lay to the east and south of the chancel. At Durham we are told that 'after dinner daily monks went into the Scentorie (Cemetery) garth, wher all the Monnks were buried and thei did stand all bair heade a certain longe space praieng amongs the toumbes and throwghes for there brethren soules being buryed there'.

A word may here be said about places of burial in a medieval monastery. From an early stage it was usual to bury the founder of a monastery in a place of honour in the sanctuary, often on the north side of the high altar as at St. Bartholomew Smithfield where the founder's tomb remains. But in general, for some time after the Conquest, burial in church was not usual, though the Cistercians used their narthex for burials, as we see at Rievaulx. However, as time wore on, the practice became more usual, and by the time of the Dissolution the process of cluttering up the church with elaborate monuments was well under way. Most brethren of a monastery were buried east of the church in the cemetery garth, but specially important members might be interred in the chapter house (as at Rievaulx and at Jervaulx where tombs of early abbots can still be seen *in situ*), or in the east walk of the cloister as at Tintern and Coggeshall. At Rievaulx, by an astounding piece of lawlessness, the brethren established a shrine for their first abbot at the entrance to the chapter house. Where a parish altar existed, the land on the north side of the nave was used as a lay cemetery, entered from the church by a spacious porch. In some cases this porch was evidently also used in the marriage service, which partly explains its elaborate nature. Good examples are to be seen at Selby, Tewkesbury, Great Malvern and Bridlington, but the finest of all is at Malmesbury where it is on the south side, owing to the monastic cloister here being on the north. Signs of a simple Cistercian one are to be seen at Kirkstall.

In some cases the slype seems to have been converted to other uses in the Middle Ages, notably a sacristy, and perhaps occasionally into a library. Books were so very expensive that most monasteries only possessed several hundred and these could easily be stored in a few cupboards. It is known that four cupboards sufficed to hold the books of Titchfield abbey and five those of Llanthony by Gloucester. Since so little space was needed for a monastery's books, it is not surprising that for most of the Middle Ages English monasteries did not have a special room as a library. Books were kept in cupboards or presses in various parts of the monastery. The side of the cloister nearest the church and the eastern cloister alley were principal places for these, as they were convenient for the use of brethren who, as we have seen, studied in the cloister. From about the late fifteenth century we find some of the older and richer monasteries building special libraries. We have few details but they seem often to have been smallish rooms built over some part of the east side of the cloister or perhaps in the south transept, as at Ely where the chapter was kept in this area till recently. They would seem to have been mostly book-stores rather than libraries in the modern sense.

Some books were evidently kept permanently in the church, notably the books used during the services, certain of which were very large and awkward to move about. A few specially venerated books had covers of precious metals and jewels which might even incorporate relics. These might be displayed on the high altar but were also housed in a treasury. A selection of books suitable for reading at meals might be kept in the refectory. By the time of the Dissolution, in some places, books were also stored in the church, perhaps through lack of space elsewhere.

The principal building in the eastern range of the cloister was the *Chapter House*, used for a variety of conventual business, including a daily meeting to discuss spiritual faults and commemorate benefactors, the hearing of confessions and discussion of business matters.

The chapter house was generally rectangular and projected east of the eastern range as at Buildwas, Beaulieu, Forde and Kirkstall. In some cases it had an apsidal east end, as at Rievaulx, Llanthony, Castle Acre and Durham. At Worcester a circular chapter house was built about 1170, and within the next century various polygonal ones appeared, notably at Westminster, and on a smaller scale at Abbey Dore, Margam (both twelve-sided) and Cockersand; plans of others survive, as at Bolton and Carlisle. Since a good deal of communal business was done in the chapter house it was an advantage to have good audibility and visibility, and for this the polygonal plan may well have been found very suitable.

It was probably the same factor which led many houses to have a chapter house without aisles, as at Bristol, St. Frideswide's Oxford and Haughmond. But the Cistercian chapter houses generally had spacious aisles, as at Buildwas, Kirkstall and Furness [Pl. 18a]. When a chapter meeting was held, the brethren sat in seats ranged against the wall with the abbot placed in the middle of the east wall, facing west, and his brethren ranged to his right and left in order of seniority. In front was a lectern supporting the necrology, a book in which were recorded and read out daily the names of friends, benefactors and past members of the house who were to be commemorated in the worship of the day.

The chapter house was entered by an elaborate doorway set in its western wall, i.e. the one next to the cloister. It was usual for this door to have on either side large unglazed openings of similar design, as at Winchester, Haughmond, Hardham, Bristol and Laycock, occasionally continuing to ground level as at Fountains [Pl. 18b] but generally in the form of windows. It has been suggested that these openings were inserted to allow the participation in chapter business of lay brethren and laity, who were technically forbidden to enter a chapter meeting but who on certain special occasions might fruitfully be associated with it. Whilst this is feasible, it is more likely that they were made to furnish extra light, and the same reason probably explains the portico so often found in front of the chapter house. As this room was built across the breadth of the eastern range it would be very dark if there was only a door in its west wall, since, unless it had a portico, much of its north and south walls would be masked by the east range and would have to be windowless.

The cheapest remedy for this, and not a very satisfactory one was to put side openings in the west wall and as many windows as possible in the eastern part of the chapter house as at St. Frideswide Oxford. Rather better was to have a small portico, as at Furness or Fountains, which in effect meant that the chapter was moved somewhat to the east and so was rather less masked by the eastern range. Best of all was to make a large portico which engrossed the whole thickness of the range and thus left the chapter house completely unmasked and allowed the insertion of ample windows in north, east and south walls. This expensive solution we find at Chester and Westminster, and, of course, wherever a polygonal chapter house was planned, except in the primitive example at Worcester.

Adjoining the south side of the chapter house, and parallel to it, in non-Cistercian houses, might be a parlour or slype or both, and at about this point in the eastern range generally comes the *Day Stair*. This was a staircase to the dormitory mostly used by the brethren when they retired for a siesta after their midday meal, an admirable custom borrowed from the Mediterranean and very advisable in view of the early hour at which, as we shall see, the monastic day began. In some cases, as at Furness, this stair was in the eastern cloister alley, but generally it was built inside the eastern range, which saved space, though it might involve having rather a steep stair, as at Kirkstall, Chester, Cleeve and Tintern. These day stairs have often been demolished.

South of the chapter house and at right angles to it, ran a room which was probably a sort of common room. It was generally vaulted and had two aisles. In some cases, as at Furness and Fountains, this is of considerable length, because of the large number of monks in the house at the time it was built. At both these places the south end of this range ends in two bays which had open arches east, west and south, thus constituting a sort of *loggia*, and this feature occurs in the much smaller house of Ixworth where it evidently forms part of the superior's apartments.

Originally all members of a convent were expected to live together, but from the thirteenth century onwards it was usual for the head of the house to have private apartments. In some cases these had annexed to them a large guest hall and stood not in the eastern range, but either south-east of the cloister, or in its western range. When these apartments were built at the south end of the eastern range, as at Walsingham and Ixworth, they generally consisted merely of a living-room below and a bedroom and chapel above. In this position they were very accessible to the monks' refectory, and it may well be that the superior took a number of his meals there, at least at first. In other cases, like a headmaster or the captain of a ship, he lived largely apart from those over whom he had the heavy responsibility of ruling.

In this area was the *Treasury*, a strong-room in which were kept many of the valuables of the monastery and the deeds of its various properties. This had no uniform position but was fitted in where convenient. At Fountains it was on the first floor at the east end of the southern range. At Durham money was counted there and in it were kept 'the Evidences [deeds] of the house, and the Chapter seale, as also the Evidences of several gentlemen's lands in the country who thought them safer there than in their own custody'.

The whole, or almost the whole, of the upper floor of the eastern range was devoted to the *Dormitory*,* or Dorter, though this did not always cover the whole of the chapter house where this projected eastward of the range. A short passage at its northern end connected with the dormitory door in the south wall of the south transept. The dorter was a long room running north and south. Originally it was ordered that there should be no partitions between the beds. But in the later Middle Ages, a perfectly legitimate wish for rather more privacy frequently led to the construction of cubicles. The dormitory was lit by lines of small windows in the east and west walls—one to each bed—such cubicles, in effect 'bed-sitters', seem to have been sometimes used for study, perhaps when weather made the cloister too cold. At Durham each monk and novice had his own cubicle, 'a little chamber of wainscott, very close', with a boarded floor and a separate window and by it a 'desk to support their books for their study'. Bedclothes, like that insufficiently explored field, monastic underclothing, seem to have been plentiful, doubtless in view of the lack of heating. It is possible that in some cases the superior originally slept at the south end of the dormitory and gradually had his quarters partitioned off, which would account for the sort of arrangement we have seen to prevail at Walsingham and Ixworth.

Near the dorter, generally on its east side, but sometimes to the south, and parallel to it, was the *Reredorter*, or monastic lavatories, which were thus easily accessible at night. The cabinets were generally arranged along both sides of a long narrow building, with a passage in between; they were at first floor level, the ground floor area covering the great drain. The large arches supporting the walls of the reredorter sometimes remain, but often little is left.

The buildings of the eastern range have survived intact comparatively seldom, partly because they were not easily adapted for domestic purposes after the Dissolution, but partly because care was taken, by Henry VIII's minions, to destroy the main living quarters of the monks (see page 138), most of which were in this area. Dormitories seldom retain more than their outer walls, though those at

---

* In a very few places, principally big Benedictine houses on awkward sites such as Worcester, Norwich and Durham, the dormitory was on the first floor of the western range, evidently because the drainage of the reredorter or lavatory (which adjoined) could not be contrived on the east side.

Cleeve [Pl. 19b], Forde and Westminster abbey still remain, the last two much altered. Few chapter houses have survived outside ex-monastic cathedrals except in Cistercian ruins.

The Southern Cloister Range

The arrangement at the east end of the south side of the cloister varied somewhat. In some cases, as at Durham, Westminster, Worcester, Waltham and Walsingham there was another slype or passage leading to an outer court (which generally contained the infirmary). As it could not be lit along either of its long sides, because of adjoining buildings, it was dark.

In Cistercian houses this south-east corner was the normal position for the *Warming house*. In all monastic orders the amount of heating was strictly limited to certain parts of the monastery and certain times of the year. The Cistercians were particularly severe about this at first, but provided a special room to which, at strictly specified times, the brethren would resort for warmth. The finest example of this is at Fountains, where the room has enormous fireplaces in the east and west walls. Few other examples of warming houses have survived but a gigantic fireplace at Lanercost, at the west end of the undercroft of the refectory, shows that this part was partitioned off as a warming house. Though this lack of heating was certainly severe, it was to some extent remedied later. In any case it is to be remembered that some use was made of braziers and that the medieval monk seems to have worn a considerable amount of clothing.

The *Refectory* was, of course, the place where meals were taken and was sometimes known as the frater. It lay on the south side of the cloister. It is sometimes found on ground level, especially in Cistercian houses, and in houses in areas where stone was scarce, e.g. Walsingham, or where the site was solid rock, as at Chester, but quite often had a stone vaulted undercroft beneath it. In some large houses a passage might connect it with the Kitchen. This is shown on the old drawing of Christ Church Canterbury where there are also two hatches marked 'The window where dishes are served out' and 'The window through which plates are put out for washing'. The refectory is almost always rectangular in shape and in most Augustinian and Benedictine houses its longer axis was parallel to the cloister walk it adjoined, that is to say it ran east and west. Its south side was always well provided with lofty windows through which such sun as medieval England got would pour in as the brethren took their midday meal. It was a spacious building, so would take up most of the south side of the cloister and was entered by a door at its western end, inside which was a flight of steps up to the frater, in cases where the latter was at first-floor level. Cistercian houses were often populous in their early days and rather short of space in the cloister area, through having to provide considerable accommodation for lay brothers (see page 74) as well as monks. Accordingly they found more space by putting their refectories at right angles to the cloister walk, i.e. running north and south, with an entrance in the middle of the north wall of the building as at Rievaulx [Pl. 2a, cf. p. 145]. Merevale and Cleeve follow the older pattern, but the latter is an unusual case of extensive Cistercian rebuilding at a time when the size of the house was much reduced.

The refectory was large and spacious and was often not vaulted but roofed with timber. This was probably because of the bad effects of vaulting on acoustics, for though conversation was normally forbidden in the refectory, reading to the brethren from some edifying book during meals was specifically ordered. The reader stood in a pulpit at first-floor level that projected from near the right-hand far corner of the room (looking towards the far end from the entrance), and was reached by steps in the thickness of the wall. Good examples of this pulpit remain at Beaulieu, Chester [Pl. 14a], Carlisle and Walsingham. At Shrewsbury the pulpit stands oddly on its own, the rest of the refectory having disappeared.

On the far wall of the refectory, confronting all who came in, might be painted or sculptured a crucifix or similar subject. Only one English painted example of these survived till modern times, a painted one in the refectory of Cleeve, which has unhappily now been completely ruined. The refectory at Worcester has a sadly damaged but magnificent sculptured figure of Christ. Beneath the figure ran the high table which was set on a dais, similar to those in Oxford and Cambridge college halls. The head of the house sat in the centre with his back to the wall, and senior brethren on either side. Other tables were set against the long side walls, the brethren facing inwards and being seated in order of seniority. There were cupboards for the table-cloths and utensils at the bottom end of the refectory, and a wall hatch or hatches to the adjacent kitchen.

The *Cellar* (*cellarium*) or undercroft, which often existed below a monastic refectory, was almost invariably a stone-vaulted room of two bays. As it had no windows in the long wall next to the cloister and only slits (as at Hardham and probably St. German's) in the other one, with next to no lighting at either end, it was a distinctly gloomy place. Its main entrance was at the western or kitchen end. Its purpose seems to have varied somewhat, but probably it was chiefly used as a store, amongst other things, for the poorish beer that was the staple drink of medieval England. It was certainly close to the kitchen and this would be why at Titchfield, at least, it was used to provide additional table accommodation for special festivities. Sometimes it was partitioned as at Lanercost (see page 34). Examples of cellars with refectories above survive at Durham, Worcester and Carlisle, and ones where the refectory above has been demolished at Herringfleet, Lanercost [Pl. 20b] and Torre.

Near the refectory was the *Laver* (*Lavatorium*), the monks' washing place. The standard of cleanliness attained by the monks was much higher than most of their contemporaries, and their firm regulations on this subject show a devotion to ablutions not unreminiscent of public schools or the armed forces. To the laver the brethren came to wash at the beginning of the day and before meals. Because of this, it was always close to both the refectory and the dormitory; near it were receptacles for towels.

The most usual type of laver was a long shallow trough having pipes with taps above it, the whole being generally set in the refectory wall under a blind arcade. In cases where the refectory was set at right angles to the cloister alley, there would be a trough in the wall on both sides of the refectory door as at Fountains [Pl. 11b]. Where the refectory ran parallel to the cloister alley, its entrance was at the west end, and the laver was often a single trough in the wall to the east of the door as at Peterborough or occasionally at the south-western corner of the cloister as at Norwich and Westminster. The taps and pipes were quickly pillaged at the time of the Dissolution and none now remain, but the trough with its arcade or the arcade alone is frequently still visible as at Chester, Fountains, Whalley and Hexham. At Gloucester a laver of this type was built, not in the usual position, but jutting out from the inner wall of the alley into the cloister garth; perhaps it was thought undesirable to break the internal lines of the superb cloister.

The second type of laver was a polygonal one which projected into the garth from the cloister alley. A classic description of one of these is given in the *Rites of Durham*. It was 'for the Monncks to washe ther hands and faces at, being maid in forme round, covered with lead and all of marble saving the verie uttermost walls. Within the which walls you may walke around about the Laver of marble, having many little cunditts or spouts of brasse, with xxiii cockes of brasse rownd about it.' This type was uncommon, perhaps because of the expense, but remains of those from Sherborne (now in the market-place), Much Wenlock and St. Nicholas Exeter are worthy of note. Christ Church Canterbury had a special 'shaving house' near the Laver, but this was probably a rare luxury. The *Rites* also tells us that 'adjoyninge to the est side of the cundit door, ther did Ring a bell to geve warning, at a leaven of the clock, for the Monncks to cumme wash and dyne'. At Westminster this was done by a gong which still survives [Pl. 28c]; the place where it hung, by the old refectory door, is still visible.

Cistercian monks, and to a lesser extent other Benedictines, had strict rules against eating flesh meat, but these were later relaxed, and, in some cases at least, an additional room was built where certain brethren could eat meat. At Canterbury about 1300 a special room was built, there called the *Deportum*, but more generally known as the *Misericord*. Here, ampler meals including flesh seems to have been available, evidently for convalescent monks; these were bound to go to church or cloister after meals and not 'while away their time with idle tales and wanton jollity'! The archaeology of this misericord requires further study; it seems to have been a simple rectangular room near the cloister.

As we have seen, the conventual *Kitchen* adjoined the refectory. It was generally on its western side. It had a series of troughs and hearths set against its outer wall and often a central hearth with a chimney above. For this layout a polygonal plan was quite suitable, but rectangular ones were also common. This type of kitchen has very seldom survived except in plan. A polygonal one is shown on the old Canterbury drawing and has an appendage marked 'The room where fish is washed'. At Ely the Norman kitchen had a square plan and lay to the north of the refectory to connect easily with the great guest hall. But many others must have resembled the abbot's kitchen at Glastonbury [see Pl. 22b and page 41 below] and Durham.

Even less remains of the subsidiary domestic buildings which clustered round the kitchen. Sometimes two or more of these would be under a single roof. The main ones were generally a bakehouse where bread was made, a brew-house for brewing beer, a buttery where drink was stored and a pantry for food. A boulting house where corn was sieved in a boulting hutch is also frequently mentioned. The surveys of English monasteries at the Dissolution threw invaluable light on the minor buildings, often giving not only their names but an inventory of their contents. Thus at Dieulacres a nunnery in Staffordshire, there was recorded *inter alia* a buttery with five table-cloths, five napkins, three pewter salt-cellars, eight hogsheads, six candlesticks, one old chest and one short trestle board with two trestles. The larder's equipment included one trough, four (table) boards and two tubs. The kitchen had five large brass pots, four small pans, one cauldron, three spits, one skillet (cooking vessel), two cupboards, one fire-fork, one flesh hook, one frying pan, two cressets, one gridiron, thirty-eight plates, dishes and saucers, one mortar and pestle, two chopping knives, one dressing knife, a cupboard, one grater, two dressing boards, two warming pans, 'chafing dishes' and sconces of brass. The brew-house had three ladles, one wash-tub, twelve 'kelers of ledde', two vats, one table before the oven and a cistern. The boulting house had a boulting hutch and 'certain old troughs and tubs'.

Quite often there was a slype or passage on the west side of the refectory and leading to the outer court as at Durham and Gloucester and Norwich. The *Rites of Durham* shows us there was a porter there to guard the entrance.

The Western Range

In a few English Cistercian houses we find a long alley adjoining the usual western cloister alley of the monks on the west side, and running parallel to it. No English example survives perfect, but there are considerable remains of the one at Byland, and traces of those at Kirkstall and Abbey Dore. This alley would allow free access to all parts of the ground floor of the western range without disturbing the privacy of the monks. At Byland one side of this alley has a long series of niches, which may have been intended as seats, perhaps for use in time of recreation. However, this additional alley seems to have been rare.

Among the Cistercians the purpose of the western range differed from that of other orders. A notable feature of Cistercian life in its early centuries, was the very extensive use it made of lay brethren (see page 74). In their largest monasteries these were numbered in scores and even, for a time, in hundreds. Their principal employment was in the manual labour necessary to maintain the monastic estates but they had also a modified round of prayer. They thus required a place of worship and a good deal of accommodation. The Cistercian order assigned to the lay brethren the part of the conventual church west of the rood screen. This was free from the parochial responsibilities of some Benedictine and Augustinian churches, since, perhaps without exception, Cistercian abbeys were founded on sites where no parish church existed. For their domestic accommodation the lay brethren were normally given the western range of the cloister which tended to be long and was subdivided into appropriate sections.

In such cases the upper floor was largely given over to dormitory accommodation which might be reached direct by a stair on the western side as at Fountains. There was a night door leading directly into the church, like that of the monks, a good example of which may be seen at Fountains. Here the magnificent lower floor of the western range [Pl. 21] is the finest of its kind in the country and perhaps in Europe; the removal of its original partitions has given it a glory not fully displayed in the Middle Ages. The part of the lower floor nearest the church seems to have been a common room, and south of it was the lay brothers' refectory. In general, the kitchen at the south-western angle of the cloister would serve both the refectory of the monks and that of the lay brethren. The reredorter of the lay brothers was generally at the extreme southern end of the western range as at Furness and Fountains.

As time went on, the number of Cistercian lay brethren appears to have shrunk to very small proportions and much of their accommodation was put to other uses. What these were is not always clear, and they were probably not always uniform. But in some cases living accommodation for seculars was provided in the form of small apartments, a few of which had a fireplace. Occasionally, as at Coggeshall, in the later Middle Ages, we find unwanted domestic accommodation (in this case a building south-east of the cloister) being let out to seculars, but it is unlikely that this would have been done on any large scale with buildings that adjoined the cloister. Normally a passage across this western range would provide access from the cloister to the outer court and would have a parlour near by. By a curious irony the western range at Rievaulx is far smaller than was usual in such a case, though the number of lay brethren recorded there is the largest known in any English monastery; considerable accommodation for them must have existed somewhere else.

The Augustinian and Benedictine orders had only a very small number of lay brethren. It is not clear where they lodged. In some cases, at least, they also may have lived in part of the western range, but they would only have required a small part of the space there available.

What was the rest used for? In a number of the small and medium-sized houses, principally it would seem for guest accommodation and for the apartments of the head of the house, who in these cases was usually a prior. The prior's apartment normally had at least a living room with a bedroom and private chapel overhead. A good example of a small set of rooms of this type remains at the southern end of the range of the little Augustinian priory of Michelham. It has a handsome dining-room adjoining the canons' kitchen with a fine room above.

The head of the house was expected to entertain important lay guests at his own table, so that a substantial living-room such as we have at Michelham was by no means purely for the prior's personal use. Sometimes these guests might be very numerous, as when the king or some great baron with his family and retinue descended on the unfortunate monastery or when an archbishop or bishop arrived with a swarm of officials about him, to carry out a visitation. For most monasteries many days must have passed without the presence of such outsiders, but due arrangements had to be made to receive them and in a rich house on a major road accommodation for travellers absorbed much monastic space. Because of this, in some houses the prior's apartments in the western range often adjoined a large dining hall, where he could play the host in time of need.

We have a full account of this arrangement at Bridlington priory, though all the buildings concerned have gone. They were largely built at the injunction of the archbishop of York, who used them as a base when visiting the eastern side of his far-flung diocese. Here, at the north end of the western range, was 'a great Chamber where the Priour alwayes dyned', with a small bedroom, chapel and closet adjoining. Then came the great hall and beyond it 'butterie and Pantrie under one Office' and 'a chamber called the Audytors Chamber' (perhaps a sort of estate office where accounts could be paid), two small parlours and three small servants' bedrooms.

What seems to have been a magnificent wooden hall on the west side of the cloisters was demolished at Great Malvern a century ago. An interesting example on a small scale survives in the west range of the little house of nuns at St. Katharine's Exeter. Here we have a hall with a private apartment on the church side and the traditional pierced screen leading to the kitchen and allied offices on the other. An example of the same rare thirteenth-century woodwork remains at Muchelney, and at Little Bricett a most interesting screen of this period, perhaps separating the prior's rooms from the hall, has recently been found. Quite often the hall was on the first floor, as a ground-floor room would have been dark owing to its long eastern wall being next to the cloister and its northern and southern ends being blocked by other buildings. In such cases the ground floor was sensibly given over to a parlour or parlours and a collection of bedrooms.

The hall of this western range is of a type commonly found in domestic and baronial use at this time and which has survived in the older colleges of Oxford and Cambridge. It had a high table at one end, behind which a door leads to the private room. In later days big projecting oriel windows on either side provided abundance of light and convenient spaces for tables from which the food could be served. Tables for lesser folk ran at right angles to the high table, lengthways down the hall, and at the bottom end were two doors, beyond which lay the draughty but ubiquitous 'screens passage'. This went across the full breadth of the building and had doors at either end, sometimes reached from outside by steps. On the far side of the passage was the kitchen with the pantry and buttery, two small rooms separated by the passage to the kitchen. Where this large hall occurs (and we find very frequent mention of it in Dissolution Surveys) the adjacent prior's lodging proper generally lies on the side near the church. This allowed the hall to adjoin the general monastic kitchen, and had the further advantage of making it more convenient for the prior to join his brethren in church. In a few cases his bedroom was perhaps on a second floor, traces of a lofty chamber remaining here at Lanercost, Bolton, and Newstead.

Quite often an external stair adjoined the west side of the western range and led up to the hall on the first floor, as in the magnificent western range of Bradenstoke priory [Pl. 22a], now destroyed. Almost always a slype led across the range at ground level to provide easy access to the cloister from the outer court. Near it were guest rooms and a parlour where visitors might converse with each other or with the brethren in time of need; the doors to these two could be seen at Bradenstoke [Pl. 22a]. The guest rooms can seldom now be identified individually, but their existence is very amply witnessed by the Dissolution surveys. Thus the Suffolk Surveys show us that at Herringfleet, evidently in the western range, on the first floor *inter alia* were two rooms:

> 'The chamber called the guests' hung with old 'steyned clothes' (painted cloth) a bed, table, settee, two old chairs, two old chests and a form. An anonymous room next to it had a bed and an old chair and hangings of 'old painted cloth', the whole valued at 3s. 9d. Beneath these apartments was the parlour furnished in the same spartan way. There was also 'another chamber called the guests chamber' against the hall and next to it a small room with two beds and sets of bedclothes 'all old and ner worne'.

Lilleshall being richer and in an area where accommodation was very scarce, had appreciably more guest rooms. There were two beds each in Dorrell's Chamber, 'the inner chamber', 'the long chamber', one in 'the chamber at the Hall door', three in 'the newe lodging' (perhaps new accommodation adjoining the western range), two in 'the Knight's Lodging', 'the Second Chamber in the Knight's Lodging' and in 'The Third Chamber in the Knight's Lodging'. The Parlour had a table, three chairs, a form and 'olde paynted clothes' all valued at 12d. These surveys often give a picture of very simple living with much antiquated furniture and bed linen.

At the Dissolution it frequently happened that these smaller rooms and the great hall, where it existed, disappeared. But in quite a large number of cases the prior's apartments were deliberately preserved, (see page 139) as at Wigmore and Castle Acre, where they run westward from the north-west corner of the cloister, an unusual position.

The Infirmary Range

Outside the main cloister range lay the *Infirmary*, sometimes called the Farmery. Its principal use was for the sick, but here lived also the elderly monks, who could no longer maintain the arduous round of the normal monastic routine, and were allowed a régime that gave them more sleep and better food. The infirmary also housed those monks who had recently experienced the slightly doubtful benefits of blood-letting. Medieval medicine was distinctly primitive and attached great value to periodic blood-letting; the patient had a vein opened and a quantity of blood removed to get rid of evil humours, and was then allowed a short period of recuperation.

In the largest monasteries the infirmary hall had side aisles and a high vaulted roof. It often ran east and west. The beds were set along the sides of the hall and sometimes partitioned off. Probably the main aisle was normally unencumbered except for a fireplace and was used for meals and recreation. At the western end might be the lavatories, at the other projected the chapel and perhaps a store-room. The rite for the dying monk was curiously elaborate, ending with his anointing. The Cistercians provided that the cloths used in the anointing should be burnt in a special aumbry, a rare example of which survives at Furness, where one of the finest surviving infirmary chapels remains intact. Here the brethren who were not confined to bed could hear mass and say their office. Sometimes the infirmary was an unaisled rectangular room with a wall fireplace, like the early infirmary of Furness abbey, later converted into the abbot's house. At the Dissolution this building was very seldom preserved intact. But aisled buildings had often been subdivided in medieval times and could easily be made into small residences. At Peterborough and Ely the centre aisle was written off, and converted into a road.

Where space permitted, the infirmary seems generally to have been built in the quiet area south-east of the main cloister, away from the main gate. But it could be elsewhere.

Though the smallest monasteries would only have a single kitchen for all their brethren, a number of larger ones had at least two—the conventual kitchen which we have already mentioned, and another which often served both the infirmary and the private lodging of the head of the house. This second kitchen is found regularly in Cistercian houses, though few have left any extensive remains. The foundations of the polygonal one at Furness have still the bases of its troughs, fireplaces and the chute from which rubbish was dispatched to the stream below. At Glastonbury, however, the abbot's kitchen [Pl. 22b] remains intact and is perhaps the finest in England. It is of the usual polygonal type, with eight sides, and has a central lantern. Here the richness of the house and the number of the guests would justify a special kitchen for the abbot alone, for his duties in the field of hospitality were evidently very considerable.

As we have seen, it was very common in small and medium-sized houses for the superior to have a private set of rooms in the main cloister range, generally either at the south end of the eastern range or, more often, in some part of the western range. But in the larger houses, especially the Benedictines and to a lesser extent the Cistercians, we find the superior's apartments constitute a distinct building, nearly always close to the conventual dormitory and reredorter. An early example of this is the thirteenth-century abbot's house at Kirkstall. It is a simple, rectangular building south-east of the cloister close to the infirmary, with a little kitchen between the two. It has three floors with the main hall on the first floor. Here, as at Michelham and other places, the upper room has been the superior's parlour, the one beneath it the dining-room where he entertained guests. The destroyed prior's house at St. Bartholomew's Smithfield had been built shortly before the Dis-solution and adjoined the east end of the church with a window through which mass could be seen without entering the church! It was connected by a passage to the dorter and infirmary.

At Ely much of the prior's apartments remain, including an exquisite little chapel south of the cloister range, and a small private kitchen. It was often found con-venient to have the infirmary and the superior's lodging ranged round a common courtyard, but quite often the two are unconnected, though both tend to be found south or east of the main cloister court. At Haughmond [Pl. 2b] is one of the best surviving examples of a small infirmary, a handsome hall with fine airy windows looking south; the abbot's lodging adjoining it at its eastern end. Here there are not two kitchens, but a single large one (whose vast chimney stacks still remain [Pl. 2b]), which connects with the infirmary at one end and the conventual refectory at the other, a rare but clearly convenient plan when, as here, the cloister court and infirmary court were in alignment.

The above pages have aimed to give a picture of the sort of buildings to be found in most Augustinian and Benedictine monasteries. Space does not allow anything more than the briefest mention of the ways in which very small monasteries differed from those considered. It will be obvious that the not insignificant number of English religious houses which had around half a dozen members, could not afford and did not require the elaborate complex of buildings such as we have sketched. Little research has been done on these minor houses, but it is clear that they had a highly simplified version of the elaborate architectural layout to be found in richer houses. In some cases at least, a simple L-shaped building may have sufficed for the main needs of the house, one wing having a refectory, dormi-tory and living rooms, another the chapel. Some such scheme seems to have pre-vailed at the interesting little priory of Peterstone and perhaps at the insufficiently appreciated Bedfordshire priory of Bushmead near Eaton Socon. At Alnesbourn there is what looks like the remains of a small L-shaped domestic block and a free standing chapel of stone, very largely rebuilt. Such houses would have a small enclosure with a modest gatehouse similar to that at Letheringham, and most of the subsidiary buildings already mentioned built according to their minor needs. In some cases these were made at least partly of wood, especially in south-eastern areas where stone was expensive.

A large number of these smaller houses were not independent but were mere cells of mother houses. Amongst these were the so-called alien priories—English monasteries nearly all founded as daughter houses of French monasteries in the century after the Norman Conquest of 1066. Frequently a wealthy parish church was the nucleus of their endowment and would provide financial support for the handful of brethren maintained there. In such cases they would normally have a rather more elaborate church than usual, the east end having a capacious chancel where the brethren might say their offices. But even at the start their conventual buildings were small and simple and if, as often happened, the brethren were withdrawn before the Dissolution (see pages 121-2) and the place let out, these buildings were very likely to disappear. Churches or parts of them occasionally survive. At Isleham survives the fine church of brethren from St. Jacut de la Mer.

A final point may here be noted in passing—the building changes which often occurred when, in the later Middle Ages, the size of a convent had been drastically reduced. Up to the opening of the fourteenth century the number of inmates in English monasteries was well maintained, but the Black Death in the middle of the century seems to have cut the figure by about half. Slowly a considerable improvement was effected but less than half the gap had been closed by the time of the Dissolution. The gains were unevenly spread and some of the small houses were sadly reduced.

Under such circumstances it was natural enough to reduce the size of their buildings, especially if (as happened not unfrequently in the fourteenth and fifteenth centuries) the burden of upkeep had proved too much for minor communities and some of their buildings had become semi-ruinous. There are various signs of this architectural tightening of the belt, though they do not follow any stock pattern. At Cleeve some unusual Cistercian rebuilding produced a comparatively small refectory running parallel to the cloister, at Creake abbey after a fire, various portions of the church were walled off and at Bourne there is some evidence that the canons built a smallish cloister adjoining the chancel in the fifteenth century. However, we must not think of the monastic orders in England being in anything like a state of architectural decline in the fifteenth and early sixteenth centuries. There is abundant evidence of much rebuilding and building on a scale that was often adequate and sometimes grand. The prosperous century before the time of the Dissolution saw a building achievement fully comparable with those of earlier days.

CHAPTER FOUR

THE BUILDINGS OF THE FRIARS, THE CARTHUSIANS AND THE NUNS. THE MINOR ARTS

THE Augustinian and Benedictine orders whose buildings we have considered above, constituted some two-thirds of the total monastic population of medieval England and included almost all the very wealthy houses of the times. The minority we have not yet considered was made up of several elements, which are worthy of attention if only because of their special characteristics. These were largely due to their programme of life differing markedly from that of the old Augustinian and Benedictine orders.

Much the most numerous and important orders not yet considered were the various orders of Friars (see pages 87-94), which brought a very modern strain into medieval monastic life. Their principal aim was evangelisation in the modern sense, strengthening popular religion by personal intervention, preaching the Word of God and administering the Sacraments of the church. Associated with this was a considerable attachment to poverty, a word the friars interpreted much more severely than the older orders. In general, the only property they held was their own monastery. Tithes, churches, lands, rents, secular buildings were all forbidden, and for their livelihood the friars relied on alms, bequests and such small produce as they could cultivate for themselves.

At first their buildings were expected to be very simple (they were often of wood rather than stone) and elaborate decoration such as stained-glass windows was forbidden. However, as with the Cistercians, experience fairly quickly suggested that this sort of artistic puritanism was not very edifying. The medieval world thought in terms of artistic splendour and the urge of the faithful to give beauty to the churches of the friars they so valued would not be denied. Soon after the death of St. Francis (the founder of the Franciscan order), spontaneous love of his memory had swept people into erecting at Assisi the great basilica which bore his name, and which quickly became one of the greatest artistic treasure houses of a land rich in artistic treasures. Although some conservatives fought a rearguard action against this tendency, by the late thirteenth century it was clear they had lost the battle. However, their defeat was not complete, for to the end the architecture of the friars retained a real simplicity. Not for them were the massive churches of the great Benedictine abbeys with their long but largely useless naves, and their elaborate transepts, towers and façades. Down to the days of the Reformation everything was on a modest scale.

The site of a medieval house of friars was almost always very small, partly because of their idea of poverty, partly because almost all the houses started in crowded towns, where space was scarce and difficult to obtain. Friars often originally took up residence in the slums, and when experience showed the need for more room they found this difficult to acquire.

Their first living accommodation were simple dwelling-houses which in England were almost all of wood. The early buildings they added were equally mostly of wood, like the chapel constructed for the Franciscans at Cambridge which a contemporary described as 'so very poor that a carpenter in one day made and set up fifteen pairs of beams' (by which latter phrase is evidently meant the whole of the chapel rafters). Whilst the fact that here the house was next to the jail and that there was but one entrance for jailers and friars very understandably proved 'intolerable'. This was in or about 1224. A century later things had changed considerably at Cambridge and elsewhere. The great increase of numbers of friars, the crowds that flocked to their sermons, the growing wish for burial in their churches, all made a more capacious site essential, and led also to more permanent churches. But the precincts of friaries remained small in comparison with those of other orders. Largish sites were exceptional and occur in one or two minor towns where the scarcity of alms required augmentation by agricultural self-help. Exceptional also was the Franciscan house of Walsingham situated outside what was little more than an overgrown village. Here the brethren apparently augmented their income by maintaining a large guest house for pilgrims to the illustrious shrine of Our Lady of Walsingham, down the street.

There were four main orders of Friars: Franciscan, Dominican, Augustinian and Carmelite. A new stage in our knowledge of their architecture here opened with Mr. A. R. Martin's survey of that of the English Franciscans, and recent work has tended to show that the other orders of friars largely built on similar lines. Unfortunately, no systematic study of the architecture of the Augustinian and Carmelite friars has yet been made.

There is the very considerable scarcity of architectural remains of English houses of friars, their buildings having very frequently been demolished to make place for others. Nowhere in England, for example, can be seen a complete friar's cloister and we have only one complete church. In far too many cases nothing or next to nothing remains. Thus none of the six houses of friars at York has left significant remains and the same is true of the London houses of friars (apart from the nave of the Austin friars, bombed out in World War II). Gone also are the great churches of Dominicans and Franciscans at Cambridge, which the University unsuccessfully sought to secure for its own use at the time of the Dissolution. Of sixty-one Franciscan houses in England a mere thirteen have left appreciable remains.

There is no reason to believe that the houses of friars had generally an extensive outer court or courts. They had no great estates to manage and most of them had not great hosts of visitors to accommodate. Nor did their gatehouse need a room for the manorial court, as they could not own manors, and largely lived in towns where manors did not exist. One of the few friars' gatehouses to survive is that of the Carmelites at Burnham Norton [Pl. 24a] which illustrates the architectural simplicity we have noted. This is a minute building, being nothing more than an arched passage-way with a small room over it. The west wall of the church stands only a few paces away, though the friary stood in the open country where plenty of space was available had a courtyard been desired. No doubt this sort of arrangement was usual elsewhere.

The friars' churches were the first English churches to be built with public preaching as a major consideration. Because of the throng of laity that frequented them, it was useful to have their main (west) door of the church on or near a public street. Accordingly often the west end of the church adjoins the road, as was the case with the Dominican and Franciscan churches at Cambridge. In some of the great towns of Italy (the richest and most populous part of Western Europe in the later Middle Ages) the friars drew enormous congregations and built for them astoundingly large churches such as we can still see at Siena, Florence and Venice. These were often enormous rectangular halls with chapels at the east end and sides. By comparison medieval English towns were very small affairs, with the exception of a minute handful which included London and York. Hence friars' buildings here were on a comparatively small scale. The London Franciscan house was much larger than most other friars' churches in England but smaller than many Augustinian and Benedictine houses.

The earliest surviving friars' church in England is probably the Franciscan building at Lincoln. This was a simple, unaisled, rectangular structure (which retains most of its original roof) built towards the middle of the thirteenth century. It was originally of one storey and was intended to be longer than at present. But the extremely cramped site prevented extension and doubtless to utilise existing space more fully a vaulted undercroft or crypt was inserted a little later. It measures 101 feet by 21 feet 6 inches.

By the time this building was finished, the prosperity of Lincoln was clearly on the wane. Had it been otherwise this interesting little building would almost certainly have been rebuilt like most of its contemporaries on the interesting plan which English houses of the order quickly developed, and which seems to have been much used by other orders of friars here. This interesting native plan, first definitely established by Mr. Martin's work, had a simple unaisled choir (normally rectangular), and a large nave, generally with two aisles though a few houses had only a single aisle. Separating these two units and giving access to each was a small transverse passage known as 'the walking place', over which was a very simple belfry tower [Pl. 23a].

The eastern chapel was used for the brethren's private use. It had an altar at the east end and choir stalls arranged in the usual fashion, with a simple sedilia as can be seen at the Franciscan chapel at Chichester. At Atherstone the eastern chapel and tower of the Austin friars survive. A fine Franciscan example of the eastern chapel survives at Chichester [Pl. 24b] and an odd polygonal-ended one at Winchelsea. It is notable that transepts occur very rarely and then only singly on the side away from the cloister.

The 'walking place' gave access not only to both eastern and western parts of the church, but sometimes also to the cloister and to the public street. In London the little street known as Church Entry was originally a continuation of the line of the 'walking place' of the Dominican church at Ludgate, and led from it to Carter Lane. The tower over the walking place was inevitably a small one and was not meant to support the great peal of bells usual in great Benedictine houses. It was often of wood, but some attractive examples in stone have survived, notably Franciscan ones at Coventry, Richmond (North Riding), King's Lynn, a Dominican one at Coventry, and an Augustinian one at Atherstone.

The nave of the church had slender pillars and ample lighting and was primarily intended for preaching, though there might be side altars in the aisles. The one major friars' church to survive almost intact in England is the superb Dominican church at Norwich [Pl. 23a], now known as St. Andrew's Hall and used for secular purposes. Its magnificent nave with its wide centre aisle [Pl. 23b] must have been admirably suited to the work of the Order of Preachers, and gives us some indication of the nature of the great friars' churches that formerly existed in almost every major town of medieval England. This church is some 254 feet long with the nave 77 feet wide. The largest of all the friars' churches was evidently the Franciscan church of London, 300 feet long and 90 feet broad. There were usually two or three altars against the screen that enclosed the east end of the nave, and others elsewhere. The Dominican church at Salisbury had no less than twelve side altars and 'one large altar with St. Barbara in the midst'. Various people of high and low degree were buried in friars' churches but in England next to nothing of their tombs has survived.

The Conventual Buildings of the Friars

There is very little precise information that can be given concerning the layout of the conventual buildings of the Friars, partly through lack of evidence, but principally because of the complete lack of system which inevitably prevailed here on the awkward and cramped sites with which many houses of friars started. At the end of the thirteenth century a famous Dominican noted the uniformity of plan in older orders and the disunity of his own order—'we have nearly as many different plans and arrangements of our buildings and churches as there are priories'. In our own day Mr. Martin comments to the same effect—'In the planning of the domestic buildings of a friary, a marked disregard of the normal monastic arrangement is frequently noticeable. The principal buildings were arranged round the cloister without any well-defined rule, while the position of the cloister itself varied considerably in different houses and was no doubt determined by the general topography of the site.'

In general, it may be said that we often find a rough resemblance to the plan of the older orders in so far as the main cloister is concerned. The same major buildings, the refectory, dormitory and chapter house are usually found there, frequently in the same sort of position. But we do not find a fixed infirmary court and the whole scheme of things is on a much smaller scale.

The friars' cloisters show various points of difference from those of older orders. Thus the Franciscan cloister frequently did not directly adjoin the church wall, but was separated from it by a narrow court. This occasionally appears elsewhere, and was probably mainly done to allow the insertion in the church wall of larger windows than would otherwise have been feasible. The cloister itself was frequently very much smaller and narrower than in the older orders. Smaller because the buildings around it were smaller, narrower because in the Franciscan, and probably in other orders of friars, the cloister does not seem to have been used as a place of study, a function for which its often dark and poky nature made it ill-suited. Another unusual feature was that quite commonly in houses of friars the first-floor buildings of the cloister range projected some way over the cloister walk, evidently so as to economise in space. The cloisters themselves were often simple affairs of wood or stone sometimes unvaulted. Nearly all of them have disappeared. But fragments of good Franciscan ones remain at Yarmouth and Ware, of a Dominican one at Norwich, and a Carmelite one at Coventry.

As with the older orders, the chapter house is frequently near the church in the eastern range. It was usually a simple rectangular room and sometimes retained the old habit of having a rather grand door flanked by two unglazed windows. The refectory turns up in various positions, but does not differ notably from that of the older orders and likewise has a refectory pulpit. The best surviving example is that of the Greyfriars at Canterbury; another can be seen at Gloucester (Franciscan friars).

An important feature of the Dominican ideal was the stress laid on study and this had interesting architectural repercussions. The Dominicans seem to have quickly instituted in the dormitories a series of small 'bed-sitters' in which certain brethren could both read and sleep, small alcoves in the outer wall replacing the old carrels already noted as places of study. These did not exist in dormitories of the older orders, at least till later days, and then probably only on a small scale. The Dominican cubicles were allotted to select students, other brethren, including novices and lay brethren, sleeping in the rest of the dormitory, which was laid out in the ancient communal manner. The dormitory of the Dominican house at Gloucester is an almost unique surviving example of this type of dormitory and is therefore of major interest. One end of it was used as a library. For much of their medieval history the friars had a keen interest in learning and cared for their libraries accordingly. A fourteenth-century traveller in England tells us how he visited friars' libraries here and found 'heaped up amidst the utmost poverty, the utmost riches of wisdom'. To what extent the other orders of friars shared this Dominican habit of combining library and dormitory is not clear.

Little can be said of the buildings outside the main cloister court which were even more haphazardly arranged than the others. The head of the house had a simple apartment of his own and in some houses another was reserved for the local head of the order, the provincial prior. The infirmary, like the chapter house, was evidently on a notably simpler scale than those of the older orders. Few remain but there are probable examples at Hulne (Carmelite) and Cardiff (Dominican), a curious structure at Clare (Austin) south-east of the main cloister may have served this purpose. The picturesque little building set up across the stream by the Franciscans at Canterbury is thought to have been a guest house originally. The Dominicans, like the Austin canons, frequently had guest accommodation in the western range of the cloister, but at Canterbury their guest hall was an independent building cut off from it by the stream. What may be another guest hall survives in the Dominican house at Boston, a long building next to the street with three early fireplaces. Some friars' houses in the big towns seem to have been frequently used as hotels by lay magnates, who must have been a considerable nuisance.

The Carthusians

As we shall see, the Carthusian order was small and strict. Although it never had more than nine houses in England and most of these have left little or no remains, its architecture was so unusual as to be worthy of note. The Carthusians were essentially hermits living in separate cells and meeting only on comparatively rare occasions for common life and worship.

The main feature of their monasteries was a great court round most of which was built a string of tiny separate abodes for the brethren. These consisted of a tiny rectangular plot of land completely enclosed, on the inner side of which was built a small stone hut, entered by a small door in the wall next to the cloister alley. Beyond, nearer the main entrance to the monastery, lay a second court which housed the lay brethren. The monks spent most of their time in their private cells and did not aim at an elaborate round of common worship. Because of this and because of the strict poverty of the order, the churches of the order were minute by contemporary standards, and of at least Franciscan simplicity. The obvious position for the church was on the side of the main court nearest to the outer court, so as to allow easy access to it from both. It was so small that it did not take up more than part of one side of the court, and the space east of it in two of our main examples was occupied by additional cells and a chapter house, near which was the laver and the brethren's entrance to their choir. In the same range might be a

5

parlour and a slype. The three sides of the main court furthest from the outer court were completely given over to cells, which stood cheek by jowl the whole way round.

Much the best preserved remains of an English Carthusian house is the priory of Mount Grace near Northallerton (North Riding). The outline of the two courts is clearly to be seen and considerable remains of the main court survive, notably much of the church (to which a simple belfry of the friars' type was added) and the inner wall of the court. Here can be seen the entrances to the cells and by each door a little L-shaped hatch in which dishes of food were placed in due season [Pl. 25a].

The best documented house of the order is the London Charterhouse, whose history is known in a quite exceptional degree of detail. There has survived a curious drawing of the main court, showing each cell duly lettered in traditional Carthusian fashion and a great conduit in the centre of the court whence pipes run out with water to the cells (see page 51). At Witham (Som.) the chapel of the lay brethren survives. At Hinton (Som.) the main outlines of the monastery have recently been established and several buildings remain intact including the simple frater and the chapter house, above which is a room with recessed windows that may have been the library. By an unusual arrangement, houses of the Carthusian order had an altar in the chapter house; traces of this can be seen at Hinton, whilst the present altar in the London Charterhouse chapel is on the exact site of that which formerly existed in the medieval chapter house.

In conclusion, a word may here be said about the buildings of medieval English nunneries, though these were never very numerous or important, and have suffered at least as heavy destruction as English houses of friars.

One of the curious and major differences between medieval and modern monasticism is that in the former the vast majority of religious houses belonged to communities of men, whereas nowadays the reverse is the case (on this see pages 83-5). With a handful of exceptions, English medieval nunneries were not rich and many of them were frequently living in penury or near it. This poverty means that their buildings were often on the small size and that not a few of them continued to build in wood long after stone had become usual in houses of men. A curious feature sometimes found in nuns' churches is a double nave, one for parishioners, one for nuns; this remains at St. Helen's Bishopsgate, London and Minster (Kent). The churches were, in general, simply planned, often being without aisles or transepts, since in houses of women side altars for private masses were not needed and most English nunneries had little or no parochial responsibility. Romsey is a unique example of a major church of English nuns surviving largely intact as a parish church; here the church also served a biggish parish. In several cases part of the church remains as at Nun Monkton (Yorks.), Elstow (Bedfordshire), Goring (Oxfordshire), Fairwell (Staffs.), Bungay (Suffolk), Polesworth (Warwickshire).

Considerable remains of the nunnery of St. Radegund at Cambridge survive

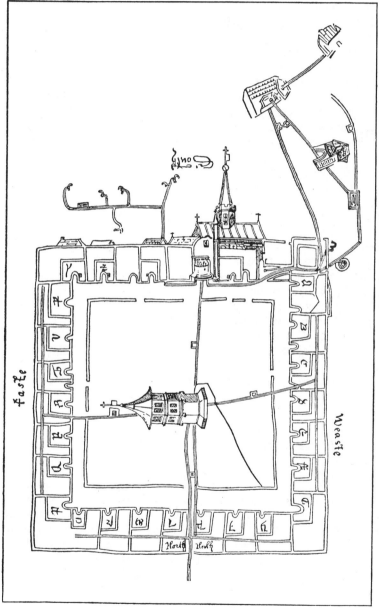

WATERCOURSE DRAWING OF THE LONDON CHARTERHOUSE
From G. S. Davies, *Charterhouse in London* (John Murray)

since it was dissolved before the ruthless days of Henry VIII to be quickly converted into Jesus College. Here can be seen most of a simple cruciform church with
unaisled transepts, and much of the main cloister buildings, though these have
been greatly transformed in the interests of college life. They are on the north of
the church. The east range was laid out on the normal pattern with sacristy, slype,
chapter house, common room, and reredorter. Most of the chapter house except
its entrance has been destroyed, and a great many modern partitions have transformed most of the refectory and cellar beyond easy recognition. The kitchen
projects from the end of the western range, and has south of it the old guest
hall, a slype (now blocked) and living rooms which include part of the prioress'
apartments.

This and other evidence show, in general, the layout of medieval nunneries to be
very like that of the Augustinian and Benedictine orders to which the great majority
of houses of nuns belonged, though the buildings were usually small and simple.
Such a view is corroborated by the layout of Lacock abbey, the only large house of
nuns to preserve most of its main cloister court. Here much of the old buildings
(but not the church) was curiously remodelled as a dwelling-house. The cloister
alley now exists only on three sides, but the plan resembles that of a small Augustinian house of men. The east range has a chapter house, sacristy and day room,
with dormitory overhead and reredorter adjacent. On the side opposite to the
church was the refectory on an undercroft, with the kitchen adjacent. The abbess'
lodgings and guest accommodation were in the west range.

Elsewhere mostly only fragments of the cloister court survive. The east range
remains at Easebourne (Sussex) and here and possibly at Redlingfield, the refectory. Denney (Cambs.) has a very large refectory though its pulpit has been lost.
The western range survives, little damaged, at Davington (Kent), Kington St.
Michael (Wilts.) and St. Katharine's Exeter, whilst the old superior's lodging
remains at Carrow (Norfolk). Few English nunneries still have remains of buildings
outside their cloister court, but gatehouses of simple design can be seen at Polesworth (Warwickshire), Cornworthy (Devon) and Malling (Kent).

The Minor Arts

Space does not allow more than passing reference to the minor arts which were
associated with medieval monastic architecture. But these were so important, and
made the monastic buildings look so very different from what almost all of those
remaining look like today, that notice of them cannot be omitted. They were
principally, but not solely, concentrated on the conventual church and gave it a
rich and colourful appearance which cannot easily be visualised from the few relics
of them still visible.

In very many English monastic remains clear signs have been found of internal
walls having been whitened. This was almost certainly done to increase the lighting

of the interior, but incidentally could provide a very impressive effect as can be seen today in the majestic French abbey of Pontigny (Yonne), one of the few major medieval monastic churches to retain a completely whitewashed interior. In some cases this whitewashing had red lines depicting bogus masonry. Quite often something much more ornate was used. The detail of the arches might be picked out in colour—(in England often red and yellow) as can be seen at such places as Chester, Ely and above all, St. Albans [Pl. 32].

To what extent elaborate wall-paintings of the type so extensively visible in Italy were to be seen in medieval England is not clear, but they were certainly fairly numerous. There is plenty of documentary evidence for them, and recent investigation has shown considerable traces of them in some of the places where they were most likely to survive, such as the cathedrals of Canterbury, Norwich, Rochester and St. Albans. At Westminster—admittedly a house exceptional in its wealth and its flood of benefactions from the English kings—the wall-paintings were both extensive and elaborate and an unusual number of them survive. In 1936 it was found that part of the wall of St. Benedict's chapel there had been painted with fleurs-de-lis on a red ground, the capitals of the wall arcade had been copper green, the roll mouldings red, and the spandrels of the arcade decorated with a pattern of green leaves and red berries. The little chapel of Our Lady of the Pew was also elaborately painted and had a door delicately picked out in red, black and white. Though we must not assume this sort of thing existed in the hosts of small monasteries of England, there must have been a very great deal about. The recent discovery that the hall of the steward of the abbey of Peterborough at Longthorpe was completely covered with wall-paintings (now mostly restored to view) shows that this form of art was far commoner than the paltry remains of it known in Victorian England would suggest.

Paintings not done on a wall, but on wooden panels, were certainly also very much more common than is generally realised, and were particularly common as altar-pieces. They explode the hoary myth that there was no good painting before the Italian Renaissance. A great triptych from a house of Dominicans in East Anglia painted about 1325 and now preserved in the tiny church of Thornham Parva [Pls. 31a, 31b] is a salutary reminder of the beauty in this field that once existed. Equally remarkable is the portrait of king Richard II in Westminster abbey, which is certainly today our greatest monastic treasure-house.

In Italy the use of mosaic for wall-pictures, pavements, tombs, etc. was widespread, partly through the strength of old Roman example, partly through the existence there of a fascinating variety of coloured stones. In England this work never caught on, though we have a handful of Italian examples of it brought to England doubtless at great expense. Here again Westminster is the prime example, with the inlaid tombs of Edward the Confessor and king Henry III, and the great inlaid pavement of the presbytery installed by the abbot of Westminster in 1268.

The flooring of English monasteries in the later Middle Ages was often of tiles.

In the case of the early, austere Cistercians these were small and plain, but brighter things quickly followed and by the end of the century Cleeve indulged in a sporty piece of tiling, showing knights in combat. Tiles were usually decorated by a yellow slip being let into the red clay of which they were made. These tiles were very popular in the fourteenth and fifteenth centuries, especially in areas like East Anglia where stone suitable for paving was scanty. They were generally a few inches square, and were made in a considerable variety of designs, heraldic devices of benefactors being very common as at Butley. In many cases immensely elaborate series of tiles are known to have existed, some portraying scenes from contemporary romances in the manner of strip cartoons, though with finer workmanship. Some of these survive at Westminster abbey but the most remarkable collection (sadly damaged) comes from Chertsey abbey, and is now in the British Museum. Its masterpiece is an astounding triple portrait of a king, a queen [Pl. 27b] and an archbishop depicted on gigantic tiles with a delicacy worthy of a drawing in a psalter. Great Malvern retains a fine collection.

Two English specialities in the Middle Ages were needlework and wood carving. The former—known as *opus anglicanum*—had an ancient history and was used notably for ecclesiastical vestments. These became extremely elaborate as time wore on, some being embroidered with golden thread and set with precious stones —copes, mitres and chasubles were the main items, but next to none have survived. Extant documents show the enormous quantities of these owned by rich monasteries. Thus by 1316, Christ Church, Canterbury, had no less than fifty chasubles, one hundred and twenty copes and twenty-three pairs of tunicles and dalmatics. Some chasubles given by Archbishop Lanfranc were so precious that when the fabric was worn out they were burnt to recover the gold they contained; one of these had fifty-one silver-gilt bells round the edge and a fastening set with a great topaz and four emeralds. This use of jewels was far from rare even on amices.

Woodwork developed rapidly and by the late Middle Ages had attained a remarkably high standard. Specially impressive are the elaborate carved roofs, often supported by a series of angels, to be found notably in areas like the West Country and East Anglia, though very few monastic examples of this survive. Equally notable were the wooden screens, as at Dunster [Pl. 29] and the main screen or *pulpitum* of which we have examples at Carlisle and Hexham—the latter being one of the few monasteries to have retained much of its ancient woodwork. The remarkable canopy at Milton is a reminder of the beauty attained in other objects of which next to none have survived. As the *Rites of Durham* shows, there was also much use made of small wooden screens and wainscotting. The choir stalls of the brethren were frequently very elaborate with lofty wood backs and richly carved pinnacles. Beneath were the seats and misericords to which we have already referred (see page 21) and in front desks, the ends of which were usually also richly carved. There is little doubt that much of this woodwork was painted and gilded, as were the bosses (whether of wood or stone) which were set at the intersections of vaulted roofs. These roof bosses have been the subject of exhaustive study by the late Mr. F. J. P. Cave, whose remarkable photographs have brought out the high degree of artistry and technical skill which often characterised them. Rather oddly, a number of the best sets occur in non-monastic churches.

More spectacular was the figure sculpture of post-Conquest England, used principally for the statues of saints or the tombs of dignitaries. However, post-Conquest England never got very interested in sculpture, and major examples of its use here are not remarkable either for quantity or quality. Fanatical Protestant outbursts in the sixteenth and seventeenth centuries did appalling damage to statues of saints, as witness the work of the infamous Dowsing in the Lady Chapel at Ely. Almost the only major monastic collection to remain is the entrancing assembly in the Henry VII's chapel at Westminster. But a fair total survives, including some interesting ones at St. Mary's York, and some exquisite work at Westminster. Effigies on tombs were quite numerous and have been more kindly treated by posterity, as they did not have the religious associations that aroused Puritanical ire. They were, however, expensive things which only the well-to-do could afford. Early ones like the twelfth-century figures amongst those at Ely and Peterborough are somewhat on the crude side, but by the middle of the thirteenth century a high standard of skill had been attained and for the next three centuries the industry was a thriving one. Several cathedrals such as Carlisle and Worcester have good examples. Most such effigies were made of stone, a small number of wood and others of alabaster which was extensively quarried in Derbyshire, from the fourteenth century on. These effigies were nearly always elaborately painted. Few surviving ones retain anything of their original colour, though a craze to supply what the Reformation destroyed there is now sweeping the English Church. These effigies were very often only the key-piece of an elaborate memorial. They often rested on a painted and sculpted stone chest which contained the body of the deceased and had over it a great painted tester supported by an elaborate canopy. The whole tomb in some cases formed part of a small chantry chapel, founded by the individual concerned, and had a small altar on its eastern side at which masses were said for his soul. Good examples of such chantry chapels may be seen at Winchester, Worcester and Tewkesbury: Hexham has one founded by a prior of the house, which has been well preserved. Such chapels were heavily painted and gilded and at their best must have been brilliant, at their worst gaudy. Much the greatest and finest collection of surviving medieval effigies is that in Westminster abbey.

Yet another source of colour in the medieval church was stained glass. This seems only to have been used in an extensive way after the eleventh century. At first it was rather austere, mostly consisting of what is known as 'grisaille' white glass painted with patterns in black relieved, perhaps, by some odd bits of coloured glass. The greatest collection of this is at the secular cathedral of York. Very rapidly in the course of the thirteenth century this was discarded in favour of extensive use of coloured stained glass. The windows were large but the pieces of glass small. Red and blue were the favourite colours and glowed with a brilliance the future was not to surpass, partly through subtle differences of shades caused by the glass being made in small quantities with slightly varying proportions of ingredients. Attractive as it was, it produced a gloom which may have been religious but was certainly irritating to anyone desirous of reading a service-book. Though the size of church windows steadily increased, this scarcely helped a situation which was only remedied when new techniques allowed the construction of less obscure glass made in larger pieces and so needing less lead to hold it together. By this time windows took up an enormous part of the available wall space and a late English Gothic church had often a mass of stained glass of great variety.

Stained glass requires a skilled attention seldom accorded it until modern times, and much old glass has been lost through lack of this, as well as by deliberate destruction, notably under the Commonwealth. Few old monasteries in England have retained much of their original glass. Canterbury, Gloucester and Great Malvern are amongst the select band that still have medieval glass worth seeing.

Although these minor arts were principally displayed in the church of the monastery, they were also utilised elsewhere, notably in the cloister, in the refectory and the superior's apartments. Thus the cloister of Norwich has a complex series of carved bosses and that at Durham had a good deal of wainscotting. The noble roof of the refectory at Cleeve can still be admired, as can the curious paintings in the prior's apartments at Shulbrede. The prior's apartment at Bradenstoke with its superb fireplace is now destroyed and a richly worked roof lies dismembered elsewhere.

A word should be added about the plate of a medieval monastery. From an early date this was very splendid, partly because plate was a usual way of preserving cash in days before banking developed, partly from human ostentation, partly through that wish to do everything to the greater glory of God. From an early date it was laid down that only precious metals were to be used for the altar vessels used at the Communion service for the Body and Blood of Christ. For these silver was very commonly used and gold by no means rare, jewels sometimes being added. Altar crosses might be equally sumptuous, as also the covers of certain precious liturgical books, notably the Gospels. Candlesticks might also be elaborate, as an example originally from Gloucester cathedral shows [Pl. 30a], though these were comparatively rarely of precious metal. The same is true of censers, one from Ramsey abbey being amongst the few still surviving [Pl. 30b].

From what we have seen, it will be clear that a medieval monastery was colourful to a degree which could never be deduced from the very scanty remains of original decoration which survive today. The monasteries of France suffered a similar deprivation in a later age, so that to see in actuality the colour that ran riot in a medieval cloister it is necessary to seek out some more fortunate area, such as Italy.

PART TWO

THE MONASTIC ORDERS

CHAPTER FIVE

CELTIC AND BENEDICTINE MONASTICISM

EARLY English monasticism derived from two sources, the Celtic monasticism of Ireland and the Benedictine monasticism of Italy. These arrived almost simultaneously, the first in the north, the second in the south of the country.

Celtic Monasticism

The origins of Celtic monasticism are very obscure, but probably derive ultimately from Egypt by way of French monasteries. By the end of the sixth century the monastic life had been given a welcome by the Irish, which it has never since outstayed, and there were large and numerous communities dotted over their country.

Life was simple but austere, with a frugal diet and a good deal of fasting. Immense stress was laid on the virtue of instant obedience; it is said that when, on one occasion, the head of a large monastic working party ordered 'Colman jump into the river', twelve brethren of that name instantly obeyed! A number of exercises to toughen the will were cherished, such as saying psalms or prayers whilst standing in a pond or stream, or praying at length with arms extended like a cross. That there was nothing neurotic or individualist about Celtic monasticism was shown by the great respect for 'white martyrdom', leaving one's home to work in foreign parts for the sake of Christ. This 'white martyrdom' was the basis of an enormous surge of that intense Celtic missionary endeavour in the sixth and seventh centuries which constitutes one of the most remarkable pages of Christian history. Steadily bands of Irish monks worked their way down the Continent to pagan or de-christianised areas. Several of their most famous foundations are in modern Switzerland, notably Luxeuil (c. 590), Bobbio (612) and St. Gall and some of their missionaries worked and died in Italy, like San Frediano, whose body still rests at Lucca. When some Celtic monks visited such distant regions it is not surprising that they descended on near-by England and Scotland. The latter area had been largely pagan hitherto and the former had lost much of its early, rather skin-deep Christianity in the turbulent generations which followed the collapse of Roman rule there in the fifth century.

At least in the first stages of their evangelistic work, the Celtic monks were aided by their peculiar organisation. This was as simple as it was unusual. By this time elsewhere the great mass of Christendom had long been divided into territorial areas known as dioceses, each ruled over by a bishop, who, amongst other things, kept an eye on any monasteries in his area. But Celtic organisation was closely interwoven with the primitive society that prevailed in Ireland at the time of its conversion. Here there were no towns to provide the normal cathedral centres and the greatest church bases were usually the monasteries with their many inmates and considerable influence. Monastic life so dominated Irish life that the monastery became the focus of local church life. Here, as elsewhere, it was recognised that bishops alone could carry out ordinations of clergy and certain other functions, but in Ireland they were not given dioceses to rule in the usual way, being kept merely as useful appendages to the monastic household, like the conventual cat. However odd or undesirable this might seem to some, it had at least the advantage of freeing the Celtic monks from an undue respect for officialdom. In their missionary journeys they went where the need seemed to call, and their intense zeal and self-sacrifice won them ready support.

The immensely important missionary work of the Irish monks in Britain began in about 563 when St. Columba, a notable Irish monk, set up a missionary base in Iona. This monastery quickly became the centre of a network of other houses, and, as an early writer noted, to it 'by an unusual arrangement the entire province, including even the bishops, is subject'. In 633 the exiled king of Northumbria (one of the largest of the several kingdoms into which modern England was then divided) returned to his kingdom. He had been baptised at Iona and now summoned brethren from there to convert his people (a little earlier, missionaries from the south had started this work but without success owing to a pagan reaction). The monks set up their main base at Lindisfarne (Holy Island) off the Northumbrian coast and near the royal residence at Bamburgh. The first leader soon proved unsuitable and was replaced by St. Aidan (d. 651), a magnetic personality who won the instant admiration of all and sundry. Under him Lindisfarne became an immensely vigorous centre of evangelism, first in northern England and later under his successor, farther south, where other Irish had arrived meanwhile. The evidence is far too scanty to allow us to trace with precision this penetration of England by Celtic monks, but there is no doubt that through their efforts a large part of the country was established in the Faith. With them they brought a very important literary and artistic tradition.

Meanwhile the Benedictine monks originating from Rome had landed in Kent, and steadily pushed into other parts of England. Their work suffered some severe setbacks, and in the result their missionary achievements were not quite so impressive as those of the Celtic monks. But by the middle seventh century they had got well rooted in much of southern England. Their continental connections gave them considerable advantages, which included a sense of the universality of the Church, not always apparent among the Celts who were bred on a distant doorstep of Christendom.

Once the country was converted, the luxury of dissension could be indulged. The effective crisis in the relation between these two Christian traditions came at the so-called synod of Whitby in 664. Though Celtic and Roman monks were agreed on all the major points of the Faith, they came from different backgrounds and had different mentalities. Hence there was the same tendency to suspicion and misunderstanding as arises today between the similarly separated Russians and Americans. As the seventh century wore on, various controversies arose. Most of the points at issue were of very minor theological importance, such as the shape of the monks' tonsure. But there was at least some practical importance as to the method by which the date of Easter should be calculated, which now became a matter of dispute. The preceding period of Lent was a time of strict fasting, and it was clearly awkward to have one lot of Church folk fasting, whilst another were celebrating the joys of Easter. But the fundamental problem lay in the friction bred by two parties with different outlooks and local loyalties having to work side by side.

At the great monastery of Whitby a heterogeneous assembly of clergy and laity assembled to hear the arguments for Celtic and Roman forms of Christianity agreed before the king of Northumbria. In the crude state of contemporary society it was almost impossible that the debate should reach a high level. As a Roman Catholic scholar points out 'both parties displayed equal ignorance and equal reliance on illusory authorities'. In the end the king gave his support to the Roman side, and, though no persecution of the defeated party ensued, the Celtic monasteries in northern England gradually withered away for lack of official support. The south was not concerned in the decision at Whitby, but the Celtic church was not strong there and steadily lost ground to Rome. With the general results of this we are not concerned, but from the monastic point of view this was of considerable importance, in that it led to the triumph of Benedictine monasticism, by then so important in Western Europe. For almost five hundred years Benedictine life ruled unchallenged. For another four hundred it was the dominant influence in English monasticism.

The Benedictine Monks in England

Benedictine monks take their name from St. Benedict of Nursia, who created the rule which they follow. He was born at Nursia (the modern Norcia, near Spoleto in central Italy), about 480, of a well-to-do family. After studying in Rome, he felt called to a life of seclusion and withdrew to a cave at Subiaco, some thirty miles from the city. The fame of his sanctity spread steadily and numerous followers arrived, whom he organised into several communities before he himself moved southward to establish what was to be the most famous monastery of the order.

This was Monte Cassino, built on the site of a heathen temple about 525. Here St. Benedict lived till his death a quarter of a century later.

Although his life is very obscure and was very uneventful, St. Benedict was certainly one of the major formative influences of the Church life in the medieval West. This is because of the immense sagacity of the monastic rule he compiled which, with little beyond its own merits to commend it, spread steadily through the monasteries of Western Europe, finally replacing almost all the other local monastic rules, though not, of course, those of the Eastern Church, with which it had little effective contact. At the time at which St. Benedict lived, the monastic life was spread widely but very thinly over Western Europe and its devotees followed various rules. Most of them gave very little regulation of detail, thus depending a good deal on the will of the individual or of the superior. The severe and somewhat unprofitable primitive tradition which regarded the monastic life as primarily an individual combat against the forces of evil, was still very potent.

St. Benedict's rule, based partly on past experience but principally on his own profound insight, was, above all, notable for its sanctified common sense. Its keynote was moderation. 'A school of the Lord's service in the institution of which we hope we are going to establish nothing harsh, nothing burdensome' was how he described the *Rule's* purpose in its prologue. The ancient stress on being tough for the sake of being tough, and the old unedifying competitions in bodily austerities, were now eliminated in favour of a régime which was neither harsh nor luxurious; thus the food allowed was much the same as that of a contemporary Italian peasant.

Equally notable was the systematic character of the *Rule* which has been termed 'a monument of legislative art'. Much previous monastic regulation had consisted of unsystematic and shortish rules, lists of faults to be avoided or abstract spiritual advice. The *Rule of St. Benedict* covered the whole field. The various needs and problems of the monastic community are dispassionately considered and detailed regulations laid down on them, together with advice on how the requisite, underlying spiritual gift was to be acquired. The various elements of the monastic day were carefully balanced, some four hours for communal worship through public worship, four hours for meditation or private prayer, and six in domestic or manual labour of some kind. Well aware of the dangers of individualism, St. Benedict laid immense stress on the importance of obedience to the abbot who was 'the representative of Christ', though this he characteristically balanced by equal stress on the heavy responsibility of the abbot to take advice and 'not to teach, establish or order anything contrary to the spirit of the Lord's revealed will'.

The primary purpose of the Benedictine life was the offering of an unbroken round of communal sacrifice to God by men who had given up all for that purpose. There was nothing anti-social about the rule, which, for example, laid immense stress on hospitality. 'Let all guests that happen to come be received as Christ, because he is going to say "A guest was I and ye received me"'; the singular delicacy of Benedictine hospitality is still remarkable today.

Perhaps the most fundamental difference between the monks of East and West, and one which rebounds to the credit of the latter, was the western conviction that true piety must be balanced by sound learning. The Benedictine life did not aim at providing anything like a university education, nor did it allow more than a limited time for study. But in an age when the society of Western Europe was steadily involving itself in the bog of illiteracy, the Benedictines insisted firmly on a precious modicum of study. To some extent this was essential if their worship was to be properly maintained, for by this time the daily offices had become quite complex as had the form of the Mass, and this complexity steadily increased. Not only was an ability to read and understand Latin needed here, but it was required for the reading which went on at meals and the private study which was enjoined. 'Idleness is harmful to the soul' said the rule, 'and therefore the brethren ought to be occupied, at fixed periods, with manual work and also at fixed periods with spiritual reading.' This limited but clear insistence on the pursuit of literacy had unexpected and immensely important results. Down to the twelfth century the monasteries of Western Europe were to guard learning at a time when most of the rest of society were very ready to ignore it.

The *Rule of St. Benedict* was not written for a monastic order in the modern sense, that is to say a collection of monasteries united by a single rule of life and a common machinery of government. As a modern scholar has indicated, it seems to have been intended by its author for 'his own monasteries and for any others in Italy or elsewhere that might care to accept it, foreseeing that such was likely to be the case'. It spread steadily on its own merits, but it was in England that it received its most celebrated, early impetus. That this was so, was due to the initiative of one of the most attractive popes of the Dark Ages, Gregory the Great (590–604). Of rich and noble family he had given up his great possessions to become a monk and, probably when an abbot in Rome, had seen English slaves sold in the market there. Later as pope, touched by their plight, he sent missionaries to convert England. For this purpose he chose Benedictine monks from his old monastery, under one Augustine who finally landed in Thanet in 597. The kingdom of Kent was chosen as their base because the king there had married a Christian princess from France who could give them the necessary initial backing.

At the time, this must all have been found very startling, for there was no effective precedent for using monks in foreign missions. But, despite some setbacks, the experiment proved abundantly successful. In 597, a monastery was established in Canterbury, the Kentish capital, on the site of the present cathedral of Christ Church, and the following year another was founded near by dedicated to St. Peter and St. Paul. This became a favourite place of burial for the early archbishops and, Augustine's fame greatly increasing, this church became known by his name. Various other monasteries sprang up including Rochester (604) and Sheppey (670). Kent was quickly converted to Christianity and missions sent out elsewhere though an attempt to convert the great Northumbrian kingdom quickly broke down owing to a local pagan reaction.

Steadily monastic expansion went on. The great Celtic monasteries of northern England gradually turned Benedictine after the 'synod of Whitby', and new ones were added, partly through a renewed vigorous contact with Rome, effected notably by St. Wilfrid, who evidently instituted the Benedictine rule at Ripon and Hexham, and his friend Benedict Biscop, who founded what were to be most famous houses at Wearmouth (674) and Jarrow (685). Both the number and dates of foundations of these early English Benedictine monasteries are imperfectly known, and are likely to remain so, because of the very inadequate evidence that has survived. But, by the end of the eighth century, several dozen monasteries of some size and an indeterminate number of smaller ones, mostly dependent on large houses, had come into existence.

In northern England major houses were few in number for the region was poor, thinly populated and disorderly. But much of Kent had now passed to Benedictine hands and there was another important cluster of their houses in the cheerless, deserted fenlands, notably Peterborough (c. 655), Ely (c. 673) and Crowland (c. 714). The lands around the lower Severn now saw the beginnings of what was to be an influential company there, including Bath (676), Pershore (c. 689), Evesham (c. 701) and Worcester (c. 743). Probably about 673 under the influence of St. Wilfrid, the Benedictine rule was instituted at Glastonbury, 'both the most ancient and the most famous monastery of our whole island', as a Tudor antiquary very properly noted and one whose origins really are 'lost in the mists of antiquity'. Elsewhere in the country the chief foundations were Winchester cathedral (c. 604), Chertsey (666), Abingdon (675), Winchcombe (798) and possibly an eighth-century foundation at Westminster. Besides there were various lesser monasteries of which next to nothing is known, like those at Carlisle and Dacre to which we have casual references. Besides these were fairly numerous daughter houses or cells of the great monasteries (mostly small) such as those which Peterborough is known to have had at Woking, Bermondsey, Breedon (Leics.) and probably Brixworth (Northants).

Within two centuries of its arrival, the monastic life had won for itself a place in English affections which it was not to lose for the best part of a thousand years. 'Every ecclesiastical statesman of the seventh century regarded the monastic order as essential to the life of the Church' writes a leading authority on Anglo-Saxon England, and he adds significantly, 'the motive of escape from a violent world will not explain the enthusiasm with which men and women of all classes entered religion . . . it was the appeal to the imagination of the ordinary man which gave vitality to early English monasticism' (Stenton).

The monastic life of England at this time had important by-products including considerable literary interests and notable artistic achievements in the minor arts. Most important was an extensive missionary activity, which falls outside the scope of this chapter, that led to the evangelisation of important parts of Northern Europe and much ambulance work elsewhere, including the revival of monastic life at Monte Cassino itself through an Anglo-Saxon monk. The modern historian of English Benedictinism, Professor Knowles, notes that 'during the greater part of the eighth century the monasteries of England possessed a life and exercised an influence more powerful than those of any other monastic bloc in Europe'.

But at this stage when all seemed set fair for the continuance of one of the golden epochs of English monastic history, a violent and unexpected catastrophe shattered this reasonable hope. In 793, out of the blue, Viking pirates landed on the island of Lindisfarne, sacked the monastery and massacred some of the monks. 'It was not thought possible that they could have made the journey' wrote a contemporary Englishman, 'never before . . . has such a horror appeared in Britain.' Horror it was indeed. The monasteries were obvious centres of attack for they were completely defenceless and had valuable plate and other treasure that could be easily transported in the shallow draught boats with which the Vikings now proceeded to terrorise the coasts and great rivers of Northern and Western Europe. Within less than a century of the sack of Lindisfarne, the structure of English monastic life had almost completely perished. Some monasteries were reduced to charred ruins, others continued to house a few inmates but the life they led was not monastic. From time to time attempts were made to restore the damage, as by king Alfred who founded new monasteries (a house of men at Athelney, and a house of nuns at Shaftesbury), and renewed old ones. But one cannot repair a house in a storm and it was only in the mid-tenth century that the storm had abated sufficiently to allow of this.

The Benedictine Revival (c. 943–1216)

Throughout the darkest days of the Viking invasions one great product of early English Benedictinism had gone undestroyed. This was a great *Ecclesiastical History of the English nation* written at Jarrow by the Venerable Bede, the most eminent scholar of his day. Inevitably this recounted, amongst other things, the memorable works of early English Benedictines. This seems to have been a constant inspiration in later times and is one of the main reasons why Benedictinism was given a prominent place in the new order that was erected, once the tempests had abated sufficiently to allow of reconstruction.

The process of monastic revival began with the restoration of conventual discipline at Glastonbury about 943. This is rightly reckoned 'a turning point in the history of England', and from then onwards to the Reformation the course of English monasticism was unimpeded and unbroken. The new abbot of Glastonbury was St. Dunstan (c. 909–88), a local aristocrat who had been educated at Glastonbury and later became a monk. The state of the old monasteries at this time varied. Some had been completely destroyed during the Viking disorders and were never revived. But almost all the larger ones and some others had retained most of the property which served as their endowment. However, the common life had often ceased or was no longer monastic, a band of clergy living a life which allowed them to hold private property and did not involve either a common dormitory or a common refectory. Yet rehabilitation was quite feasible, and rehabilitation came.

The old veneration of the monastic life now flared up afresh. Laymen, from the king of Wessex—the leading local ruler of this time—downwards, gave it their fullest support and some of the most self-sacrificing men of the time took monastic vows. Of the latter Dunstan was the chief and his merits led to him being made successively bishop of Worcester, bishop of London, and archbishop of Canterbury (960–88). He had two principal assistants in the work of monastic revival, St. Ethelwold (c. 908–84), a monk of Glastonbury who became abbot of Abingdon and then bishop of Winchester (963–84), and Oswald who, after becoming a monk abroad, was bishop of Worcester from 961 to 992 and archbishop of York from 972 to 992. His very unusual step of holding two bishoprics together, was only to be justified by the extreme poverty of the see of York. Northern England at this time was poor and undeveloped and the Church there had suffered particularly severely from the Vikings. Because of this, and because of the strong support available in the south and west, the centre of monasticism now shifted radically. The old monastic glory of Northumbria did not revive and the chief houses of the order all lay well south of the Humber, notably in the Fens, Kent, Dorset and the lower Severn valley.

The list of places where the monastic life was established at this time is lengthy and impressive. A notable feature was the number of Benedictine cathedrals established then. To hand over a cathedral to a monastic community was a very unusual thing throughout these centuries, and normally only approved because of exceptional circumstances, although at all times it was common enough for a monk of notable holiness to be extracted from his monastery (often protesting vigorously) and consecrated a bishop. Exceptional circumstances had inspired the Benedictine mission to Kent and the establishment of a Benedictine cathedral at Canterbury and this precedent lay behind Ethelwold's and Oswald's establishment of monastic communities at their own cathedrals of Winchester and Worcester, and the introduction of Benedictine monasticism at Sherborne cathedral (993).

Amongst the old monasteries now revived were Malmesbury, Bath (944), Westminster (958), St. Augustine's Canterbury, Abingdon (964–5), Peterborough (966), St. Albans (969), Winchcombe (? 972), Hexham (c. 975) and Ripon (? 980). Some new monasteries were also founded, Winchester [Hyde] (965), Ramsey (969), Cerne (987) and Burton-on-Trent (1004). Amongst late-comers were two founded by king Cnut—St. Benet's Holme (1019) and Bury St. Edmunds (1020). The latter quickly came to the fore, owing partly to the reputation of the saint whose name it bears.* Later came Coventry (1043) and Abbotsbury (c. 1044). However, by the

---

* St. Edmund was a king of East Anglia who was killed by the Danes in 870. His remains were installed in a shrine at Bury in 903, moved away for safety a little later and finally returned in 1013 to a new church specially built for them.

time of the Norman Conquest the number of English monasteries was a tiny fraction of their ultimate total. They numbered about sixty, including twelve nunneries, but the combined wealth of these was already enormous. The *Domesday Survey* of England of 1086-7 has certain omissions, so must not be taken as a complete guide to English wealth of the time, but it is notable that in it the property in monastic possession constituted no less than a sixth of the whole, almost all of which had been acquired before the Conquest. Monastic wealth was, however, very unevenly distributed, both over the country and among the monasteries themselves. All the existing monasteries in 1066 lay 'east of the Severn and south of a line from Burton-on-Trent to the Wash'.

Anglo-Saxon monasteries did not incur the problems (so common in later days) which resulted from having large numbers of houses which because of their small-ness found it hard either to make ends meet or to maintain an effective common life. By the time of Domesday there were, indeed, some smallish houses such as Athelney, Buckfast and Horton, none of whose incomes exceeded twenty pounds a year. But at the other end of the scale were a number of giants with three-figure incomes which under the conditions of the day would normally leave them immensely wealthy. At the top of the financial tree, as ever, was Glastonbury with an estimated annual income of £828, followed by Ely with £769, six others with over £600, eight others had an income over £400, and another seven an income of between £100 and £200. Economists are not prepared to translate these sums into modern equivalents, but there is no doubt that most of these richer houses must have been very comfortably off, and some of them already far too rich to avoid the danger of scandalising at least some men in the street. As we shall see, the wealth built up in England by the medieval church in general and its monasteries in particular was to create deep-rooted problems which were only finally abolished by the undiscriminating destruction of the monasteries by Henry VIII.

The English monasteries would not have reached the strong position they had attained by 1066 had it not been for the profound popular respect for the monastic life as such which existed. As we have seen, this was very deep-rooted, and as we are to see, it was to become even more pronounced. To account for it is not easy but it was certainly nurtured by several factors. Very important was the profound popular belief that the full common life of the monk, with its rejection of the world and the flesh was the highest form of Christian life, the kind of life which had prevailed amongst early Christians (here men went beyond the rather hazy evidence of the times), the kind of life to which the out-and-out enthusiast would naturally aspire. Further it was a simple passionate age to which the monk's simple spec-tacular rejection of the claims of the world and the flesh spoke with immense power, exercising an evangelical influence incomparably greater than that possible in the muddle-headed society of modern times.

Another important factor in the immense power of monasticism in the life of the times, was the enormous belief in the value of the intercession of holy men and

6

women in enabling the individual soul to reach Heaven and avoid Hell. In most of
the Middle Ages rather naïve ideas of hell-fire religion were as much a reality as in
nineteenth-century America, though they were not found in subtler and sophisticated sections of society. But all agreed with the New Testament dictum 'the
prayer of a righteous man availeth much before God'. Those who could afford it
would found monasteries, and those who could not, would give benefactions to one
already existing, in return for a clear defined obligation of prayers by the convent
for them and their family, prayers that might save them from Hell.

The monasteries would not have been established and maintained unless the
man in the street found them to be 'righteous' and this they would not have been,
had not great attention been paid to the details by which their life was governed.
Great though the merits of the *Rule of St. Benedict* were, it was not left as the one
and only monastic text but was steadily expanded by the use of fresh 'customs' or
'observances'. Some of these were made because of local conditions, others
because of changing life of the Church (especially of its worship which steadily
grew more complex) others to the passion for titivating which throbs so powerfully
in most ecclesiastical breasts.

The re-establishment of the monastic life in England in the mid-tenth century
was an obvious juncture at which to reassess the details which governed it. On the
Continent an important revision of this type had taken place over a century before,
at the council of Aachen of 816–17, where *inter alia* monastic constitutions for the
monasteries of the great Carolingian Empire had been drawn up. In these the
Rule of St. Benedict was still the core of the life, but there were a few fresh developments. New rules recognised the habit of brethren normally undertaking manual
work of various kinds within the monastic precinct, but did not allow any extensive
involvement in agricultural labours. They were now to give up teaching any but
oblates (the young children given to monasteries by their parents in the hope they
would become monks). Conventual worship was lengthened, notably by the addition of an Office for the Dead and a collection of prayers and psalms said thrice
daily and known as the *Trina Oratio*. In the following century and a half, various
monasteries in Western Europe became famous. Most of them had no influence in
England, but certain houses in the Lorraine area and in the Low Countries were
exceptions to this rule, notably Blandinium (St. Peter's, Ghent) and Fleury at both
of which English monastic reformers studied. The need for a modernised way of
life for the new monasteries was evident in England, and to satisfy this, about
970 a great assembly of bishops, abbots and abbesses promulgated the 'Monastic agreement of monks and nuns of the English people' (*Regularis Concordia
Anglicae Nationis monachorum sanctimonialiumque*) generally known as the *Regularis
Concordia*.

As Professor Knowles points out, this document represented in effect the normal
use of Western Europe with some local English variations. It includes permission
for the brethren to work in shelter, not in a cloister when the weather was cold, a

much prolonged pealing on bells on great feasts and special stress on prayer for the royal family. More notable was its assumption that the public would attend the major monastic mass on Sundays and festivals, and the stipulation that, where cathedrals were monastic, the bishops elected should be monks if possible, or at least should conform as closely as possible to the monastic life. This last provision is 'without any parallel in the Western Church of the time' as Professor Knowles points out, and is a conscious adherence to local tradition. In fact not only in cathedral sees but elsewhere in England it was now the tradition to elect monks as bishops. It has been calculated that in the seventy years after 970 'probably the overwhelming majority of the (English) bishops were monks'.

This remarkable fact is a real tribute to the high moral standards of English monarchy. In many other parts of the West, now and later, medieval rulers tended only too often to treat high ecclesiastical offices as a cheap way of providing for members of their family or rewarding their major officials. It is further testimony of the high regard for Benedictinism now prevalent in England. There can be little doubt that their monastic bishops conferred a considerable benefit on the Church, through their high spiritual standards. Abroad very many magnates of the tenth and eleventh centuries were prepared to sell their Church appointments and sell away the lands of their bishopric or abbey—a practice known as simony. This was very widespread in Italy and south France at this time, but it is a very notable fact that there is very little indication of its existence in contemporary England, partially because so few bishops were of the type likely to consent to this practice.

There are various other signs of a flourishing monastic life in England on the eve of the Norman Conquest, which can be merely noted in passing. Their architecture was not ignoble, their patronage of other arts consistent and crucial, whilst within their walls flourished a remarkable interest in vernacular literature of which the most important illustration was the production of the *Anglo-Saxon Chronicle*, a complex composite work, on which, with Bede's *Ecclesiastical History*, an enormous part of our knowledge of pre-Conquest England depends.

Benedictine Monasticism after the Norman Conquest (1066–1215)

In 1066 the battle of Hastings led to the crowning of William duke of Normandy as king of England, and, though his reign of twenty-one years was uneasy and battle-strewn, he and his family were never afterwards dislodged. From the Benedictine angle the new royal house had advantages and disadvantages. William and his sons were tough rulers in constant need of money. Because of this they were very apt to utilise the immense resources of the plutocratic Benedictine group of monasteries to whose wealth we have already referred. There were various ways of doing this. One was to get a wealthy cathedral to elect a successful civil servant as its bishop, and this was now increasingly done, the good old days of plentiful monastic bishops steadily receding, never to reappear. The practice was not quite as bad as it sounded, since all civil servants were churchgoers and were likely to be able to cope efficiently with the great feudal responsibilities with which the cathedrals and abbeys of these days were inevitably encumbered. On the other hand, such people had not often the spiritual insight to inspire the monastic community entrusted to their care, and, instead of living with their convent, fairly quickly developed households of their own.

Another financial practice of Norman and other kings was to delay election of a new bishop or abbot for as long as possible, when death or resignation or removal had led to a new head being required. This was a very lucrative practice in the case of really wealthy abbeys, since feudal custom gave the patron of the house (in most of such cases the king) the right to run the estates of such a community during a vacancy and pocket the profits left after running expenses had been paid. It did not affect poorish houses for obvious reasons, and even the plutocrats could not claim it was an irreparable blow to their salvation, for a great medieval monastery, like a modern battleship, had a great hierarchy of officials who were perfectly capable of running the establishment effectively in the absence of the official head. Lack of a bishop was more important, but even here much of his work was done by his deputies anyhow, and there were always local bishops who could be called in to perform strictly episcopal functions such as the ordination of clergy. Royal practices like these were fairly common in England after the Conquest, but for long gross abuses such as simony continued to be rare, thanks to the real if middle-of-the-road piety of the kings of the time, with the notable exception of William II (1087–1100).

On the other hand the Norman Conquest brought certain definite gains to Benedictinism. By a curious turn of the wheel, the new king came from an area whose connection with Benedictinism was more potent than that in any other part of Western Europe except England itself. Although the Duchy of Normandy had only begun in 911 when it was created for a great Viking chief, the ducal family settled down to Catholic life with remarkable speed and regularity. By 1066 the duchy was very thickly studded with Benedictine abbeys which had recently benefited from an effective reform movement, whilst William's trusted ecclesiastical adviser was one Lanfranc, who was abbot of the great Norman abbey of Bec.

Thus the Benedictine monasteries of England were likely to gain as well as lose, and gain they did. One of the most remarkable developments was the considerable extension of the Benedictine hold over English cathedrals. In 1066 there were four cathedral monasteries—Canterbury, Winchester, Worcester and Sherborne. The latter was lost about 1075, when the see was moved, but important gains completely outweighed this loss.

Benedictines were installed in the small cathedral of Rochester in 1077 and into the highly important cathedral of Durham, six years later. Durham owed its power and prestige to its connection with the most beloved of all the saints of northern Britain, St. Cuthbert. His body had been faithfully preserved in a remarkable series of journeyings during the Viking disorders, to find a permanent home at

Durham, with those of other saints of the golden Northumbrian age, notably the Venerable Bede. By the Norman Conquest the place was already rich and the steady popularity of the cult of St. Cuthbert in later times augmented its considerable wealth. The cathedral of the land of East Anglia was settled at the Benedictine monastery of Norwich in 1089. About 1088 the bishop of Wells moved his see to the Benedictine abbey of Bath, though the two places ran jointly in episcopal harness for some time, as did Lichfield and Coventry after 1100, when the bishop of the former established his see in the abbey of the latter. Finally in 1109 a new diocese was cut out of the gigantic diocese of Lincoln, the venerable and rich abbey of Ely being chosen as the new cathedral. In 1122–33 a new diocese of Carlisle was created, with a priory of regular canons for its cathedral (see page 81). In all, no less than ten English cathedrals were now in monastic hands. Non-monastic ones were hereby reduced to a mere seven—York, Lincoln, Salisbury, Exeter, Chichester, Hereford and London. We must not, however, be too sentimental about the creation of these new Benedictine cathedrals. A main motive in the choice of some sites was economic, the revenues of those abbeys chosen providing amply for the needs of both bishop and convent. Yet, even in this age, popular admiration for monasticism was not universal, and it was not outside the bounds of possibility for a king so inclined to convert a monastery into a chapter of secular canons. That this did not happen in Norman England is worthy of note.

For nearly half a century after 1066 the foundation of new monasteries was slow, at least by later standards, partly because William I was much involved in subjugating his new country, and his immediate successor, William II, was one of the very few anti-clerical kings of the age. But by 1100 there had been founded about a hundred new Benedictine houses. A good number were 'alien priories' cells or dependent houses given to foreign monasteries (mostly in the north of France) by the *nouveaux riches* barons of the Norman Conquest. Some of these cells were so small as to be largely useless; no proper communal life could flourish there nor did they offer much financial aid—Professor Knowles roundly asserts that ' they served no religious purpose and were a source of weakness to the house that owned them'. William the Conqueror himself founded two notable houses—Battle abbey (1067) in thanksgiving for his momentous victory, on the battlefield itself, the high altar being, it is said, on the spot where his rival Harold fell, and (perhaps in thanksgiving for the safe birth of his son, the future Henry I) the abbey of Selby (1068). His followers founded important houses at Shrewsbury (c. 1085), Chester (1093) and Colchester (1095).

Understandably, a certain Normanisation of English monasteries followed the Conquest. The great abbeys were far too important in national life to be allowed to go their own way and as their abbacies fell vacant they were steadily given Norman heads. Some of the new prelates were somewhat muscular Christians, like the Norman abbot of Peterborough who informed the monks of Ramsey that unless they returned the body of St. Oswald which they had purloined he would burn down their monastery forthwith, or the abbot of Glastonbury whose novel and distasteful ideas of plainsong had to be enforced by archers against a convent who resisted unconventionally with candlesticks, benches and commendable courage.

But Norman vigour found more profitable channels. The churches of Anglo-Saxon England were not generally impressive in size or workmanship, though some little attempt had been made to build in the grand Continental manner now developing, notably at Westminster abbey by Edward the Confessor. The Norman abbots and bishops initiated a passion for building on the grand scale which was to give the English Church some of her most remarkable buildings, and which was not to die away for centuries. The resources available in cash and labour services were very considerable, so far as the famous few dozen monasteries were concerned, and the resultant buildings very elaborate, thanks also to contemporary readiness to wait half a century or more to have a great church rebuilt. The greatest English Benedictine cathedral of the age, that of Durham, was begun in 1093 but only finished about 1130; other churches took even longer. Specially remarkable were the long naves—longer than those of northern France—begun at such places as Ely, Peterborough, Norwich and Gloucester, whilst the same generous scale is seen in the massive lantern towers of Tewkesbury and St. Albans, both of which belong to a Norman rebuilding scheme.

It was not surprising that the business-like Normans checked up on the Benedictine observances and found them capable of some improvement. Lanfranc the Benedictine archbishop of Canterbury drew up a new set of Observances for his cathedral church, which were quickly copied in various other English monasteries. They represented contemporary continental practice and are not remarkable for any important innovations.

The year of the death of William II (1100) roughly coincides with the opening of a new era in the history of English Benedictinism. Hitherto the order had long been, in effect, the only monastic order, though particular houses might be particularly important at particular times, and at intervals new ideas from across the Channel might be absorbed. Its progress did not die out but was comparatively unimportant. Between 1100 and 1215 the number of English houses increased from about 150 to about 226 but only a handful were abbeys of any size and most of the rest were small, some very small. The future lay with the new orders which were of two types. Some were not Benedictine, but were of entirely new types with new houses and new rules. Others were independent orders or congregations created within the Benedictine family, each with its own scheme of government and collection of observances, though retaining the *Rule of St. Benedict* as their basis. It is these latter that we shall now consider.

The New Benedictine Orders

Although Christian experience had shown that hermits living alone created various tricky problems for themselves and for others, the old veneration for their life remained, and some of the problems could be solved by having hermits living together and not on their own. In the eleventh and twelfth centuries various communities of hermits came into existence, but only one had any important effect on the English Church.

This was the *Carthusian order*, so called from the Latinised form of its mother house, the *Chartreuse* or Charterhouse, founded not far from Grenoble in 1084. The founder was St. Bruno, a famous teacher of Rheims who gave up an attractive career to lead a life of great severity in solitude. The observances of the house were largely formed a generation after the first foundation, and were thereafter little altered: 'Never reformed because never deformed' was the reasonable claim of later Carthusians for their order.

Little stress was laid on a common life. Brethren lived most of the time in separate cells, each with a small garden, grouped round a cloister court. They met in church for only a limited number of services and at first did not even have a regular, conventual mass. In the interests of solitude there was no manual labour inside the cloister or outside it, with some very minor exceptions. Nor was there a common refectory, brethren taking their meals in their private cells. Common recreation was strictly limited. The main objectives were solitude and silence in which the brethren could give themselves freely and continuously to contemplation of God. Allied with this was considerable severity of régime notably in regard to silence and diet. The former was largely unbroken and the latter austere. Lay brethren lived near by in an adjacent court and did the heavy manual work of the estate. But this was not extensive, for the Charterhouses lived simply, mostly well away from society. They never undertook any parochial work and their own church was of the simplest type.

This sort of life has never been the vocation of more than a very select few, and the English Charterhouses numbered only nine. The first of them was founded comparatively late (about 1179) at Witham in Somerset. Unlike most monastic orders whose foundations had largely been accomplished by the end of the thirteenth century, a high proportion of English Carthusian houses came late, five being founded in the fourteenth century, including a notable one at London. Of this house there are still important remains and recent excavations revealed *inter alia* the lead coffin and skeleton of the founder.

Much more conventional and popular was the Cluniac order, so called from its mother house at Cluny in Burgundy. It began as an important Benedictine abbey founded by the duke of Aquitaine in 910. Cluny—quickly noted for its fervour—was in the heart of France, at one of the cross-roads of West European culture, on a major road to Rome, and rapidly became immensely important and attracted followers, donations and privileges in a way unparalleled at this time.

It was subject directly to the pope and, with the aid of various papal privileges, gradually became, in theory, the despotic head of a separate order. The abbot of Cluny was supposed to profess all novices and could visit any daughter house, and his abbey received small annual payments from the other houses of the order. In practice, however, because of the widespread expansion of the order, this direct control by Cluny had to be limited. Houses of the Cluniac order varied a good deal in size, a few being large and venerable and many middle-sized. The vast majority of them ranked as priories and not as abbeys.

The distinctive aspect of Cluniac life was the immense stress it laid on worship. The primitive Benedictine balance of public worship, private study and manual labour was overthrown, in the interests of a highly complex and artistic round of public worship. By the middle of the eleventh century so much of the daily Cluniac round was given up to services in choir, that an Italian visitor commented that it was scarcely possible for the brethren to commit any sin save one of thought! This length was partly due to various additions to the text of the service, partly to the increased complexity of singing. Immense visual splendour accompanied this. The wealth of Cluny enabled her to rebuild her conventual church and the new one, completed in the twelfth century, has been claimed as the largest in medieval Europe. Including its western narthex it was no less than 750 feet long. The English churches were less elaborate but show the same high workmanship, as witness the west front of Castle Acre [Pl. 6b] or the fine capitals which survive from Reading abbey. A similar attention was shown to the auxiliary arts—sculpture was profuse and elaborate, and metalwork, painting and stained glass lavishly employed. Cluniac worship was thus offered in a setting of intense splendour, well calculated to appeal to the eye of the visual-minded public of the day.

To England the Cluniacs came late, their first house here being the important priory of Lewes founded in 1077 by a great Norman noble, William de Warenne, after he had stayed at Cluny on his way to Rome. Other English houses included Much Wenlock (c. 1080), Bermondsey (c. 1089), Castle Acre (c. 1089) and Pontefract (1090). The final total here fell just short of fifty but most of them were not large.

Much more spectacular was the popularity of the *Cistercians* who arrived half a century later and in one or two major respects challenged the Cluniac way of life. Both orders took the *Rule of St. Benedict* as their foundation, but not surprisingly they disagreed on what was the correct interpretation of a document now five centuries old.

The mother house of the Cistercian order was Cîteaux (*Cistercium*) not far from Dijon in northern Burgundy. The house owed its origin to a party of monks under one Robert, who in 1098, had left their mother house of Molesme to found a stricter one, under the conviction that the interpretation of life prevalent at Molesme was too easy-going. Their life was a hard one and at first showed no great signs of prospering. But fairly quickly the situation improved out of all knowledge. This was partly due to the wise abbacy of the Englishman Stephen Harding who ruled Cîteaux from 1109 to 1134, but very much more to the order's acquisition of the most influential churchman of the century, St. Bernard of Clairvaux. This was a man of immense sensitivity and unyielding self-sacrifice, with a golden voice that spoke so fascinatingly of the glory of monastic life, that, it is said, mothers hid their sons when they heard of his approach, lest they straightway gave up all to follow him. 'To see him was the whole world's desire' wrote a contemporary, and this fascination St. Bernard exerted made him all unwillingly a public figure of the first rank, corresponding and consorting with ecclesiastical and secular rulers of the highest rank, and preaching far and wide over Western Europe. It is indicative of the power of his personality that when St. Bernard presented himself at Cîteaux to become a monk, he brought with him a whole troop of male relations inspired with the same intent. Led by him the Cistercian movement surged through the Western Church like flood water through a broken dyke.

By 1115 Cîteaux had four daughter houses, including Clairvaux of which Bernard was made abbot. By his death in 1153 there were, it is estimated, 343 Cistercian abbeys and between 1134 and 1342 some 600 houses were founded. Eventually St. Bernard's own abbey produced no less than eighty daughter houses, far more than Cîteaux itself.

What was the Cistercian ideal which swept so many hundreds of men of every degree into the cloister? It claimed to be a re-establishment of primitive Benedictinism and was certainly intensely conservative in nature. Like many of the early monks of the Church, the Cistercians strove to withdraw as completely as possible from the world. Their abbeys were ordered to be 'in places remote from human habitation', so desolate valleys and lonely forests were sought. They were to have no parish responsibilities, a chapel for the visitors and dependants of the monastery being the only place of worship apart from that of the brethren. Originally, it was logically laid down that the Cistercians should not own such ecclesiastical sources of revenue as advowsons or tithes. Their isolation from the local church was increased by papal privileges which exempted them from the usual visitation by the local bishop.

In their worship they cut away some of the luxuriant liturgical growth which the Cluniacs so favoured, such as various litanies, processions and the office of All Saints, but they retained the historic outline of western monastic worship.

There was a similar simplification of the visual aids to which western worship had been so long accustomed, and which the Cluniacs so greatly cherished. It was thought that the rich Romanesque art of the time had become distracting, so some rigorous simplification was ordered. The stained-glass windows now coming into vogue were forbidden in favour of plain glass. Forbidden also was the use of gold and gems in church plate, and the use even of silver was much restricted. Crucifixes were to be of painted wood only, and animal and human carvings forbidden, in favour of plain foliage and geometrical designs. The richness of vestments was similarly under suspicion. Such artistic Puritanism was not confined to the Cistercians, nor did it prevent them erecting churches characterised by a dignity and beauty none the less real for being austere. As time went on it proved as transient as most artistic reactions, and by the end of the thirteenth century this Cistercian fussiness was largely extinct.

A notable feature of Cistercian life was its stress on manual labour, which, as was rightly perceived, was a fundamental element of the original Benedictine life. To this theoretical point in its favour were added two practical ones. In the first place many Cistercian abbeys at first had very little endowment, and as they had also little or nothing coming from ecclesiastical revenues, living remote from the towns where alms might have been procured, they were at first much dependent for subsistence on the work of their own hands. Secondly the Cistercians developed enormously the use of lay brethren, which thus gave them a labour force far beyond the usual domestic needs of the monastery.

The immense appeal of the Cistercian life in the twelfth and thirteenth centuries meant that many wished to lead it who had not the qualifications to become a choir monk. But at this time most laity of every social level were illiterate, so many recruits would not make the educational grade needed for the normal conventual life and in any case many were not suited to it. Yet such people could be of great use if they took monastic vows and, with a diminished round of worship, concentrated their main energies on manual labour. The monastic site had to be cleared, its buildings erected, gardens and fields laid out and drained, land reclaimed, crops and flocks to be tended. Such work was rapidly and effectively undertaken by the thousands of lay brethren who flocked to Cistercian cloisters. One unexpected result of this was that the marked poverty which usually characterised early Cistercian houses often rapidly changed to considerable wealth. The great labour force of the Cistercians and their early privilege of exemption from paying tithe on lands which they cultivated with their own hands, all helped to develop Cistercian wealth. In England by the late thirteenth century the Cistercians had done not a little to develop the wool trade on which so much of England's wealth in later medieval times was to depend, whilst one or two Cistercian abbeys played a prominent part in the English iron industry at this time.

A final feature of Cistercian life remains to be noted—the strict uniformity which it laid down and enforced. The *Rule of St. Benedict* was to be 'interpreted in one way and observed in one way'. Thus all Cistercian houses were dedicated to Our Lady, the old custom of choosing a local or some other saint being ruled out. Their buildings were laid out on a remarkably uniform plan and their worship based on a uniform use. All houses had to have at least thirteen brethren and no two of them could be founded close together. Much medieval legislation tended to be pious aspirations rather than established facts, but this Cistercian uniformity was very strictly enforced by means of a *General Chapter*. This was an assembly of the abbots of Cistercian houses which met annually at Cîteaux, to legislate for the order and enforce its regulations on errant houses. Distant abbots might be excused annual attendance, but had to observe the legislation, and all were liable to be visited annually by the abbot of the house from which their monastery had drawn its first brethren, Cîteaux itself being visited by the abbots of its first four daughter houses. Medieval transport was too slow and the expansion too rapid to allow this visitation to be very effective, but it did something to hold the order together.

It would be unfair to say that the Cistercians took no interest in study. But they certainly gave it a minor place. Devotional reading was much more stressed than theological speculation and private prayer was allowed at certain times instead of reading. The order produced few notable theologians and at first was hostile to contacts with the new universities. But in this, as in other things, time brought experience and their interest in study increased somewhat, though, like so many religious people with a touch of puritanism, they never got really enthusiastic about matters intellectual.

The first Cistercian house in England was founded at Waverley (Surrey) in 1128 but the major early centre was Rievaulx founded three years later with William, St. Bernard's secretary, as its first abbot. Excavations showed that his fame led to an entirely unofficial shrine to him being put up in the chapter house at Rievaulx. This abbey quickly founded daughter houses, and is said to have had 140 monks and 500 lay brothers by the time of the death of its most famous member St. Ailred (1165). A year after Rievaulx was established, came the foundation of Fountains abbey, not far from Ripon. Its early years were marked by abject poverty but conditions rapidly improved. In twenty years it colonised a dozen daughter houses, including one in Norway. It ultimately became the richest English house of the order, with considerable properties in Yorkshire and the Lake District. The Cistercians took England by storm, no less than fifty-one houses being founded here between 1128 and 1154. After this the pace slackened markedly, the total number being seventy-six. In 1147 the Cistercians absorbed a little order of Savigny (a Benedictine house in Normandy) which had a score of houses in England, of which the most important was that of Furness (N. Lancs.), which vied with Fountains for primacy and was second to it in wealth.

By the middle years of the thirteenth century Benedictine expansion of all kinds in England had died down to a trickle, but the progress made had been very notable. The total number of houses of men was now about seven times what it had been at the time of the Conquest (about 345 against 48) and there had been an even greater increase in houses of nuns (now about 140 as against 12) in 1066. It is true that nearly all the new houses were smaller than the Benedictine giants of pre-Conquest days, and many of them appreciably so. But the fact that the number of monks had risen from about 850 to about 6000 is sufficient indication of the continued potency of Benedictinism in one form or other. What renders this expansion even more remarkable is that it was accomplished in an age of exceptional competition from new monastic orders.

CHAPTER SIX

THE REGULAR CANONS

THESE formed the second great family among the religious orders of the medieval Church, and are also known as the 'regular canons of St. Augustine', or as 'Austin canons'. In the Middle Ages their use of a black cloak when outside the monastery, led them to be also known as 'black canons'.

Technically it is incorrect to call them *monks* or *monachi*, the latter word being reserved for those leading the Benedictine life and other forms allied to it. But long before the end of the Middle Ages, in popular if not in legal language, this term was applied to them and it can scarcely now be withheld.

The Origins of the Order

A canon was originally a priest on the official list of diocesan clergy, as distinct from one serving in a monastery or at a private chapel. For most of the Dark Ages the majority of such official clergy lived in large clergy houses or collegiate churches known in England as *minsters*. Canon came to be the name of a member of one of these large institutions, as distinct from one living by himself or with only one or two brethren. In the centuries before the Norman Conquest, the official rule for such canons was that they should have a common refectory and dormitory and not private houses, and should draw their stipends from a common fund. It was understood that they should be unmarried, but they were under no obligation to live under any kind of a vow of poverty.

In the mid-eleventh century, however, in Italy and northern France especially, there arose a movement to make life in their minsters or collegiate churches more severe. It was vigorously urged that in the time of the apostles there was a complete lack of private property among Christian folk and that clergy, especially, should set an example by giving up private possessions. And at the same time much stricter recognition of the rule that clergy should not marry was demanded. This movement attracted much attention and won the support of some of the chief reformers of the day, one of whom, the future pope Gregory VII, brought up the matter for official consideration at the Lateran synod of 1059. This created a difficult question, as the Church had never insisted on her clergy living under vows of poverty. In the end a very reasonable compromise was reached—the council warmly commended the idea of clergy living what was in effect the monastic life, i.e. being unmarried and living without property under obedience to a fixed rule of life and a common superior. But it did not attempt the unwise step of enforcing such a programme on the clergy of the day.

Those who followed this way of life had now got it officially approved, and various communities of this type came rapidly into existence in Italy, Austria, Flanders, certain parts of France and neighbouring regions. Clearly some way of distinguishing such houses of canons from those following the old method of life had to be found, and by the early twelfth century it had become usual for the former to be called 'regular canons' (i.e. canons living by a *Regula* or rule) and the latter became known as 'secular canons' because they lived in the world (*seculum*) and not in a strict community. By this time it was usual for those living the monastic life to have a fixed written rule, that of St. Benedict by now having long reigned almost unchallenged in Western Europe. Largely to answer criticism in this respect, the regular canons sporadically but steadily adopted the so-called *Rule of St. Augustine*. The origins and history of this document have been much discussed, but it was probably a masculine version of a letter to a house of nuns written by St. Augustine of Hippo about 423 and adapted for use in a house of men not very long after. The later version had added to it a short preliminary part enacting specific rules about several practical points. These were necessary, since the *Rule of St. Augustine* unlike that of St. Benedict, was not a detailed and systematic consideration of the regulations that should govern the daily life of a monastery, but a short document giving some useful spiritual advice but very few concrete regulations. By the mid-twelfth century most of the preliminary part was found inapplicable to western conditions, and it was generally henceforth largely or wholly omitted.

Because of all this the regular canons who adopted the *Rule of St. Augustine* had to reinforce it with various rules or observances if their daily life was to be regulated with the detail and precision desirable. For long there were no official series of observances imposed on them by authority, but houses were left to fend for themselves, subject to official approval. As they had no immediate predecessors, the regular canons inevitably borrowed much from the Benedictine monasteries who had so long practised with success the sort of common life to which the new order aspired. But the Augustinian ideal was rather less severe than that of the Benedictines, with a rather shorter round of worship, and rules over fasting and silence were notably less exacting than those of such strict Benedictine orders as the Cistercians. Indeed the regular canons of the twelfth century claimed that their life was a *via media* between the excessive austerity of the monks and the excessive interest in the world of the secular canons. However, it must be admitted that in the end there was little important difference between the régime of many Augustinian and Benedictine houses. Because of the lack of a common origin, early observances in Augustinian houses varied a good deal in detail. Under the influence of the early Cistercians, a certain number of Austin canons adopted a quite severe form of life, but these were always a small minority.

It used to be thought that early regular canons undertook considerable pastoral work, but it now seems very unlikely that this was the case. In general, the regular canons were not interested in missionary work in the modern sense. They rather strove, like the monks of old, to influence the world indirectly in two ways—firstly, by their own disciplined lives in community to display rejection of the world, the flesh and the devil, which would inspire the outsider to a renewed attempt to seek perfection in the Christian life. Secondly, by their maintenance of a majestic and unbroken round of worship to offer up prayer and praise to God on behalf of the outside world, more especially for their benefactors and their relations. It is, however, true that from the end of the twelfth century onwards, we do find a trickle of instances of regular canons taking duty at parish churches, a practice which was most rarely copied by the Benedictines of these days. Occasionally the altar thus served was that of the parishioners, which stood either in or very near to their conventual church. But increasingly it was more usual to be that of a distant parish church of which the house was patron.

From an early stage in the existence of the order there were a number of houses of regular canons which were founded with little or no connection with a local parish church, either on a completely new site outside a town, or very far from it, or, in some cases, on the site of a hermitage where a hermit or band of hermits had been living a life of retirement. In some other cases we find regular canons serving hospitals. As we shall see, medieval hospitals were of three main types, serving travellers, the sick, and the aged. They had normally a largish body of clergy attached and it was quite common for these to be bound to a fairly strict rule of life. Such being the case, the sober discipline of the regular canons was understandably adopted in some cases—one of the most famous of these was the Hospital of St. Bernard up at the top of the Alpine pass of that name.

The regular canons were clergy in theory and because of this were normally under the supervision of the bishop of the diocese in which they lived. But a few of the houses got the special privilege of being subject directly to the pope. After 1215, the regular canons had to hold general chapters, assemblies at which all houses of the order were represented, which legislated for the common good and strove to enforce law and maintain good discipline. These general chapters were organised on a regional basis. Thus in England there was at first one chapter for the whole country but from 1233 onwards this split into two bodies, one for the province of Canterbury, the other for the province of York. However, their activities were not impressive; a writer at Barnwell priory wrote that their decrees were 'easily published and rejected with equal ease'!

By the time the general chapters went into action, an important minority of the regular canons belonged to independent congregations of the order that had grown up. These had their own rules and regulations and their own machinery for enforcing them. As we shall see, a few of these had English daughter houses; most of them were never very influential.

The Introduction into England

The new order made very slow progress in England for half a century after its confirmation at the Lateran council of 1059. The first house did not come until about 1086 when Archbishop Lanfranc established a small community in a church of St. Gregory which he built at the north gate of his cathedral city of Canterbury. The brethren were to tend inmates of a hospital for the poor, hear confessions and live a common life. About the same time a house of regular canons came into existence at the church of St. Mary's Huntingdon, which in 1092 sent regular canons to establish a small house in the church of St. Giles' Cambridge. But this intention was not fulfilled and finally in 1112 the brethren were moved to a much more suitable site at Barnwell, outside the city of Cambridge.

It seems unlikely that any of these houses had adopted the rule of St. Augustine, which at this time was little known in outlying areas of the Western Church. The first English house of the order to adopt it was probably the priory of St. Botolph's Colchester. This had originated as a little house of secular canons, but at the opening of the twelfth century the brethren decided to join the new order. About 1103, with the help of Archbishop Anselm, two of their brethren went to France and studied the life of the regular canons in the abbeys of St. Quentin at Beauvais and St. Jean-en-Vallée at Chartres. Then they returned and taught it to their brethren. Soon after this, a small house of the order was founded at Little Dunmow (1106), not far away. But the first major step in the order's progress here came with the foundation of Holy Trinity priory Aldgate. This was established by the queen of England, Matilda, probably in 1107 and rapidly became wealthy and fashionable. Quickly Aldgate established daughter houses at St. Osyth, Plympton, Launceston, St. Frideswide's Oxford, Dunstable and possibly Llanthony. Meanwhile Huntingdon had founded daughter houses at Barnwell, Hexham, Bolton, Merton and probably Worksop. Much the most important of these was Merton priory which quickly vied in importance with Aldgate. It was founded by Gilbert the Sheriff, an important civil servant in 1114 on a new site not far out of London. From it colonies soon went out to Taunton, Bodmin, Cirencester, Holyrood, St. Lô in Normandy and Christchurch (Hants.).

King Henry I of England was a notable patron of the order. His biggest foundation was the abbey of Cirencester and the houses of Carlisle, Cirencester, Dunstable, St. Denys-by-Southampton and Wellow-by-Grimsby claim him as their founder. By the year in which the king was alive and dead (1135) some forty houses of regular canons had sprung up in this country. For a full century thereafter expansion continued, being longer maintained than that of any other order. By 1215 about 140 houses had been added and by 1349 some twenty-nine more, the total figure being about 208.

Impressive as these figures are, by themselves they are somewhat misleading, for few of the English houses of Austin canons were very large and a good number were very small. The Benedictines had some houses with between fifty and a hundred monks. The Cistercians insisted on a minimum of thirteen brethren per house and often had more. No English house of Austin canons is known to have reached fifty, the largest convent certainly known being Cirencester though a few bigger ones probably existed. A useful proportion seemed to have started with the traditional thirteen. This was not an official minimum and a fair number of houses had fewer, in some cases substantially fewer. Thus Charley at one time had only three brethren, Breedon and Wymondley five, Royston and Buckland seven. There is no doubt that the establishment of such very small houses was far from wise. They had not the resources of money or manpower to establish a really thriving common life. As time went on we find some of them maintaining a protracted and not always successful struggle to stave off bankruptcy whilst their spiritual well-being was sometimes equally in danger.

A number of these houses were in East Anglia where, in the twelfth and thirteenth centuries, there existed an extensive upper middle class whose members were anxious to ape their betters by establishing monasteries of their own. Their resources were often inadequate for this, but some were able to ease the problem by establishing their priory in a fairly wealthy parish church of which they owned the patronage. The revenues of this would maintain a few canons, and as such endowments could not be held by laymen, this saved the founder considerable expense. To what extent he increased this pre-existing endowment depended on his inclination and resources. There is no doubt that the founders of a number of these houses established them in the hope that other benefactors would increase what they had begun. It is equally certain that this expectation was normally not realised, owing to the intense competition for bounty brought about by the arrival of so many new orders in England.

Not all houses established in old churches were small. A number were medium-sized and a few large. To the latter category belong, some but not all of those founded by converting ancient secular colleges such as Launceston, Bodmin, Taunton and St. Oswald's Gloucester. Cirencester, the wealthiest house of the order at the time of the Suppression, had been a college, but at the time Henry I established regular canons there its endowments were held by a single priest. This was also the case at Hexham, formerly a monastery of renown, which Archbishop Thurstan of York made into one of the larger monasteries of northern England. These two at one time had forty and twenty-seven canons respectively.

As we have noted, where a major church formed the nucleus of the endowment the new convent might share the church with the parishioners. A large number of churches of Austin canons, probably the majority, had no parochial connection, but were founded afresh and had the right to maintain a place of worship only for themselves and their dependants. Some of such houses were on the outskirts of towns, like Llanthony by Gloucester, but some were well clear of it like Bolton, Launde and Lanercost. In some half-dozen cases this remote site was due to the house having been established on the site of a hermitage, as at Bushmead and Llanthony. Some communities of hermits became regular canons, partly because experience showed the value of leading a properly organised monastic life instead of the rather haphazard life of hermits with no fixed position or rule, partly also, probably, because the adoption of the rule of St. Augustine did not tie down the new community to a set of complex rules like those of the *Rule of St. Benedict*. These non-parochial houses also varied a good deal in size, but did not include many of the largest houses; Merton priory is one of the exceptions here.

A few other houses of English Austin canons were hospitals at one time or another. In cases like Anglesey, Newstead by Stamford and Creake a hospital was converted into a priory, which again, of course, cost the founder little or nothing. The resources of one or two more English houses of the order were pretty equally divided between regular canons and those in need and were known sometimes as 'hospitals' sometimes as 'priories'. We shall consider medieval English hospitals later, but may here note in passing that two of the most famous of these—St. Bartholomew's Smithfield and St. Thomas's Southwark—originated under the auspices respectively of the London houses of St. Bartholomew's priory at Smithfield and St. Mary's Southwark.

Two English houses of Austin canons are worthy of special note. At Carlisle a priory had been established about 1122 in a very harassed Border city. At this time north-western England had long been a no-man's-land between the kingdoms of England and Scotland, though recently the Norman kings had had some success in their attempts to attach the area to England. To assist in this process, a new diocese covering most of Cumberland and half of Westmorland was now set up, the priory of Austin canons at Carlisle being made the cathedral. The first bishop was consecrated in 1133 but Border warfare went on fiercely for some time, Carlisle temporarily passing into Scottish hands soon after. The see was extremely poor and when the first bishop died a long vacancy ensued; the second bishop was a not very inspiring person who had been archbishop of Ragusa and then wandered loose for some time. However, after this things settled down somewhat. Carlisle was the last English diocese to be founded in the Middle Ages, though the number might profitably have been much increased. It was also the only cathedral to belong to the Austin canons.

Ultimately wealthier and more famous was the Augustinian priory of Our Lady of Walsingham. This originated as a chapel about 1130* built after the manner of the long-destroyed Holy House of Nazareth. Not long after, a small priory of canons was founded at the chapel, the first prior evidently taking up office in 1153. For some time the priory was of no more significance than the other small religious houses with which East Anglia was so liberally peppered. In the course of the thirteenth century, however, popular devotion to the statue of Our Lady at

* The idea that it was founded before the Conquest has not been accepted by any reputable historian for a century, but still lingers in uninformed quarters.

7

Walsingham made the priory something of a pilgrimage centre, and the cult steadily developed in the fourteenth and fifteenth centuries. Our Lady of Walsingham was one of the few English pilgrimages to attract some following from abroad and on the eve of the Reformation was easily the most popular shrine of its kind. King Henry III (1216–72) went there first in 1226 and made a number of later visits. A great proportion of the later English kings and their queens were pilgrims there including even Henry VIII who seems to have hoped to gain an heir through his visit.

By 1216 the English house of Austin canons numbered about 180. Though, as we have seen, they continued to gain new adherents for some little time to come, very few of these were of any size, the majority evidently having not more than one or two dozen brethren, and far too many having a convent that did not reach double figures. The vast majority of these houses were priories though thirteen independent houses at one time or other had abbatial rank. Their organisations differed notably from that of the new Benedictine orders. The great mass of houses of regular canons had no unified machinery or customs, each house worked out its own salvation, subject always to the approval and due control of the local bishop. Only two English houses got the special privilege of exemption from this, St. Botolph's Colchester (where English regular canons probably first practised the *Rule of St. Augustine*) and Waltham abbey (which had acquired this as a royal foundation of the first rank).

A small minority of English houses of regular canons belonged to separate congregations, though the latter were generally much smaller than such great Benedictine orders as Cluny and Cîteaux.

Of those founded overseas, the order of St. Sepulchre of Jerusalem had half a dozen small houses in England, including St. Sepulchre's Warwick and Caldwell. These were all subordinate to their famous mother house in the Holy Land, and when this was lost by the collapse of the Crusading kingdoms, they were left stranded. Less insignificant were the daughter houses of Arrouaise, a house near Bapaume in northern France, whose strict observance owed not a little to Cistercian influence. First to be founded was Missenden (1133), quickly followed by Bourne, Dorchester, Lilleshall and Notley. In the Cistercian manner all these were known as abbeys. But the final total did not reach double figures. The little house of Arrouaisian nuns at Harrold (Bedfordshire), like most English nunneries, ranked as a priory. The middle of the twelfth century saw an unsuccessful and short-lived attempt to make Carlisle and one or two other houses Arrouaisian. The order of St. Victor originated in the great Parisian abbey of that name and had half a dozen English houses mostly in the Bristol area. The first of these was Wigmore priory whose founder had seen St. Victor when staying in Paris on the way back from a pilgrimage to the famous Spanish shrine of St. James of Compostella. Next came the most important abbey of St. Augustine's Bristol, which was destined to become a cathedral at the time of the Reformation.

Much more influential than any other foreign order of Austin canons in England was the order of Prémontré. It was founded by St. Norbert, an aristocrat who threw over a secular career to become an itinerant preacher. He attracted followers and was given a site for a monastery in a forest near Laon, in 1120. The house became known as Prémontré and its inmates as Premonstratensians. The early Premonstratensians, unlike almost all the other regular canons of the time, showed some interest in preaching and early took on mission work in east Germany. But this interest was very limited. It did not prevail at Prémontré itself which seems to have led a secluded life, and the order fairly quickly stressed the monastic at the expense of the missionary side of their work.

Under Cistercian influence the Premonstratensians set up a system of annual general chapters and by the end of the twelfth century they had divided their houses into regional groups known as circaries. These had annual visitors appointed by the general chapter and might be visited by the abbot of Prémontré. After 1247 the order was exempt from episcopal visitation. There were soon appointed local visitors for the various circaries, whose activities were apt to be more effective than those of mother houses, whose heads might well find it difficult or impossible to visit daughter houses if these were numerous or very distant. Again imitating the Cistercians, the Premonstratensians insisted on a considerable degree of uniformity, notably in such matters as service books (which at this time elsewhere varied considerably in detail), dress and diet, and observed a stricter rule than the general run of Benedictines.

In 1152 the general chapter of the order forbade further foundations although there were exceptions made. The expansion of the Premonstratensians in England has been fully investigated by Mr. Colvin, and can be referred to only briefly here. The first English abbey of Premonstratensians was founded at Newhouse in Lincolnshire about 1143, and from the first this was immensely important, quickly colonising no less than eleven other houses. By 1267 the order had here thirty-one abbeys and three nunneries in England. Nearly all were founded in the twelfth century, only three English Premonstratensian abbeys being established after 1200. The houses were spread over most of England, mainly in secluded spots and were nearly all of moderate size.

These foreign orders of regular canons were joined by an English one, the only medieval monastic congregation to originate in this country. This was the order of Sempringham, founded by St. Gilbert in the Lincolnshire village of that name; its members were sometimes called Gilbertines. The mother house was begun about 1131 when Gilbert, then parish priest at Sempringham, established seven local maidens in a little convent by his church, adding some lay brethren to do the rougher out-of-door work. By 1154, to Gilbert's surprise, Sempringham had been joined by another ten monasteries. Progress continued for some time, the final total being twenty-six. Twelve of these, headed by Sempringham, were double monasteries, i.e. they had a house of nuns and one of canons in the same precinct but strictly separated. Although, for some time, certain of these double houses probably had a large number of inmates, none of them was very rich, though Sempringham and Watton had a good deal larger income than most Augustinian houses in England. The rest were houses of men only and almost all were poor. Originally St. Gilbert had hoped to make his young congregation Cistercian but this proved impossible as they were given Augustinian observances with a Premonstratensian flavour. The appeal of the order was very limited, most of the houses being in and around Lincolnshire.

The Nuns

To the modern mind, one of the most unexpected aspects of medieval monastic life is the very minor rôle played in it by women. Today the great majority of Christian monasteries are houses of women, not of men; in the Middle Ages the exact reverse was the case. It is difficult to explain why this was so, but it was certainly due to a combination of factors. Influential was the conservatism of medieval society, which took over with little question the ancient assumption that women were naturally inferior. This belief had been very strong in ancient Greece whose civilisation was essentially a male civilisation and one which greatly influenced medieval thought. Then there was the suspicion of women that reigned so early amongst what one may term the left-wing Christian ascetics, as well as the very crude social conditions of the Middle Ages which made it undesirable for nuns to attempt the sort of social works they have done on such an important scale since the sixteenth century. And in the late Middle Ages in the Western Church an important consideration was the fact that women could not be ordained to priest's orders, and could not, therefore, offer the masses in whose efficacy the man in the street so greatly believed. Certainly there was a widespread assumption, even in pious circles, that the woman's place was not the cloister but the home, and was a subordinate place even there.

However this may be, medieval nunneries were a minor feature of English monastic life. In Anglo-Saxon times there had been monasteries where houses of monks and nuns shared a common church but had strictly separated living quarters. Sometimes the ruler of such a double monastery was a woman, the most famous of these being St. Hilda (d. 680) who ruled the great house at Whitby. But after 1066 authority was steadily hostile to double monasteries and very few of them existed, though the order of Sempringham had some.

A very notable feature of English houses of nuns was the considerable poverty of all but a tiny minority of them. Famous and rich was the nunnery king Alfred had founded at Shaftesbury, which at the Dissolution had an income of over a thousand pounds a year and in the thirteenth and fourteenth centuries had over a hundred sisters. Barking was even older and also richer. Below these—mostly a long way below—was a handful of mainly moderate-sized houses like Wilton, Amesbury, St. Helen's Bishopgate, Malling, Nuneaton, Romsey, Wherwell and

Buckland, most of which had inherited endowments from pre-Conquest times. Very few sizeable houses of nuns were founded in the later Middle Ages but to this category belong Dartford, the only English house of Dominican nuns, and the Franciscan nunnery in London. A good three-quarters of English nunneries certainly lived in the poorest way with a revenue which, even at the Dissolution, only amounted to a few dozen pounds a year. Those who believe women to be more sacrificial than men or believe in the power of poverty will note with satisfaction that, despite this poverty, the average size of a house of nuns at the time of the Dissolution was apparently slightly larger than that of a house of monks.

It was doubtless largely because of their poverty, that houses of nuns seem quite frequently to have taken ladies as paying guests and sometimes to have maintained what were in effect small boarding schools. The new orders of friars with their stress on priestly work could not be copied by houses of women and only five houses belonged to their orders, four of which were Franciscan, in which order a separate section with entirely different functions from its houses of men was created. Almost all the other houses were Augustinians or Benedictines of some kind and observed much the same pattern of life as their male namesakes.

The exact number of houses of English regular canons of all kinds established by the opening of the thirteenth century was in the region of 270, being some eighty fewer than the total of Benedictine houses, of one kind or another. Together the combined total of Augustinian and Benedictine houses by 1216 seems to have been well over 600, to which we must add about 140 houses of nuns, giving a combined total of towards 800. A rough estimate of the number of inmates of these monasteries suggest a grand total of some 14,000, of which 3000 were nuns. This compares with a total of sixty monasteries and about 1000 monks and nuns in 1066. However, this prodigious increase was not the end of the story. Within a very few years began the last great wave of monastic invasion, that of the Friars, which demands separate consideration.

CHAPTER SEVEN

THE FRIARS, THE MILITARY ORDERS AND THE HOSPITALS

The Friars

B Y the opening of the thirteenth century Augustinian and Benedictine monasteries were so widespread in England, that, except in the desolate parts of the north and west, a man could not walk many miles without passing near one. That the former zeal of these houses by this time had now much decayed has occasionally been alleged but has never been proved, and the view is probably to be rejected as one of those gloomy suspicions that has often led the modern Anglo-Saxon student of monasticism astray.

Popular respect for the monastic ideal and its exponents remained a very real thing, but was not untempered with criticism. Just as today many criticise the parish clergy who would be sorry to lose them, so then (as, indeed, before and after this time) criticism of particular aspects of monasticism was entirely compatible with loyalty to it, indeed some of it sprang from that loyalty.

One main question that led to such criticism in the late twelfth and early thirteenth centuries was the wealth of the monasteries at this period. As we have seen, this was most unevenly distributed, and many houses were very far from affluent, but the aggregate of English monastic wealth was now very considerable. One or two dozen old Benedictine houses invited severe criticism by their considerable affluence, and recently the same sort of charges were being levied against some Cistercians. These had acquired much land and wealth from benefactors and exploited their estates with great vigour and skill. They had the capital the ordinary farmer lacked, as well as an unpaid labour force in their lay brethren, and the privilege of paying no tithe on lands they cultivated by their own hands, besides an intelligence and foreign connections which enabled them to show a trading initiative the simple backwoods farmer of contemporary England would never exhibit. On top of all this came the Cistercian regulation that its monks should support themselves at least in part by their labours. All in all, therefore, it is not surprising that the English Cistercian monks practised agriculture with an unparalleled and instructed vigour which, amongst other things, was destined to do much towards laying the foundations of the wool trade, upon which, from the late thirteenth century, the foreign trade of England for long mainly depended. Inevitably their success infuriated their unsuccessful competitors, and the keenness with which they added field to field gave them an understandable if not entirely justified reputation for avarice, which increased the popular feeling that monasticism was too closely linked with money, a sentiment as keenly felt on the

Continent as in England, despite the somewhat different economic conditions there.

A second factor at this period was changing the old society in which traditional monasticism had been born. This was the steady spread of education, at all levels. Its most spectacular effects were the establishment of universities in Western Europe at this time and the growth of a literate middle class in certain areas such as Italy and Flanders. By the late twelfth century in these areas at least, the clergy and laity alike were taking a much greater interest in the intellectual side of the Christian life, questioning and discussing things which for some centuries had been little questioned or discussed. One result of this was the rise of heretical movements on a scale unknown in the West for a long while. These rejected one or other aspect of the Catholic faith. Their success in some areas brought home to the far-sighted the need of theological study if orthodoxy was to be properly understood and wisely defended. Another result was the revival of preaching, which for some time had dwindled to very small proportions in western parish churches. By a process which it is almost impossible to disentangle, there developed an important change of attitude to the monastic life. Hitherto, as we have seen, the history of monasticism had been very largely, if not completely, dominated by the conviction that monks should live outside the bounds of everyday society, and influence their members not primarily by direct intervention in its affairs, but by their prayers and by their manifestation of a disciplined Christian life. By the early thirteenth century this ideal was very much alive, and was, indeed, partly responsible for the great expansion of the Augustinian and Benedictine orders which we have just noted. But alongside it seems to have grown up the sentiment which has dominated western monasticism in modern centuries. This sees the monastic life as a way of evangelising the world by the direct intervention of its members in everyday society. It was this idea which inspired the friars and explains why they remain so important a force in the modern Christian world. As we shall see, they tended to specialise in this pastoral work, had a fresh concept of the nature of monastic poverty and produced a highly flexible organisation of a type hitherto unknown.

The Orders of Friars

There were four major orders of friars in medieval England, of which two—the Franciscans and the Dominicans—were particularly important.

The Franciscans take their name from their founder, St. Francis of Assisi, one of the most remarkable and challenging exponents of the Christian life that the world has seen. He was born in 1181 or 1182 at Assisi, the son of a wealthy cloth merchant. The Umbrian hills of his home region are one of the most exquisite areas of an exquisite country, and his father gave him plenty of money wherewith to enjoy the good things of this life, so it is not surprising that Francis' youthful years saw him enjoying to the full the delights of the world. But behind it all nagged feelings of doubt; doubt as to whether these delights were not being enjoyed at other people's expense; doubts as to whether this was the sort of life that would save his soul at the last. In the end the doubts triumphed. The old life was thrown over and a new one begun, marked pre-eminently by prayer and poverty. Prayer in desert places and poverty involving living entirely on the alms of others. With it went a passionate wish to aid the afflicted, especially the lepers, those outcasts from the medieval body politic. Concerned with souls as well as with bodies, Francis started to preach a simple call to repentance, of acceptance of Catholic religious duties.

He had never intended to found a religious order but the unexpected happened. Followers came, first in driblets, then in scores, till within a short space his society was numbered in thousands. The problem of organising this host of helpers to the highest advantage of their Church was pressing and difficult in the extreme. Difficult because of the founder's passionate views on poverty, privilege and learning. Francis had found peace of mind through a view of poverty which involved the complete rejection of living for the day after tomorrow; no property was owned and nothing stored up against an evil day. Money he found to be something most likely to inspire covetousness and selfishness, to deflect man's eyes away from his essential function, to love God, Man and Nature. As for legal and other privilege, it tended to excite selfishness in the individual and hostility in his neighbour. Whilst there were those whose vocation it was to pursue learning, this was not for Francis. The esteem accorded to university men in these first days—as great as that accorded to the Victorian scientist—was apt to breed conceit and to cut off such a man from one of St. Francis' great loves—the man in the street.

Such refreshing views as these constitute a valuable warning to most Christians most of the time, when expressed in the lives of the select few. But the Church had to preserve and canalise the work of St. Francis in such a way as to make it fertilise the future. For this, some considerable degree of organisation was necessary. If the heretic was to be converted and the faithful illumined there must be learning as well as piety—there must be houses and libraries, rights to preach to the people and hear their confessions, rights to use when bishops and clergy proved hostile to new order. Some degree of friction with the secular clergy was almost inevitable, human nature being what it is. Both for psychological and financial reasons (see pages 91-2) many priests would object to their congregation flocking off to the new friars— people more eloquent and highly trained than many clergy—to hear their sermons or to make their confessions and hear mass in friars' churches. Because of these factors the first century of Franciscanism was much more contentious and disturbed than that of any other great monastic order. The question of the nature of their vow of poverty especially, split the order before St. Francis' death and long after it, and this internal struggle was contemporaneous with trouble with the parish clergy, and also a certain amount of rather jealous criticism from the older orders. It was typical of St. Francis' respect for his Church and his sweetness of character that he refused to be involved in dissension or protest, and spent the last few years of life (1220–4) in miserable health and complete serenity, largely in solitude.

What was the constitution which was evolved for his *fratres* ('brethren') or 'friars'? A novel and valuable feature was that members were professed to the order as a whole, not to a particular house as was the ancient Benedictine custom, taken over of late by the new Augustinian orders. This gave the freedom of movement necessary for higher education and the mission work that often lay beyond it. Friars' houses were grouped into 'provinces' which were subdivided into 'custodies'. The heads of houses were known as 'ministers' to stress the element of service of others that St. Francis felt so passionately. Representatives from the houses attended annual provincial chapters, above which were triennial general chapters. Ultimately the whole order, having this elaborate machinery of its own, was freed from visitation by the local bishop. The original aim of the brethren was to preach to people and as far as possible to minister to his poor. At first this preaching was of a rather naïve type, but as time went on the value of a more sophisticated approach was felt, and friars given a long and careful training with much theological study. They developed a close connection with the universities, but, unfortunately, in the process of being educated, tended to lose a good deal of their primitive concern for the poor.

If the out-and-out poverty of early days was understandably early abandoned, the Franciscans always lived in a state of very real financial austerity. In effect friars owned little except the houses they lived in, and these were of very simple character, lacking completely Cluniac or Benedictine grandeur. Friars held no benefices, living largely on alms they begged and the offerings of the faithful. St. Francis had preferred living by manual labour as costing others less, but experience showed that this, when exercised on any considerable scale, tended to interfere seriously with their major work, and it quickly came to play a minor part in the friars' attempt to make ends meet. Because of the nature of their work and their need of alms the friars almost always settled in towns.

Their descent on England was planned in a very intelligent way. This began late in 1224 when a small party which included three Englishmen landed at Dover and went straight to Canterbury cathedral, where they were evidently expected. Within a few weeks they had set up small houses in London, Oxford, Cambridge and Northampton; they had thus pin-pointed the capital of England, its ecclesiastical centre, its two university towns, and (in Northampton) a major medieval meeting-place for northerners and southerners. Twelve other major towns were colonised in the next five years, with a speed and religious enthusiasm comparable to that generated by the Cistercians, a century before. By 1240—within sixteen years of their arrival—no less than thirty-four Franciscan houses had been founded, including fifteen in cathedral cities and twenty-five in county towns. A century later the total had risen to about fifty-three.

The second major order of friars, the Dominicans, had been founded and spread to England almost simultaneously. Their founder, St. Dominic (1170–1221), contrasts vividly with St. Francis, indeed the personalities of the two show little in common beyond an intense self-sacrifice for the good of the Church. St. Dominic was born about 1170 and became an Austin canon at Osma in Spain, where he was made prior at the age of twenty-four. The problem which was to guide him to his destiny was the problem of heresy which had recently broken out in certain areas, notably southern France, where St. Dominic was to be much engaged.

It is not easy to discover the exact nature of the views held by these heretics, but, at least in their extremer elements, they were socially dangerous and very anti-Catholic. Cistercian missionaries in the area proving of little use, St. Dominic and some companions were called in. Dominic had one of those intensely shrewd minds which was never clouded by cheap emotionalism. He who, from his early years, had prayed for a true love of souls and ability to help others, perceived at once that this new problem required radical new methods, which he proceeded to develop in the magnificent, cold-blooded way that made him and his order so effective.

Poverty in the Franciscan sense was not to St. Dominic the spiritual essential it was to St. Francis. But he saw its practical utility for those engaged in saving souls, especially the souls of those who in his day were, understandably if not justifiably, attacking a Church that included not a few over-wealthy institutions. So he practised poverty himself and made it part of the life of his order.

What was, however, the most original and important aspect of the Dominican programme, was the stress it laid on study. At all times true piety and sound learning are the classic recipe for vigorous religion, but most people most of the time show little interest in the second ingredient. Though the monks hitherto had been less illiterate than most, recent developments had tended to a rather reactionary policy over learning, evident both in St. Bernard and St. Francis. St. Dominic was clear that piety was not enough. The lively but crude ecclesiastical life of his day invited misrepresentation by the hostile, and weakened the virility of the Church. Whilst if the heretics' views were to be properly refuted, sound learning and logical thinking were essential: religious emotions would not suffice.

The main purpose of St. Dominic's mission was thus the exposition and defence of the faith of his Church, more especially through preaching. Such stress did he lay on this last that his order became known as 'the Order of Preachers' (*Ordo Praedicatorum*). Because of the importance of good preaching remarkable stress was laid on the necessity for study. Indeed the Dominicans may be said to be the first monastic order to give intellectual discipline pride of place. The daily office was abbreviated to allow more time for study, learned novices were sought, a long and careful intellectual training established and close contact with university life fostered. Theological centres were established in Paris, Oxford and Cambridge and in 1224 the new university of Toulouse was put in their charge.

As remarkable as their stress on study was the constitutional machinery of the

Dominican order, which was slightly older than that of the Franciscans and had some influence on it. In Cîteaux and Prémontré the abbey was the basic unit and the abbot was the basic authority. But with the Dominicans, life was the life of the whole order not of a particular house. Brethren could be moved easily from one house to another and life appointments to high office were unknown. The houses were grouped in provinces, each governed by a provincial prior with an annual provincial chapter, the former being elected by the priors of the province and two delegates from each house. At the top was the Master and an annual general chapter, the former being elected by provincial priors and two representatives from each province. All legislation had to be approved by three successive chapters. This extensive use of election was not due to democratic ideas born out of due season, but to the conviction that it ensured the best choice. Certainly in the event the Dominican constitution worked with a silent efficiency that has lasted down to the present day and contrasts vividly with the disorders of much early Franciscan history.

The Dominicans reached England in 1221, three years before the Franciscans, after equally careful preparation. After the archbishop of Canterbury had approved a test sermon, houses were set up in Oxford in 1221 and in Holborn (London) a year or two later. Others quickly followed such as Norwich (1226), York (1227), Bristol (1230) and Northampton (1232)—all, it will be noted, major English towns of the day. By about 1260 some thirty-six houses had been established and another dozen had joined them by 1272. Their final total was fifty-three, four less than those of the early Franciscans. The similarity of their work and the simplicity of their life inevitably brought them to the same sort of centres, and no less than thirty English towns had both a Dominican and a Franciscan house. The shrewd, sophisticated Dominicans filled a very important gap in the monastic ranks; they were favourite confessors and also, on occasion, useful diplomats. It is claimed that all English kings from Henry III to Richard II had Dominican confessors and most of their queens had Franciscan ones.

The rise of these two orders was an immense source of strength to the medieval Church. At a time when lay piety was developing they nourished and trained it most notably. Until their time, preaching to the laity was neither common nor popular; now it was carefully studied and took its rightful place. Sermons were adequately prepared and afforced by anecdotes (suitably collected in reference books by the early friars).

At the same time the friars played an important part in developing amongst the laity the practice of sacramental confession, i.e. periodic confession of sins to God in the presence of a priest, who could give counsel and absolution. This practice had developed gradually and after being found valuable by monks and clergy was extended to the whole Western Church by a decree of the Lateran council of 1215. Such a delicate task as hearing confessions required an insight and training which was fairly rare amongst the parish clergy of the thirteenth century, and much more likely to be found amongst people like the Franciscans and Dominicans. It is not therefore surprising that many laity flocked to friars' sermons and went to them for confession. Nor is it surprising that this upset the parish clergy. Not only did it wound their *amour-propre*, it also diminished their often not very princely pay, since offerings made at services and confession would often be diverted to the friars, as well as the legacies made when, as tended to happen, such people left instructions that they should be buried in friars' churches.

Such a situation inevitably created tricky problems, for it would have been as unfair to deprive the laity of the spiritual understanding of the friars, as to deprive the parish clergy of an important part of their income. After much heart-searching, an official compromise was hammered out, giving the Dominicans and Franciscans the right to bury the faithful in their churches on condition that part of the legacy went to the parish, the right to preach freely in public places and their own churches and by official invitation elsewhere and the right to nominate a limited number of brethren as confessors whom the bishop of the diocese would license as such. The only really unhappy feature of the early history of the two orders was their linking with the work of the Inquisition, the most hateful invention of the Western Church, even if its effects have often been grossly exaggerated. But the Inquisition was only allowed into medieval England on one brief occasion, and does not concern us here.

A notable feature of the friars was their close connection with the papacy. Monasticism had originated in the East and for long had no very consistent link with the popes of the West, being developed and maintained largely through local initiative. Cluny was the first order to be intimately linked with the papacy and this was the case increasingly with the new orders of the Western Church. It was providential that the careers of St. Dominic and St. Francis coincided with one of the wisest of medieval popes, Innocent III (1198–1216), who gave them the support and encouragement so necessary in their controversial but invaluable work. The same papal support was a decisive factor in the two other main orders of friars— the Augustinians and the Carmelites. Like the Austin canons, and unlike the Dominicans and Franciscans, these had no single great figure whom they could claim as being their founder, though the Austin friars could properly contend that some, if not all, of their way of life was foreshadowed by St. Augustine of Hippo. But the modern members of the *Friars Hermit of St. Augustine* or Austin friars (not, of course, to be confused with the Austin canons) trace their continuous life back to a number of semi-eremitical communities of hermits in Italy, which by the end of the twelfth century had almost all adopted the rule of St. Augustine. The papacy intervened to give them cohesion by making them a single order and this process concluded in a papal bull of 1256 which allowed them to be mendicants, i.e. to live on alms like the Dominicans and Franciscans. They quickly came heavily under the influence of the Dominicans and largely dropped their original hermits' way of life to become urban and intellectual. Partly through coming rather late into the field, they were less numerous than the older of friars. Their first

English houses were in rather rustic spots like Clare (1248), Cleobury Mortimer (1250) and Tickhill (1260) but thereafter they tended to choose urban centres. There were eleven houses in England by 1272, seventeen by 1300, then an interesting expansion which finally brought them a total of thirty-four houses.

The origins of the fourth main order, the Carmelites, were not dissimilar to those of the Austin friars. They too originated in communities of hermits of the twelfth century, though they had first centred on Mount Carmel, in the Holy Land, which the Crusading movement had brought into the sphere of influence of the Western Church. In the course of the late decades of the twelfth century, western hold of the Holy Land gradually crumbled away and with it went the old footholds there of the Austin friars. But they found fresh ones in Western Europe, though they tended to alter their way of life. Originally they had lived on severe eremitical lines not unlike the Carthusians, but in the mid-thirteenth century their English general St. Simon Stock (d. 1265) carried through an extensive reform much influenced by Dominican observances, relaxing the severity, increasing the communal life and government and allowing houses to be founded in or near cities. Mendicancy had been allowed by papal privilege a little earlier. However, the order never abandoned interest in the contemplative life.

The first English houses were founded in 1240–2 away from towns. They were Hulne near Alnwick (Northumberland) and the Kentish houses of Losenham and Aylesford (where the old house has been recently restored to the Order and relics of St. Simon Stock installed). By 1272 they had twenty-two houses, thirty-seven a century later including several in major English towns. It is interesting to note that London, York, Oxford, Cambridge and seven other English towns had houses of all four orders of friars.

Besides these orders, there were one or two very minor orders of friars here with picturesque names but little support. Such were the Crutched Friars, the Friars of the Sack (or of Penance) and the Pied Friars, but their total number of houses was a bare twenty-four.

From what we have seen it is apparent that the work of the medieval friars was essentially work for clergy, and, as women were not ordained, the way of life could scarcely be adapted for use in nunneries. However, there is an exception to be made here in the case of the Franciscans. By a curious development St. Francis of Assisi, who did not intend to found a monastic order, ended by being responsible for the record number of three, though it is true that one of these was not strictly monastic.

His First Order was the one we have already considered. The Third existed only in embryo at the time of his death. It was based on a rule for laity who continued to live outside the cloister. It did not involve taking monastic vows but accepting a highly disciplined spiritual life with much more stress on prayer, meditation and good works than was normally to be noted. Because it was the Third (*tertius*) Order its members were known as tertiaries.

More important for our purposes is the Second Order of the Franciscans, founded with the counsel of Francis himself by St. Clare. She belonged to a wealthy family in Assisi, and, like so many, was stirred to the depths of her being by the Franciscan message, especially its call to complete poverty. Attractive and vivacious, she decided that her call lay in the cloister. Her family was infuriated at the idea and a series of clashes ensued which ended when Clare fled away by night to take monastic vows before St. Francis. At first given lodging by friendly Benedictine nuns, St. Clare went on to found her own community which was originally housed at the little church of S. Damiano outside the city, which St. Francis had restored in his early days. But soon it was found necessary for the sisters to move inside the walls of Assisi.

The aim of the Second Order was completely contemplative, being to worship God and to intercede for man. This was done in a régime of great severity in which fasting and silence figured prominently. St. Clare was just as convinced as St. Francis of the importance of refusing endowments. The ecclesiastical authorities had understandable doubts about the wisdom of this for a community completely severed from the world, and thereby deprived of the facilities for obtaining alms open to the First Order. But St. Clare was sure of her ground and fought the opposition with a serene inflexibility, that finally levelled all resistance, so that the utmost poverty became the rule of the Order. The vocation of the 'poor Clares' or Second Order was a very specialised one, like that of the Carthusians, and there were only three houses of the order in England at the Dissolution. All were late foundations, that in London being the first major foundation (1293–4). The only house of Dominican nuns was founded at Dartford (Kent) in 1346.

By the time of the Black Death of 1348–9 the medieval monastic orders in England had reached their major extent, totalling something between 950 and 1000 houses of which nearly 200 were houses of friars and about 150 houses of nuns. The estimated number of inmates at this time was in the region of 17,000 of which 3000 were nuns. By this time the whole face of England was dotted with monasteries of one kind or another. In the sparsely populated areas such as the Lake District, Northumberland, the Welsh Border and the West Country there were comparatively few, but elsewhere, notably in the prosperous East Anglian countryside, they were very thick on the ground. The establishment of so many houses was a testimony both to the piety of the orders themselves and to the deep convictions of their founders and benefactors. But as we shall see, it is arguable that the zeal behind the movement had pushed it further than was ultimately profitable. The maintenance at full strength of all these convents was to prove a difficult problem and ultimately raised the eternal dilemma of institutional history—whether or not it was advisable to subordinate quantity to quality or vice versa.

After the advent of the friars the establishment of new monasteries largely ceased. This was not, as is sometimes alleged, because monasticism had gone out of favour, but because it already possessed more than enough houses for those likely under normal circumstances to feel called to enter them. New monastic institutions in England during the fourteenth and fifteenth centuries were to be comparatively few, for the very good reason that few were needed.

Side by side with the great monastic orders we have considered, were various others which may be termed semi-monastic to which brief reference may profitably be made. Two of the so-called 'military orders' may be noted—the Templars and the Hospitallers, or to give them their full title 'the Knights of the Temple' and 'the Knights of the Order of the Hospital of St. John of Jerusalem'. Medieval men found it far easier than we do to believe in a Holy War, and attached far more importance to Christian possession of the Holy Land. These were two of the main forces behind the Crusading movement, which, from 1099 onwards, brought Jerusalem and surrounding areas temporarily into western hands. They also led to the formation of these military orders where, by a conjunction curious to modern eyes, military duties were combined with a severe religious rule. Both orders quickly became powerful, as well in the Holy Land as outside, and developed a professional jealousy reminiscent of some modern trade unions.

The Templars originated about 1118 in an association of knights for the protection of pilgrims to the Holy Land. They rendered valuable services in this sphere and quickly acquired much property. This they organised elaborately, their small houses being known as 'preceptories', their main ones as Temples. They built some of the most spectacular castles of the age for the defence of the Holy Land but, despite their stubborn resistance, by the end of the thirteenth century the whole Crusading movement in the West had collapsed and the Templars were left with a good deal of money and no very obvious *raison d'être*. In one way or another they incurred unpopularity and envy, and the tough and avaricious French king, Philip the Fair, took advantage of this. By a combination of intrigue and pressure he persuaded a weak pope to suppress the order in 1312, on charges of various crimes which are now recognised to be largely faked.

Their main English house of the order was the Temple in London whose church was originally built, like so many others of the order, on the same circular plan as the church of the Holy Sepulchre at Jerusalem. This had been originally founded elsewhere about 1128 but moved to its final site in 1184. The London house was essentially a great administrative centre, collecting the various moneys from the other English houses, which came to a considerable sum. Most of the other English establishments were very small with a mere handful of brethren, and, as Professor Knowles remarks, acted 'mainly as recruiting centres and farms for the support of the order'. They finally totalled just under fifty and after their suppression some of their property was held by the Crown, some went to the Hospitallers and other religious or semi-religious bodies. Its richest house—Willoughton (Lincs)—passed to the Hospitallers as did Temple Bruer, another important one in the same county.

The Hospitallers originated in Jerusalem at the end of the eleventh century with a community that cared for the sick and protected pilgrims and Crusaders. Some were 'infirmarian brothers' others 'military brothers' to which were inevitably added chaplains. The order fought to the last in the Holy Land and, soon after the final collapse, captured Rhodes (1309) and made it their centre. In England their head house was in Clerkenwell outside the walls of medieval London. Their organisation was similar to the Templars with very small houses the general rule. At the time of the suppression of the Templars, the Hospitallers had about forty houses, their peak figure being fifty-nine. They seem to have been rather more interested in dispensing hospitality than the Templars. Their houses in England were mostly country estates in places that figure but slightly on history's page. A number of their establishments had an income equal to that of a smallish house of Austin canons at the time of the Dissolution, and a good many of their wealthiest houses had formerly belonged to the Templars.

Very much more numerous than the military orders and in many ways appreciably more important, were the hospitals of medieval England. It is true that medieval man, like his classical predecessor and his Renaissance successor, showed little interest in the study of economics and therefore tended to accept as inevitable a state of poverty which the twentieth century, at long last, is scientifically abolishing. But it is also true that he had an interest in the poor and distressed which was of great intensity and showed itself in a remarkable flood of benefactions to those in need. 'Remember the poor', wrote St. Paul, and whatever Biblical maxims the medieval West neglected, this was not one of them. Poverty it revered and aided in a variety of ways, century after century. Almsgiving was an important monastic activity and was an essential feature of the life of any great noble, ecclesiastical or secular, as well as an almost inevitable feature of any important funeral. A further important and lasting expression of this concern for the needy was the foundation of hospitals.

Today we think of a hospital as primarily a place for the sick, but medieval hospitals dealt not only with them but also with the aged and with travellers, either separately or in combination. Such hospitals were occasionally founded in the early Middle Ages, but became much more numerous in England, as elsewhere, after the opening of the twelfth century which saw the beginning of much economic and social progress. Like the monasteries they varied a good deal in size.

A few became very large. St. Leonard's York maintained 200 sick as well as a considerable staff including thirty choristers. Newark hospital at Leicester provided for 100 folk. But such numbers were highly exceptional. A certain number of English hospitals catered for one or two dozen inmates, but probably a largish majority had less than ten. These figures exclude the staff which was larger and more varied than the modern mind would expect. A hospital without a chaplain would have been quite unthinkable and many had several clergy to celebrate mass and minister to the inmates. These clergy often had brethren and sisters to assist them, and all three categories frequently lived a strict rule of life which was sometimes in effect monastic. Thus in some houses the rule of St. Augustine was observed.

Some hospitals were leper houses which were commonly founded in the twelfth century; by the end of the Middle Ages the disease had become rare.* The poor and aged were obvious and perennial categories, as were the sick and travellers. Hospitals might be founded for one of these needs or for several and sometimes changed their *clientèle* as time wore on. They might serve people of one sex or of both. In some cases provision was made to feed but not lodge the needy, as at Gaunt's Hospital, Bristol, which in 1406 provided meals for 100 people twice a week.

Professor Knowles has recently estimated that the total number of medieval English hospitals was about 980, but he points out that 'in almost every period numbers became extinct or were united, whilst new hospitals were perpetually being founded'. A few of these hospitals were put under the supervision of monasteries and others originated as the organised expression of monastic hospitality. Amongst the latter were St. Bartholomew's Hospital in Smithfield connected with the priory of Austin canons there, and St. Thomas's Hospital in London connected with the Austin priory of Southwark.

The obvious social value of hospitals meant that they suffered much less severely than monasteries from the storms of the Reformation. A number of the larger ones maintained an unbroken existence and some of them still use their medieval buildings like the Great Hospital of Norwich founded in 1249 and the Almshouse of St. John the Baptist and St. John the Evangelist at Sherborne. As the remains of the latter show us, the plan of such hospitals was in effect that of a monastic infirmary (see page 41) with an eastern chapel adjoining a large aisled hall containing cubicles. Hospitals are closely linked with town life, and, because the town life of medieval England was on a very minor scale, very few of its hospitals can fitly be compared with the major ones across the Channel.

---

* The name *leprosy* seems to have covered a variety of skin complaints.

CHAPTER EIGHT

THE MONASTIC OFFICIALS AND THE DAILY RÉGIME

I. The Officials

The Abbot or Prior—The heads of the great mass of English monasteries were called abbots or priors, according to whether the house they ruled was an abbey or a priory. What was the difference between the latter? Like so many questions, the closer we look at it the more complex does it appear. In the strict sense an abbey was a house ruled by an abbot but even in the Middle Ages the word was used loosely. Thus we find Carlisle and Durham both called abbeys, though technically both were cathedral priories, whose heads were always known as priors in legal documents and nearly always, it would appear, in popular parlance also. This hazy use of the word abbey later ran wild. As knowledge of the medieval past receded, ignorance and social snobbery unofficially promoted many old sites of priories to abbatial rank, and the same privilege was accorded to mere farms that formerly belonged to abbeys. Hence England became rich in abbeys that never existed, including such famous sites as 'Bolton Abbey', a house which throughout medieval times was a priory.

If we ask what houses were technically abbeys in medieval times, i.e. were legally referred to as such, and whose superiors were termed abbots, we find that no neat answer covers all the facts. All the old Benedictine monasteries of any size were abbeys, but most of the lesser ones were priories. However, all Cistercian houses were ruled by abbots as were those of some small Augustinian orders, notably the Premonstratensians and the Victorines. Amongst the very numerous independent houses of English Austin canons, a mere handful attained abbatial rank: rather oddly these ones were not necessarily very large houses, a more important factor, apparently, being that most of them were in the royal patronage. In the English houses of the order of Cluny, the title was similarly rare, probably because the title of abbey evidently implied a degree of independence scarcely compatible with the considerable centralisation under the mother house which prevailed in the early centuries of its history. Of the thirty-seven English Cluniac houses only Bermondsey had the title of abbey.

Some monastic orders and some few independent houses, mostly of abbatial rank, became 'exempt' houses, that is to say for disciplinary purposes they were responsible directly to the pope, and exempt from the diocesan bishop. Another privilege enjoyed by some abbeys at the end of the Middle Ages, was that of being 'mitred abbeys'. This was a liturgical rather than a legal privilege, allowing the abbot of the house in question to wear a mitre and carry a pastoral staff (the normal emblems of a bishop), but it had no legal significance. Less prized at the time, odd as this may seem to modern eyes, was the privilege of being summoned to Parliament. From an early stage it was normal to summon a selection of abbots to Parliament, mostly those of the great Benedictine houses that we have already mentioned in so many connections. But in the Middle Ages attendance at Parliament was often viewed with distaste, not least by churchmen. It involved often long and uncomfortable journeys, to transact business much of which was either formal or of little direct concern to ecclesiastics, who had their own machinery of government. Accordingly it is not surprising to find medieval abbots seeking to avoid going to Parliament, and adopting manœuvres like that of a certain Benedictine abbot whose account roll includes the pleasing item, 'To the Clerk of Parliament that my lord abbot be not summoned (to Parliament) 20s'!

The above functions were very largely, though not entirely, confined to abbeys. The great majority of the English monasteries did not come in any of the categories just noted and were priories. In an abbey the second-in-command was a prior. In very big houses he might be known as first prior to distinguish him from the 'second prior' and 'third prior' who were the officials immediately below him. In houses ruled by priors, the second-in-command was the sub-prior.

What was the function of the superior? His primary responsibility was to be the father of the house. The word abbot (*abbas*) meant 'father' and knowledge of this was kept alive by St. Paul's letter referring to 'the spirit of adoption whereby we cry, Abba, father'.

The abbot was not merely an earthly father, but a father in God, chosen after solemn prayer for divine guidance. Because of this he was regarded as taking the place of Christ. Because God had sent him to the office a command from him was to be treated 'as if the command had come from God' as the *Rule of St. Benedict* put it. For the same reason he was shown an intense exterior respect. Undue familiarity with him was to be avoided and all were to rise and bow when he passed by. Special honour was accorded to him in the elaborate round of church worship and when he came back from a long journey he was met in procession by his brethren who led him to the high altar, offering thanks for his safe return and receiving his blessing.

Once elected the whole government of the house was his ultimate responsibility. He appointed all monastic officials, received and professed novices, took disciplinary decisions and alone could grant special privileges. He had a big share in the dispensing of hospitality on which the *Rule of St. Benedict* and all ways of life derived from it, laid such stress.* For this purpose, as we have seen, there might be a special dining hall close to his own set of rooms.

* Thus we find the abbot of Furness when about to be visited by a local magnate writing hurriedly to the vicar of Kirkby Lonsdale desiring him to 'send quickly' all the fish he could so that the monastery's reputation for hospitality should not be in any way belied. The vicar lived only a few paces from a fine salmon stream.

The superior's command 'ought to possess such a weighty authority over all that no one should presume to neglect or defer whatever he has directed, provided it be not against God'. So wrote the *Customs of Barnwell* and this is in the usual vein. Equally common is the stress which the *Customs* lays on the spiritual danger inherent in holding a post with such heavy responsibilities. 'It is evident that superiors, if they ever do wrong, are worthy of deaths as numerous as the deadly examples set by them to their inferiors. The loftier their station, the greater their fall.' On all matters of importance the abbot was expected to take advice from the more experienced brethren. In the Benedictine and Augustinian monasteries normally the head of the house was elected for life, and would only be removed if he was guilty of some very great offence or had become physically or mentally unfit. The friars were more cautious and, as we have seen, had officials elected periodically.

Whether he liked it or not, the head of an English medieval monastery of any size was bound to be away from his house on ecclesiastical and secular business, and even when he was in residence was greatly encumbered with administration. He could not therefore devote all the time necessary for the exacting task of seeing that the daily life of the brethren was happy and healthy. To watch this was the main task of the second-in-command, be he first prior or sub-prior. He was compared to the mother of the house, and it was understandably said that 'the peace of the house depends on him'. To foster and maintain the tightly knit Christian life of a monastic community no virtue could be irrelevant. The prior's was a strenuous day, beginning early, when he toured the dormitory with a lighted lantern to see that no one had overslept, and closing late when he toured the cloister area to see that the requisite doors were locked and lights out. For his exacting duties he generally had at least one assistant and in very large monasteries two or three.

From what we have seen, it will be understandable that the number of officials in an English medieval monastery varied enormously. A great Benedictine house might have a score or so, a medium-sized one a dozen or less, and a small house the merest handful.

In the running of the material side of the monastic life the chief official was the *Cellarer*, whose functions were not unlike those of a modern bursar or steward. 'The Cellarer ought to be wise, cautious and thrifty. Everything that belongs to the monastery, whether lands or churches, with the exception of what belongs to the other officials is to be in his charge' says the *Customs of Barnwell*, and goes on to detail his work: 'It is part of the Cellarer's duty to attend to everything that has to do with food, drink and fuel, whether for the bakery, the brewhouse, or the kitchen. Moreover all transport of goods whether by land or water, repairs of house, all purchases of iron, steel, wood, ploughs and carts and all purchases of bacon, stores of salt and dried fish, clothes, wine, together with the entire care of the whole monastery excepting the duties of the other officials, fall within the province of the

THE MONASTIC OFFICIALS AND DAILY RÉGIME

Cellarer. On this account he ought frequently to visit the manors, the ploughlands and the folds, to keep check on stores, to keep sharp watch on the character, behaviour and zeal of the lay brethren and of all servants put in charge of manors.' He had often to be away on business but 'ought to be present at the canonical Hours whenever he can find leisure'. There was much detail to be checked—thus bread was not to be too new or 'dirty, broken or burnt or gnawed by mice'. To carry out all his labours he had a sub-cellarer to assist him.

Service of meals depended primarily on the *Kitchener* whose work was to see that meals were served efficiently, punctually and cleanly, not in 'vessels that are broken or dirty, and not dirty on the under side, so as to stain the tablecloth'! The *Hosteller* was the modern guest master. The *Customs of Barnwell* thought he ought to have 'not merely facility of expression but also elegant manners and a respectable up-bringing' for 'he ought neither to do or to say anything but what sets monastic life in a creditable light'. 'By shewing cheerful hospitality to guests', said the *Customs*, 'the reputation of the monastery is increased, friendships are multiplied, animosities are blunted, God is honoured, charity is increased and a plenteous reward in heaven is promised.' The Hosteller had to see that guest accommodation was clean and attractive, beds 'pleasing to the eye', no spider webs in the guest house, no fires that smoked. He was to rise in time to see the guests off 'lest by an oversight they should forget and leave behind them a sword, knife or some other such article, and lest some of the property belonging to his charge should accidentally be taken away'.

Besides these, there might be a brother in charge of the infirmary known as the *Infirmarian*, and an *Almoner* whose difficult duty it was to dispense the monastic charity. The *Customs of Barnwell* enjoined him to give special priority to pilgrims, chaplains, beggars and lepers. 'Old men and those who are decrepid, lame and blind or who are confined to their beds, he ought frequently to visit and give them suitable relief. Those who in former days have been rich, and have come to poverty, and are perhaps ashamed to sit down among the rest, he will assemble separately that he may distribute his bounty to them with greater privacy. He ought to submit with calmness to the loud-voiced importunity of the poor and help all petitioners as far as he is able . . . he ought not to strike or hurt or even abuse or upbraid anyone, always remembering that they are made in the image of God, and redeemed by the price of the blood of Christ.'

Amongst the chief internal officials was the *Precentor* who was in charge of the books as well, 'and so might also be called the Librarian'. The chant used in medieval western monasteries in the later Middle Ages was extremely complex, and the Precentor had the responsibility of leading and correcting what was potentially 'a source of delight and pleasure to God, the angels and mankind'. 'If any mistake has been made in singing in the Church, whether in setting the tone, or on any other way, let no one set their opinion above his', says the *Customs of Barnwell*. He also arranged processions and chose those with special functions in the daily worship.

Books were extremely expensive things and monasteries looked after them with corresponding care. They were not to be lent without security of equal value and had to be carefully stored and regularly examined for signs of decay.

Like other major officials the precentor had an assistant, the *Succentor*, who was to be skilled in singing and have a strong voice: a main duty of his was to lead the singing on the north side of the choir, when the precentor led the section on the south of the choir, in those parts of the services where singing was antiphonal, i.e. verses sung first by one half of the choir, then the other.

The *Sacrist* was an important official whose main concern was 'to make the church useful and in every way seemly'. This implied custody of all the church furnishings—plate, vestments, linen, reliquaries, ornaments, altars, etc. All had to be carefully guarded, kept clean and ready for use. The church itself had to be kept clean, and the hay or rushes which served as matting to be swept up and replaced periodically. The sacrist also had charge of the lighting of the monastery. He bought the wax for the better quality candles and mutton fat or tallow for the inferior ones and oil for using in cressets. Cressets were stones in which were scooped out a semi-circular hole or holes in which fat and a floating wick formed a primitive form of candlestick, or rather of candelabra [see Pls. 28a and 28b], for most cressets had several holes. The sacrist saw to the manufacture of candles and issued supplies of them to other officers.

By the late Middle Ages any substantial monastic church was something of an artistic treasure house, containing a great many valuables, notably the altar plate and crosses, reliquaries and books in precious bindings. At least in the largest churches, it was not thought advisable to leave the church unwatched during the night hours. At Durham, as we have seen, there was a sort of ecclesiastical night porter; the *Customs of Barnwell* provide that the church was never to be left unguarded and even stipulates that 'the guardians of the Church must take their meals in it'. Here the sacrist slept in the church. As we have already noted, it was perhaps for his opposite number at Peterborough that the brethren made the little fireplace in the west wall of their south transept, near the foot of their night stair. His duties also involved the sacrist in seeing that the bells were rung at the proper times, and the church clock (on which the programme depended) kept in order. He also had to see the cemetery was kept tidy.

Clearly in any large church the sacrist's responsibilities involved an enormous amount of work of one kind or another and for this he was allowed one or more assistants. The chief of these was the sub-sacrist. On him often devolved the task of seeing that the right bells were rung at the right time, a task of some complexity owing to the elaborate nature of late medieval services. He assisted in 'sweeping the Church, hanging up curtains, preparing vestments and other ornaments, cleaning lamps and trimming or extinguishing other lights in the Church. . . . In winter he ought to supply live coal in iron dishes to warm the hands of those who minister at the altar.'

A key official was the *Novice-Master* who had to train those wishing to become monks to see the beauty and the power of the monastic life. He had to be a man of insight and discipline. The novices had a special part of the cloister, generally either part of the eastern or western alley, set apart for them and lived much of their time together working under the novice-master. He taught them the obvious details of monastic routine, how to dress, how to bow, how to chant the office and read aloud, above all how to build up the spiritual defences on which their happiness depended. Normally a man spent a year as a novice, during which, at intervals, his progress was considered and it was decided whether his continuance would benefit him and the house. At the end of the period, if all went well, he made his final vows to remain a member of the community and observe its rules, was given the kiss of peace by the brethren and became a full member of the order.

In larger monasteries there were various other officials such as the *Chamberlain* who looked after the clothes of the brethren, and the *Refectorian* who was in charge of the refectory and its furnishings. Besides these officials, there were lesser ones appointed to lesser work for shorter periods. Chief was the *Hebdomadarian*, who held his post for a week at a time. It involved leading the various canonical Hours giving various blessings and singing the High Mass during his period of office. Those who served at table and the reader of the lessons in the refectory were likewise appointed weekly.

Such were the main officials of a large Augustinian or Benedictine monastery but, as has been pointed out, their number varied much; in the numerous small houses members would often double up the various duties, whilst the largest ones had many officials and a larger series of assistants.

II. The Daily Régime

The daily routine of a medieval monastery of any size was as complex as that of a battleship or modern hospital, and, in the interests of efficiency, acquired the same sort of rigidity. It varied somewhat with the season of the year and much more according to the life of the order. Clearly the functions of the friars and the Carthusians, for example, were too different for them to have a great deal in common in the details of their routine, though these were not as different as might have been expected. Here, as in our study of monastic architecture, we shall be mainly concerned with the Augustinians and the Benedictines, whose houses comprised so great and influential a fraction of the whole.

On the monastic life as on monastic architecture, the lack of cheap artificial lighting in the Middle Ages had influence. In the long winter season, like the rest of society at this time and long after, the monks went to bed comparatively early and got up comparatively late. Thus, in the time of Dunstan, in winter the Benedictines rose about 2.30 a.m. and retired about 6.30 p.m.; in summer they rose an hour earlier and retired about 8.15 p.m. By the time that midday had come, especially under the summer routine, the monks had already put in a long period of activity which, from the purely physical angle, was a good deal more arduous than the outsider might imagine. It was, therefore, very wise to allow them after their midday meal that siesta from which the Emperor Charlemagne and Sir Winston Churchill have derived so much of their embarrassing energy. As we have noted, after the midday meal the brethren would adjourn to the dormitory for this from the near-by refectory by way of the day stair.

Our present times for meals are amongst the most recent of social phenomena, and differ very widely from those of a medieval monastery. According to the primitive Benedictine plan, in winter there was but one meal, taken about 2.30 p.m., though a couple of hours later in Lent. From Easter to Whitsunday there was a main meal at midday and a lesser one about 5 p.m. The same rule was followed from Whitsuntide until the opening of the winter régime in mid-September, except that on Wednesdays and Fridays, as fast days, the winter system of a late single meal was observed.

Pious laity of many periods have entertained dark suspicions that monks get far too little to eat, just as monks have entertained equally dark suspicions that the laity get far too much. The former suspicion has some evidence to support it, at least in the early centuries of monastic development. But monasticism has generally been ready to learn from experience, and in this case experience showed a less austere régime was desirable. Hence, as time went on, a second meal in winter became more usual, and the situation was further improved by what were called pittances. These were special endowments to provide some sort of addition to the usual monastic fare. By the end of the Middle Ages there is no doubt that the food in the richer monasteries was often very far from spartan either in quantity or quality; indeed Englishmen, whether in or out of the cloister, seem to have had a reputation for being singularly careful to avoid doing anything that might suggest a spirit of excessive self-denial over food and drink.

Another change, as time wore on, was the much greater use of fleshmeat, or rather that of animals, for that of birds was considered not to be flesh. In the extent to which this practice was allowed, orders differed very considerably. This ban of fleshmeat is perhaps one of the few religious practices of the kind whose desirability is not very obvious and today has lost much of its authority. In the Middle Ages this decline developed. The Benedictines for long made next to no use of fleshmeat, but gradually it became permissible under certain conditions. The superior had to entertain the outside world and so it was allowed in his hall, though it is not to be assumed that he himself necessarily partook of it. Whilst, as we have noted, in the last centuries of the Middle Ages, a special room was built in some monasteries where certain of the brethren might eat meat. The regular canons were less attached to the practice of abstaining from fleshmeat (see page 109).

A marked feature of monastic meals in particular and monastic life in general, was extensive use of silence, experience having shown it to possess a peace-giving quality that should not be ignored. The longest period of this was the so-called 'greater silence' which extended from Compline until well into the following morning and was as complete as was humanly possible. But in varying degrees in varying orders the same rule applied throughout most of the day in the church, refectory, dormitory and cloister. In the refectory, unless for some special reason, silence was largely unbroken except by the voice of the reader in the refectory pulpit, rehearsing some edifying work, when meals were in progress.

No organisation can be competent which bases its life on the principle of all work and no play, and the medieval monk would also have short periods of recreation during which conversation was permitted on spiritual and, to a lesser extent, on secular matters. On the timing and duration of these breaks as with so much medieval monastic detail, no great precision can be given, for, as our leading authority points out, 'it is all but impossible to ascertain the exact lengths of the periods and how far the conversation was intended or permitted to be merely recreative'.

To provide a change from the liturgical routine and to show forth the importance of study and manual labour, periods each day were set apart for these. In small houses and in primitive conditions the monks might have to do a good deal of the monastic chores, but as time wore on it was found more efficient to have the greater part of these done by others, either by lay brethren or paid labour, the brethren confining themselves to comparatively light duties which lay near to hand and concentrating their activities on whatever was the main function of their order whether it be conventual worship, evangelism or religious contemplation. An Augustinian canon of Bridlington, writing in the mid-twelfth century, has left us an interesting catalogue of the pursuits he considered appropriate for his brethren in this connection. It includes reading, preaching, teaching, choir practice, writing and binding books, making and repairing clothes, making wooden spoons, candlesticks, baskets, nets and beehives, as well as an extensive range of gardening operations. As he rightly notes, 'this provides something for everybody'.

So far as study was concerned, the regular provision for this in most of the rules of the time put the monasteries ahead of most of medieval society, especially before the rise of the universities and civil services in the twelfth and thirteenth centuries. But one must not over-estimate their intellectual interests. In the older orders such as the Augustinians and Benedictines the time available for it in practice does not seem to have been enormous and it was much broken up. In Dunstan's day Benedictines had allotted for work one hour early in the day, three hours before sext and rather more than two hours in the afternoon. Though this looks adequate on paper it was probably much eaten into by other things and in any case occurred too late in the day and in too small amounts to allow for that intensive thought which scholarship demands. At least one twelfth-century Austin canon wrote sorrowfully that he had scarcely time to get down to writing before it was time to get up and go to something else! With the friars the situation was, of course, somewhat more favourable. But even there, for various reasons, the theological output of the monasteries after the thirteenth century was not impressive and the number of writers of any note was small. Probably the monks of these times—like the parish clergy of our day—knew the obvious textbooks, but were not, in general, interested in wide reading or deep research, partly because so many other calls on their time, rightly or wrongly, seemed more pressing. One such call was, of course, the various duties undertaken by the officials and their assistants whose duties we have just discussed. These could be very time-consuming especially in the smaller monasteries.

All these monastic involvements were entirely subordinate in all monastic orders to the maintenance of a daily round of worship. It was from this that the monk drew the spiritual strength necessary to maintain the high standards of his exacting vocation. Even orders like the friars which stressed this side of monastic activity so much less than orders like the Cluniacs, had an extensive programme of worship.

In the early centuries of monasticism this worship had been un-coordinated and the corporate element had sometimes been comparatively little stressed. But as the Middle Ages wore on, worship became highly organised and predominantly corporate; the amount of time allotted for private prayer and meditation was quite small, the stress being laid on an exacting round of common worship of a very precise and complex pattern. The outline of this worship will be familiar to most Church people; its details are immensely technical and can find no place in a general survey such as this. The conventual worship common to all the orders of the medieval West had two main elements. One was the series of daily Offices which punctuated the course of the day. The first of these Offices was Nocturns (now called Mattins) which was the opening major act of worship of the day. It was followed by Mattins (the modern Lauds), Prime (which was sung at dawn), Terce, Sext, None, Vespers and the singularly beautiful Office of Compline which brought the monastic day to an end. These Offices were largely composed of psalms, short prayers or collects and versicles and responses, i.e. set ejaculations of praise and intercession each with its appropriate reply.

Clergy of all lands and ages have an apparently incurable passion for liturgical innovation, being seldom happy if they are not altering the form of worship which they have inherited. So it was in the Middle Ages, and these Offices were gradually encrusted with additional small acts of worship such as prayers and litanies. Typical of such additions was the *Trina Oratio* which by the time of Dunstan prefaced both Nocturns and Terce and followed Compline, and the Psalms for the Dead, which then followed the daily Chapter—a meeting of the brethren in the chapter house to conduct various religious and secular business.

But the major act of all Christian worship is the Eucharist or Mass, in which the Church, from the first, has shown forth the death of Christ on the cross. By the twelfth century western monasticism had adopted a comparatively recent innovation (never copied in the East)—the habit of having private masses, that is to say, masses at which no congregation was expected, beyond a server who would make the necessary responses and help the priest in certain minor ways during the service. This custom rapidly became widespread and, as we have noted, led to it becoming the rule for almost all members of a monastery of men to be in priests' orders, no lower rank being qualified to say mass—before these times many monks were either laity or in minor orders. As mass had to be said fasting these private masses were normally said in the early part of the day. But the most important mass was the conventual mass. This had a much more complex form, with not one but three officiating clergy (at least in large houses) and various other elaborations, notably the singing of the service.

The type of music used, known as the Gregorian chant or, more popularly, as plainsong, was much developed in the course of the Middle Ages. One well qualified to judge, has hailed it as 'a music wide in its emotional expression, majestic, spiritual and austere beyond all other forms of the art, exquisitely spontaneous and pure in its melody and extremely subtle and sophisticated in its technical perfection'.

Another adjunct of the high mass was incense swung in a censer, a symbolic act at certain points in the service; the beauty of its delicate blue smoke lifting gracefully heavenward would not be lost on that visually minded person, medieval man. It was at the high mass that the sedilia was used, the officiating clergy sitting there during certain elaborate parts of the singing and during the sermon, if sermon there was. From an early date western monasteries had a morrow mass, at first said but later sung at the choir altar. In Dunstan's time it was usual for the main mass on Saturday to be one commemorating Our Lady if no feast day occurred then. As time went on the growing medieval devotion to her led to a daily mass in her honour being instituted.

To have had exactly the same forms of service day in day out, would have been to encourage 'the greatest of all heresies—the belief that Christianity is dull'. It would also have failed to do justice to the richness of the Christian life. In medieval monasteries, as outside them, at this time there were utilised two great series of variations of a type still used by Eastern Orthodox and Roman Catholic and—in a more austere version—by Anglicans. But these variations were rather more complex in monastic worship for obvious reasons. Both series added much life and colour to worship and were annual cycles. One of them commemorated the various major events in the earthly life of Christ with its culmination in the foundation of the Church. First came Advent, then Christmas, Lent, Easter and Whitsuntide, with lesser commemorations between. With this cycle ran concurrently (at times with complicating effect) the second series, that of commemoration of the saints. For various reasons, especially the fact that for long canonisation* was done locally, by the eleventh and twelfth centuries the number of saints had already become very considerable. They varied both in antiquity and fame, including with the

* The official declaration that a certain Christian had the status of a saint.

apostles and early martyrs and leaders of the early Church, a whole host of later figures, notably monks, nuns and bishops of the Dark Ages not all of whom would have been classified at Advanced Level by examiners of later days.

Each saint was commemorated on the day of his death. With such an embarrassment of saintly riches, there was much scope for individual choice as to who should be commemorated on a particular day and in what degree, for there were various grades of this form of remembrance. Each monastery exercised some degree of choice, though in the more highly organised orders this was limited. Saints with local interest were specially loved, as were saints whose relics were, as it was thought, preserved in the Church. The major saints of the Christian Church were inevitably included, but otherwise there was much variation in the detail of the monastic calendars.

These two special series of commemorations led to a series of small changes in the text of the worship of the days concerned, these changes being known as the proper. In the case of major saints, these would be employed for eight days, i.e. on the day itself and during the week which followed, a period known as an octave; but lesser ones would be commemorated on the much smaller scale of a single day. The various parts of the proper cannot be detailed here; the most important was the use of a special collect, epistle and gospel in the early part of the mass. The occasions on which they were used steadily grew; by the opening of the thirteenth century at Worcester, for example, nearly half the days of the year were festal days.

Such were the ingredients of the monastic day. It is impossible to make any very precise generalisations about the time-table in which they were all combined, partly because we have little evidence over the timing, partly because of the considerable variations which occurred from time to time and from order to order, partly because little modern research has touched the point. Professor Knowles has worked out in detail the régime of the Benedictines in the time of Dunstan, and more studies of this kind are greatly needed.

There can be no doubt of the immense stress which all Benedictine and Augustinian orders laid on worship. This had become a very large fraction of their activity. But that singularly well-organised body, the Cistercian order, provides an example of the sort of variations that might occur. Though the general framework of the monastic day of the old orders was retained, a fundamental change was introduced by the increased stress on manual labour. In winter the four hours before dinner were kept clear for this, and in summer that same amount of time was allowed, but part allotted to the period after the siesta; there were special arrangements for haymaking and harvesting. The additional time thus engrossed was secured by cutting back the luscious liturgical growth. Various additions to the Offices were excised, as was a second major mass on most days of the year, while on the remainder it was permissible to be absent from this to say a private mass. At the same time the complexities of the singing and ceremonial were abridged.

So far as the Austin canons were concerned there was not a great deal of difference between most of them and the ordinary Benedictines, though their régime was somewhat lighter as the Cistercians was somewhat stricter. Thus the regular canons of the twelfth century did not abstain perpetually from the use of meat, being allowed it several days a week. Their rules of silence were less severe. Generally, it would seem, even in the church, refectory and cloister necessary speaking was allowed if done 'briefly in a low voice not causing scandal to the brethren'. The regular canons' services were also generally rather shorter than those of monks; at Mattins they had nine not twelve lessons. But a small section of the Augustinian canons borrowed heavily from the Cistercians.

To modern man with his passion for the material, the medieval monastic routine may seem the fruit of ideas almost if not quite anti-social. Medieval man did not give the same priority to 'the meat that perisheth'. He saw the monastic routine as something that proclaimed in clear, uncompromising terms the eternal truths. There was the truth that the highest form of man is disciplined man. Not man drifting in whatever direction he was pushed by his senses, but man steadied and strengthened by the manifold resources of Catholic worship. Wrote Dean Church in a sensitive study of the greatest of medieval Benedictines:

'In an age when there was so much lawlessness, and when the idea of self-control was so uncommon in the ordinary life of man, the monasteries were schools of discipline: and there were no others. They upheld and exhibited the great, then almost the original idea that men needed to rule and govern themselves; that they could do it and that no use of life was noble and perfect without this ruling.'

But there is more to do than that. Monastic worship did more than act as an agent of social reform. To most people most of the time the medieval monastic routine spoke clearly and predominantly of God and His heaven. It was God who had evoked the majestic conventual church that so dwarfed the petty houses huddled outside the precinct, God who had inspired the saints who looked down in friendly fashion from pedestal and stained-glass window, God to whom the rich round of worship with its timeless chant and dignified artistry was poured out in a great pulsating rhythm that, for the nonce at least, lifted a man far out of that savage, unkempt society of the day to give him a blissful foretaste of that realm prepared by Christ for those who loved Him. God it was whose power had enabled those figures dimly seen in the convent stalls to resist the calls of the world and the flesh, calls that were at least as insistent for medieval as for modern man. And God in the end would accord to those monks and those nuns, who despite all their obliquities had sought to be faithful to death, the promised 'Crown of Life'.

CHAPTER NINE

THE DISSOLUTION OF THE MONASTERIES

T HE two centuries which intervened between the end of the great monastic expansion which we have considered and the age of monastic suppression in England constitute a singularly uneventful age, and for that reason little will be said of them. As anyone who has worked on the history of individual monasteries at this time knows well, the most obvious fact that emerges is the lack of important developments. Though the evidence is often rather scantier than of yore it is amply sufficient to make this clear and forbids us positing major changes that have gone unrecorded.

Such uneventfulness is, after all, only what one might expect to find. By this time centuries of effort had set up a mighty network of monasteries which covered the whole country. These, like the vicarages of today, were now in action engaged in a work which, at its best, was intensive and edifying, but was scarcely ever spectacular. Just as the clerical stories printed in the cheaper section of today's Press are not typical of more than a minute section of the whole body of clergy, so also many of the monastic events which were recorded in episcopal and papal archives of the fourteenth and fifteenth centuries tend to be unusual rather than normal.

In general, the currents of English monastic life at this time flowed very smoothly. Most days were just like the one before or the one after, with events of moment breaking in only at long intervals. From time to time the local bishop with a far-from-negligible retinue would arrive at the great gate to carry out his visitation of a monastery not specifically exempted from this. This was a lumbering, painstaking affair with much examination of the brethren with a view to discovering what, if anything, was amiss in the spiritual or temporal affairs of the house; it would conclude ultimately with official injunctions which aimed at remedy where remedy was due or with the curt and pleasing note, 'All is well'. But these visitations, revealing though they are, were not very frequent, for English medieval bishops had many other calls on their time.

Attendance at general chapters of the order affected all houses after 1215. Those of the Cistercians and one or two other orders involved long and costly journeys overseas, but for the mass of Augustinian and Benedictine houses only short and infrequent trips. From time to time recourse to Rome was necessary, perhaps to acquire a privilege or contest a lawsuit. This might be a protracted and expensive affair and so tended to be rare. In any case once the brethren involved had disappeared from sight, the monastic routine went on as before.

More frequent and often more tiresome were the demands of secular magnates on monastic houses with which they were connected. It is true that a king or baron might help a monastery of which he was patron by straightening out its finances in hour of need or by occasional gifts of such things as venison or timber from his estate. But, in general, such patrons gained appreciably more than they gave. The king did well out of taxation of religious houses and developed various under-the-counter methods of utilising their wealth. In the later Middle Ages some English monasteries found themselves saddled with the obligation of maintaining some ex-soldier in need of support, whose language must often have left something to be desired. Families of importance had often to be placated by appointing one of their members to one of the rather numerous administrative posts needed to hold the often sprawling monastic estates together, or to one of the wealthier benefices of which a monastery was patron.

Whether the area was rich and populous like southern and eastern England, or sparsely inhabited like much of the north and west, monastic hospitality was in steady demand, and we ought not to dismiss as unfounded the many complaints of the strain on monastic finances thus created.

Recourse to the royal law courts was a favourite pastime of medieval England. It might be expensive and was very often intolerably prolonged, lengthy adjournments being granted because witnesses were not present or even because they had not come of age! Understandably monasteries often found it worth while to accept a compromise solution rather than fight to the bitter end to maintain their rights.

In the sphere of ecclesiastical change there was singularly little sign of movement. As we have noted, the Black Death severely diminished the monastic population but steadily some, if not all, of the lost ground was regained, even if the standards of entry tended to be lowered to achieve this. As time went on the observances which governed the monastic life were revised, sometimes by mere local effort, sometimes on the grand scale, as when in 1339 and 1336 the pope issued new constitutions for the Augustinians and Benedictines respectively. Occasionally, as we shall see, some small houses got into low water and were either suppressed or (more frequently) put under the charge of a larger local house.

An interesting development was the systematic linking of the older orders with the Universities of Oxford and Cambridge. As we have seen, the friars already had this connection and it was not now lessened. The richer Benedictine houses established joint colleges of which Worcester College, Oxford, and Magdalene College, Cambridge, retain interesting remains. The Augustinians established St. Mary's College at Oxford for their students, after considerable travail but were mostly content to use Barnwell priory as their Cambridge centre. But the results of this experiment do not seem to have been impressive. Despite the fulminations of general chapters over neglect to send suitable brethren to higher study there was a good deal of passive resistance to the project, partly from financial reasons, partly because of lack of conviction that the matter was important. Understandably the contribution of Augustinians and Benedictines to late medieval learning was not impressive. Nor, rather surprisingly, did they add much to the remarkable outburst of mystical literature in these times, though one or two individuals, like Walter Hilton, an Austin canon of Thurgarton, were influential.

As might be expected, the economic fortunes of English monasteries in these days varied considerably. A few like Walsingham flourished notably, but the great majority seem to have stayed much where they were. At the bottom of the scale a number of nunneries and small Benedictine and Augustinian houses found the problem of making ends meet a very trying one, which a certain number failed to solve. In general, monastic life was free either from great poverty or great superfluity.

The Background to the Dissolution

Before considering the process of dissolution which was to wreck nearly a thousand monasteries, it is worth considering the quantity and quality of their inmates in these latter days.

It is obviously much easier to get a rough idea of something as simple as the former, than of something as complex as the latter. Evidence of the population of medieval monasteries is a good deal less extensive than the modern man would expect, but by the fourteenth and fifteenth centuries there is enough of it to make clear the general outline of the picture, as a recent survey by an American professor has shown us. As we have already shown, the number of religious rose remarkably in the late eleventh and twelfth centuries, and continued to increase thereafter till the time of the Black Death of 1348-9—the greatest set-back the English population has ever suffered. At the time this broke out, the total English monastic population was made up of about 14,000 monks and 3000 nuns. The precise extent of the losses caused by the Black Death is not obtainable, but recent estimates suggest that it carried off about a half of the total population of England and at least the same proportion of the English monastic population. To recover from so grievous a blow was clearly a slow process, but one which seems to have begun quickly and proceeded steadily. Some, though by no means all, of the lost ground was made up, and by the opening of the sixteenth century the English monasteries had some 10,000 monks and 2000 nuns. It is doubtful if this number increased at all thereafter, and certain that from 1534 onwards it declined owing principally to government enforcement of a rule that all monks or nuns who were under the age of twenty-four, or had been professed before the age of twenty, should be dismissed.

9

As we shall see, the fourteenth and fifteenth centuries saw a certain decline in the number of English monasteries, but this was not of major proportions, a large fraction of the houses involved being very minor ones.

Much more difficult to establish is the quality of the life maintained in English monasteries in these times. This matter was hotly disputed in Victorian times, but since then the growth of historical knowledge on the subject and the decline of religious bigotry has done much to make an agreed solution of the question possible.

What are the defects which contemporary evidence exposes in English monastic life, and what is their significance? To answer these questions we have available from episcopal and other visitations a good deal of evidence, though of a kind requiring very careful and sympathetic interpretation.

A not infrequent complaint at monastic visitations is the disrepair of monastic buildings. Thus in 1439 it was reported at St. Neot's that the priory roof was in such a poor state that in rainy weather the brethren could not hold a book open in quire; at the same time the prior of Spalding said his church would soon be in ruins if the roof were not repaired. In 1440 some nuns were not sleeping in the dormitory 'because they are agreed of the the ruinous state of the same dorter' and the following year a nun of Ankerwyke said her community was storing hay and grain in the church as their barns had been allowed to fall into ruin. At Lacock in 1519 the infirmary was not fit for use, and sick nuns had to sleep in the dorter. It would not be difficult to add to such instances, but it is very important that we should not misinterpret such evidence by neglecting certain important considerations. In the first place we must remember that it is unlikely that the sum total of such cases of ruinous monastic buildings was large. It is certain that in a considerable proportion of English monasteries we have no reason to suspect any such unsatisfactory state of things, and there is much to show that many houses were able to carry out important new building schemes at this time. A very high proportion of rich houses such as Glastonbury, Christ Church, Canterbury, Westminster, and lesser ones like Sherborne, Bolton, Bath and Cerne made notable additions to their buildings at this period.

Further, it is to be remembered that complaints of buildings in urgent need of repair are very largely confined, as one would expect, to small houses, especially the perenially impecunious houses of nuns, and to other monasteries whose affairs happened to be mal-directed at the time.

The burden of maintaining our medieval parish churches today with a much richer and larger population than was available to support the multitudinous ecclesiastical institutions of pre-Reformation England, should make us chary of quickly condemning those whose repair problems were so much more difficult than our own. The truth of the matter is, of course, that this matter of disrepair was normally due to lack of money, a thing which cannot fairly be imputed as a major fault of monastic life. And it was this same financial stress that lay behind such irregularities as those which led the prior of one tiny house to neglect conventual worship by sending out his brethren to do the hay-making and the nuns of another to contemplate establishing an alehouse at their gate!

Another complaint voiced in monastic visitations at one time or another was that of mal-administration by senior officials, especially by a particular head of the house. Electing a head of any big institution is apt to be a difficult matter, with the chosen one from time to time failing to come up to expectations. If this occurred in electing the head of a monastery, a serious situation might well arise. There was no genteel dustbin like the House of Lords whither they could be dispatched, for they were mostly elected for life. Deposition was a very serious step which authority was anxious to avoid, and then, as now, ecclesiastical officials' views of human nature tended to optimism rather than the reverse. However this may be, unwise exercise of the very heavy responsibilities of being head of a monastery could upset the morale of the community as quickly and effectively as unwise conduct by a senior naval officer can upset that of his ship. Various examples of incompetent heads can be found.

At Canons Ashby (not far from Cambridge), in 1442, the situation had got so out of hand that a pathetic prior begged the bishop to 'bridle the heady importunity of the young canons who want to study at Oxford'. In 1440, at Humberstone, an abbot could not cope with a monk who answered him 'saucily and rebelliously' when taken to task for 'climbing up a gate to behold the pipe-players and dancers in the churchyard of the parish church'. At this time the great Benedictine abbey of Peterborough had an abbot who seems to have been no business man—a serious matter in view of the opportunities for waste offered by so rich a house. He was accused of 'senseless expenses' in building a windmill 'for corn and for making oil out of rapeseed . . . to no profit' and of allowing poachers to practise freely in the abbey's fens and marshes. Nunneries sometimes tried to make ends meet by taking lodgers whom occasionally the superior could not control. At Gracedieu in 1440–1 the bishop ordered the removal of a Frenchwoman who lived there, 'because of the unseemliness of her life, for she receives all alike to her embraces', and at this time the nunnery of Legbourne was plagued by 'a secular woman who lies of night in the dorter among the nuns, bringing with her birds, by whose twittering silence is broken and the rest of the nuns disturbed'. Another lady lodger 'attended church with twelve dogs which make a great uproar'. But these sort of problems were not particularly frequent or (probably) particularly disturbing to the outside world; nor did such incompetence and insubordination cease at the Reformation.

What were more disturbing were the signs of laxity over that maintenance of worship which was the *raison d'être* of so many monasteries. There were various manifestations of this, notably non-attendance and irreverence at worship. In 1437 at Peterborough, in what was admittedly one of the worst phases of the house's history, the brethren set up a scandalous shift system for church attendance. There were times when only ten or twelve out of a convent of forty-four were present in quire and even by 1519 only eleven out of thirty-five attended when they should. Allied to this are various complaints that the toughest part of the monastic routine —rising in the middle of the night for Mattins (see page 103) was neglected. In 1440 the abbot of Wellow was accused of coming to Mattins only on the principal feasts, and a monk of Gedney was said to gossip till midnight, then, after ringing the bell for Mattins, to retire to bed! Another fairly frequent complaint was that monks and nuns instead of retiring to bed immediately after Compline (the last service of the day), would adjourn for a drink and a little conversation. In 1518 it was said that the canons of Owston were given to drinking and talking in the refectory after Compline and a similar complaint was made about the canons of Kirkby Bellars at this time. Two monks had been accused of exactly the same offence at Bardney in 1439. This practice is probably not entirely extinct in modern seminaries or theological colleges, and can scarcely rank as a sign of grave iniquity.

The same relaxed standard is seen in another way—the prevalence of leaving the monastic precinct without good cause. Hunting was to the fifteenth century what football pools are to our own day, and we find various cases of monks going a-hunting. One abbot of Leicester became notorious for this, but took the age-long 'painful duty' line of defence, maintaining he engaged in this frivolous occupation 'not from delight' but only to please the king and the great lords who were his guests, and for the advantage of his house! More original was the prior of Westacre who, in 1494, was accused of spending too much time at his rabbit warren and in rearing swans which he gave to local gentry and others free of charge. Against this the canons of Bolton who were accused of going out of the monastery on bird-nesting expeditions seem unimaginative.

There are, of course, individual instances of the sins of violence and sex, but it cannot fairly be claimed that these were more than rarities, and if we look at the contemporary law courts there is plenty to suggest that, as might be expected, in such matters the laity of the time were not in a position to throw stones at those who, with all their faults, were prepared to sacrifice private property and the prospect of marriage for the cause of Christ.

In considering these and all other faults of which English monasteries were accused at this time, it is important to bear in mind the importance of a simple mathematical approach to the problem. With nearly a thousand monasteries existing in a period when lay society was far from refined in its manners, it was certain that the monastic life should be to some extent contaminated by the crudity of the age, for as a bishop once properly pointed out, the main reason for the low standard of the clergy is the unavoidable necessity of recruiting them from the laity. That some such defects as those we have listed were to be found is neither surprising nor shocking. What is crucial is to know the prevalence of these sort of defects? Were they rare, common or very common? This is the kind of question that really matters. It is easy to find a few dozen cases of the sorts of laxities just considered, but less easy to remember that there were thousands of monks and nuns at this time of whom nothing reprehensible is recorded.

It is of course true that the available evidence on this question does not give a complete picture. Some of the facts necessary for this have not survived, others have not been published. If we try and see the whole of the monastic picture it seems safe to say that life in the English monasteries in the century before the Suppression largely followed the uneventful course which most ecclesiastical institutions follow most of the time. It is notable that one of the best informed historians of this subject, Dr. Coulton, though a vigorous and rather misleading critic of various aspects of medieval Church life, did not support any very unfavourable view of medieval monasteries. In his introduction to his massive, if rather muddle-headed, *Five Centuries of Religion*, he wrote: 'The Religious Orders have been among the main force of European civilisation; at certain times and at certain places they may perhaps have been the greatest of all civilising forces'. In his final volume he reiterated this, adding: 'the monasteries (apart from exceptional times and places) were far from perfection, but the society which had bred them, and from which their influence was derived, was itself still further from the Christian ideal'. That there was a good deal that needed correction in the monastic life of our period is undeniable. That had often been true before, was to be true again and was likewise true of most other sections of the Church. As our leading authority on the English Church in the fifteenth century has put it: 'it is impossible to escape the conclusion that English monasteries in the fifteenth century needed spiritual quickening to justify their existence as a whole' (A. Hamilton Thompson). But what was needed was not destruction but reforming.

The odd idea that the monastic ideal as such was out of date is belied by the stark facts of the case. Various medieval orders still carry out considerable works for the Church and have been joined by scores of new ones which express the old ideal in new forms. But if monasticism as a Christian activity was in no way outmoded, there is no doubt that to some degree the form in which it was expressed at this time was. Looking back from our modern historical arm-chair we can see that major changes were essential if the monastic ideal was to recapture the popular acclaim it had inspired for so much of the Middle Ages.

The first need was for a radical overhaul of the monastic machinery of the day. The early Middle Ages had given such exuberant support to the conservative monasticism of its day that it had failed to guard against the dangers inherent in overshooting the mark. The passion for building railways and canals in nineteenth-century England rapidly got out of bounds and produced far more of these than could be profitably employed. It is arguable that the same thing happened with the post-Conquest monastic revival, and that more monasteries were established than contemporary society was likely to be able to man effectively, once the revivalist emotions that accompanied the birth of the monastic orders had subsided. If this were so, it would do much to explain the lowered quality of monastic life in generations before the Reformation. Certainly a considerable number of small English monasteries could profitably have been closed down and their brethren and resources transferred to those large houses where alone an effective communal life could be maintained. At the top end of the scale the plutocratic Benedictine monasteries, which so clearly had far more wealth than was necessary for the body or good for the soul, could equally profitably have had some part of their possessions utilised in other ways. Allied with this was the question of the desirability of effecting in one way or another a partial disendowment of the monasteries. This need not necessarily have implied seizure of some of their wealth by the government but merely diversion of it to other channels having a religious importance, such as education. As we have noted, there were good recent precedents for this. Within the monastic order itself there had long been a section of opinion fully aware of the undesirability of those who took vows of poverty living in luxurious surroundings. Probably in a great majority of English monasteries plain living prevailed, but, as so often happens, there were also the scandalous few whose behaviour naturally but unfairly discredited the respectable many. Unhappily at this time there was very little chance of such salutary but far-reaching changes being effected. Medieval monastic foundations were almost inextricably enmeshed in both civil and canon law and it is not easy to see how these sort of changes could have been effected. Further, there were all sorts of vested social interests involved in the existence of a monastic house, which added further obstacles to any attempt to suppress it or reduce its status. For example, local families great and small got various perquisites from local monasteries and were likely to fight hard to retain them.

Even more important for a flourishing monastic future was a reassessment of the monastic ideal. Mere imitation of the past never provides a permanently satisfactory basis of Christian life, as the friars had found, and their astounding success had been principally due to their readiness to undertake radical re-thinking. By the early sixteenth century social conditions had changed enormously from those of the days of St. Benedict or St. Bernard. A change in monastic emphasis was demanded if these changes were to be met. The spirit of the age was now what some would describe as practical, others as materialistic. 'It is an earthy, selfish, grasping age', writes Professor Knowles of England of the eve of the Reformation. Certainly there were some as unwilling to accept the traditional rather uncritical and automatic admiration of the monastic life as any Victorian Protestant. 'Shall we build houses and provide livelihoods for a company of bussing monks, whose end and fall we ourselves may live to see', wrote Bishop Oldham (1505-19). 'No, no; it is meet to provide for the increase of learning and for such as by learning shall do good to Church and commonwealth.' His assumption that monasticism was effete was not to be substantiated by future events, but the impatience with old ways which inspired his words was worth taking seriously. There is no doubt that this dissatisfaction came largely from a feeling of distaste, not for monasticism as such but for the highly conservative form in which it was practised in almost all houses of Benedictines and Augustinians. To be conservative is not the same as to be out of date, and the future of the Church on the Continent was to show clearly that such orders as these still had a useful part to play in Church life. But the new part was a good deal smaller than it used to be and demanded certain changes of rôle, e.g. over monks taking parish duty, a thing very rare in the Middle Ages, far from uncommon today. New social conditions demanded reinterpretation of the monastic ideal, and utlimately this reassessment was successfully and drastically made. Later centuries were to see a remarkable resurgence of monastic life in Western Europe. But the chief new monastic orders differed markedly from the old in the much greater stress they laid on active as against contemplative work. Under modern conditions the great mass of religious orders in the West are not primarily concerned with maintaining an elaborate round of prayer and praise in the old medieval manner. Some there are who do this, and few who have met them would doubt the validity of their vocation. But the majority have a direct concern with educational, social and pastoral work that was much less obvious in the Middle Ages.

It is, of course, true that this modern spirit with its emphasis on the market place rather than the cloister existed in medieval monasticism to some degree. It had lain behind the foundation of the friars, which explains why orders like the Franciscans and Dominicans passed from the medieval to the modern world with only minimal readjustments. But in a sense the friars came too late, and at the end of the fifteenth century in England, as elsewhere in the West, the monastic institution was heavily weighted in favour of the strongly contemplative régime of early centuries. It was this now excessive conservative strain in the monastic ideal which inspired such lopsided criticisms as that of Bishop Oldham, and provided a certain discontent with the monastic set-up which it was open to greedy rulers and their minions to exploit.

These two deep-seated problems, the over-expansion of monastic life and its too conservative spirit, are much more important in explaining the undoubtedly wide-spread criticism of monastic life in England in the fifteenth and sixteenth centuries, than the moral deficiencies, real and imaginary, about which the Victorians got so excited. Nobody who knows Tudor and Stuart England (or for that matter the courts of Francis I or Louis XIV) can derive the impression that the laity of these times were morbidly sensitive about moral lapses, nor does the court life of Hano-verian England or Louis XV suggest any change of heart hereon. There is not the slightest evidence at this (or indeed at any other) period to show that life outside the cloister was more noble than that inside. Many would regard it as reasonable to expect that the lives of men and women prepared to give up money, marriage and a career are more likely to be sacrificial than the lives of those who do not.

The trouble about the major general factors just stressed, was that they were so singularly difficult to cure. Their roots curled and twisted deep into the jungle of the past, and human nature being what it is, it is not surprising, even if it is regrettable, that in some areas the situation was left to be solved by the crude and nasty weapon of force.

However, it must not be thought that some sort of condign punishment or at least severe discipline was unavoidable if monasticism was to survive Tudor England. English medieval monasteries might have pursued their somewhat lumbering way till the eighteenth and nineteenth centuries, as did most of their Continental counterparts, had it not been for unpredictable actions of Henry VIII and his advisers. On the other hand, we must not regard the English Dissolution as an isolated phenomen. In almost every major part of Western Europe the same process took place at one time or another in one way or another, the modern state greedily devouring medieval monastic endowment.

The Process of Dissolution

Although the Dissolution of the Monasteries under Henry VIII was almost unparalleled in its motives, scope, methods and results, it was not without some small precedents which are worthy of note. The process of monastic foundation in the twelfth century was a difficult one and needed a complex legal procedure to be effectively carried out. Even at this date, therefore, a few communities, not surprisingly, failed to get established. For some the expected endowment was not ultimately forthcoming, others were thwarted by local opposition or because the first community lacked spiritual stamina. Thus a house of Austin canons planned at Wallingford never materialised and, in the face of Benedictine opposition, Archbishop William Corbeil of Canterbury had to withdraw the regular canons he had established at St. Martin's Dover. But at this time as in the thirteenth century such falling by the wayside seems to have been very rare, though there are a few isolated instances such as the priory of Canon Legh (Devon) from which regular canons were ejected for no very obvious good reason. But it is to be noted that here the regular canons were at once replaced by a house of Augustinian nuns, in accordance with what had now become the established rule—that property once given to a religious house could not be alienated from monastic use.

In the early fourteenth century came an unexpected and unusual event with the official dissolution of a whole order. This was the Order of the Temple to which we have already referred (see page 95), effected in 1312 by the weak pope Clement V acting under considerable pressure from a ruthless French king who had an eye on the not inconsiderable wealth of the order. Torture was used to extract confessions of guilt in a very modern way. But the charges of immorality, superstition and heresy then laid against the Templars are now largely admitted to have been exaggerated beyond all reason. Here, as at the Reformation, the issue was confused by the order having wealth greatly coveted by the lay power. In any case, the Templars were not a monastic order in the full sense of the term, and it was at least arguable that the collapse of the Crusading movement had deprived them of their *raison d'être.* Their suppression could only be put into effect with the help of the local ruler who, in England as in France, took the opportunity to take an unofficial commission on the proceedings. However, by no means all the property was lost to its original uses, and in England some important houses were transferred to the sister body, the Order of Hospitallers.

By the time the Templars' property had been divided out, another not dissimilar problem had arisen—that of the 'alien priories', the name given to monasteries subject to foreign houses here (almost all of which were French and Benedictine). The term did not cover full members of orders like those of Cîteaux and Prémontré, but referred to houses which were in effect cells of individual foreign houses who controlled their personnel, at least in theory, and might draw from them surplus revenue, including the order of Cluny.* The majority of these houses were not conventual at all, but were nothing more than manors (often with the local parish church attached) at which two or three brethren would reside for short periods, largely to act as estate agents for their mother house. But besides these there were also about thirty-eight houses of some size, notable among which were sizeable houses like Lewes, Much Wenlock and Bermondsey.

It was the financial tie that involved the alien priories in a whole sea of troubles with the English government starting in the late years of the thirteenth century. This was because, from this time onwards, the English and French were long at loggerheads, a rivalry which soon flared up into the Hundred Years War. War is expensive, and, at an early stage, vigorous protests were made against the existence of alien priories which were liable to send money to France, the land of the enemy. Though the total amount involved must have been small, it was understandable that government action should be taken to prevent its transfer. On several occasions in the very late thirteenth and early half of the fourteenth centuries, the English crown took charge of these alien priories.

At first the crown appointed custodians to supervise the financial side of the houses' affairs and appropriate any surplus left after reasonable expenses had been settled, though some larger houses avoided this by payment of a heavy annual fine. But in 1351 Lewes, one of the largest of the alien priories, bought a 'charter of denizisation' which in effect legally freed it from its foreign commitments, and most of the other larger houses followed its example. However, numerous small alien priories were unable to do this, and the great bulk of them were transferred to existing monasteries, either as cells or mere granges, thus respecting the ancient rule that ecclesiastical land should not be used for secular purposes. By a wide interpretation a little property went to non-monastic churches like the great secular college of Windsor, a move almost but not absolutely without precedent.

There was, however, one interesting new development. In the late fourteenth

---

* Cluniac houses evidently counted as alien priories when Cistercian ones did not, because the constitution of the order made all daughter houses subject to the mother house and liable to make smallish financial payments to it.

and fifteenth centuries education was attracting growing interest, and foundation of educational establishments increased steadily. On the grandest scale was William of Wykeham's foundation of a school at Winchester and a college (New College) at Oxford (1379). His action was imitated a century later by king Henry VI by his foundation of Eton and King's College, Cambridge (1441). Both of these included in their endowments a few, small, suppressed alien priories, whilst several existing places of education, like Pembroke College, Cambridge, were given small pickings from this not very tempting joint. Though the total amount of monastic property thus converted to educational use was very small, it constitutes a significant new departure.

A limited number of houses of Austin canons were very poor and weak, so it is not surprising that some of them failed to weather the storms of time. Their frail reserves could easily be irreparably damaged by some single calamity such as a fire, a flood, a plague or an incompetent head. In 1416 Peterstone priory was said to be in a poor way as a result of the plague of 1349 and floods in 1378 and 1387; some time later it was transferred to Walsingham priory. Similarly, the small priory of Spinney was given to Ely cathedral, following 'negligence of the priors and other misfortunes'. An outbreak of plague in 1506-7 left no brethren at all at the little priory of Bicknacre and probably none at Creake abbey either. Yet the importance of such monastic failures must not be over-estimated. The total number of houses affected was very small and all were very poor establishments. In some cases they seem to have become mere granges, in others small cells.

The extreme care and conservatism which marked the mode of their dissolution as dependent units, contrasts vividly with the methods which were to follow under Henry VIII. In these early cases there was always a careful enquiry into the state of the house, and in no case was the establishment allowed to pass into lay hands, it normally being transferred to a large local monastery.

But the tendency to use monastic property for educational purposes slowly gained ground. In 1496 bishop Alcock of Ely had converted the nunnery of St. Radegund, Cambridge, into Jesus College, employing both the old buildings and the old revenues. In 1507 the king's mother acquired the possession of several small monasteries including Creake abbey, to augment the endowment of Christ's College, Cambridge, which she had founded. But this process was soon to be seen on a much more notable scale.

By 1523 Cardinal Wolsey had decided to rival the twin educational foundations of William of Wykeham and Henry VI by establishing a school in his home town of Ipswich and a college at Oxford. Papal permission was secured to convert the priory of St. Frideswide's Oxford into the college and to endow it with monastic property to the annual value of £2000. For this purpose twenty houses were suppressed, mostly small ones. In 1528 the pope sanctioned the conversion into a school of the Augustinian priory of St. Peter's Ipswich, and a few more monasteries, mostly local ones, were suppressed to augment the endowment.

It is thus apparent that, by the accession of Henry VIII, to dissolve a monastery was no new thing, and that the number of English monasteries had been perceptibly reduced before ever the new king was casting covetous eyes on monastic wealth. By the time that the total suppression of English monasticism was being mooted, some 150 of the original 1000 independent English foundations had ceased to exist. But this large figure is highly misleading, and it would be improper to regard it as proof of widespread rottenness in the monastic tree. The very minor nature of almost all the extinct foundations makes it clear that it was a matter not of preventing mortal dangers by a major operation, but rather ineffective pruning of a tree that had been somewhat slackly tended, and grown too luxuriantly.

The Dissolution of the English Monasteries under Henry VIII

Now that religious prejudices have so much subsided and modern scholarship has demolished so many old ideas, it is not worth while exploding the view that Henry VIII's suppression of the monasteries was initiated by any lofty ideas of moral reform.* There can be little doubt that the major and immediate consideration was funds. As we have seen, down the centuries monasteries in England, as elsewhere, had innocently and almost inevitably collected a considerable amount of wealth, as a result of the spontaneous respect which millions of the faithful so long bore for the life of the cloister. From an early stage, in some cases, it had been thought excessive, and lay magnates not least the king, steadily got some share of it in practice, though not in theory. By a great variety of devices monastic wealth, property and offices were used for lay purposes, but by the time of Henry VIII it had for centuries been accepted that any direct attack on monastic wealth as a whole was improper.

Although we have very detailed information about the financial position of English monasteries on the eve of their suppression, we have unfortunately no similar details regarding non-monastic wealth. Because of this, it is not yet possible to form any precise estimate as to the proportion of English wealth in monastic hands at this time, though perhaps an estimate of a quarter may be somewhere near the mark.

To any impecunious king such wealth was highly tempting, and by the middle of his reign king Henry VIII certainly found it so. He had inherited something of his father's avarice and, as the years slipped away, this steadily blotted out his youthful liberality. The origins of the idea to proceed to so revolutionary a step as the complete confiscation of English monastic wealth, have not yet been satisfactorily established. But there is no doubt that the scheme owed not a little to the mind of the king's chief minister, Thomas Cromwell, who displayed that cold lack of scruple which the Italian Renaissance was now making so fashionable. As the

* Cf. Professor Knowles, who in his recent dispassionate and elaborate survey of the Dissolution, moderately remarks: 'It is at least permissible to conclude that neither the desire nor the hope of reforming the religion of England had any part in determining the actions of Henry and Cromwell'; it is difficult for the reasonably informed to dissent from this.

reign proceeded, a few monasteries apart from those involved in Wolsey's scheme were snuffed out, and in 1532 the suppression of Holy Trinity, Aldgate (a major house of Austin canons) without reference to the pope was something of a danger signal. By 1534 rumours and plans for confiscating Church wealth were circulating, one of the latter suggesting inroads on both monastic and non-monastic wealth alike and proposing reduced and uniform allowances for ecclesiastics with the surplus going to the king and the suppression of smaller monasteries. At the end of the year Cromwell boasted to an ambassador of his intention to make Henry the wealthiest prince in Christendom.

Cromwell was well aware of the immense opposition which such a far-reaching operation was likely to arouse and planned the Suppression with subtlety and complete lack of scruple. It was preceded by a systematic survey of the wealth of the English Church carried out in 1535 and digested into the so-called *Valor Ecclesiasticus*. This gigantic survey of Church wealth was pushed through with great speed and efficiency and by the early months of 1536 was complete. It recorded both temporalities of ecclesiastical bodies—e.g. farms, manors, houses, rents —and their spiritualities (e.g. rectories and vicarages, tithes and alms) as well as recognised items of expenditure. There seems no doubt that most of the details of the survey was substantially accurate, though like more modern financial assessments, it perhaps inevitably took a legalistic view of expenditure, only allowing for example doles which a convent was bound by law to make. On the other hand, it has recently been suggested that the valuation appreciably underestimated the potential income of monastic estate. The Survey showed the total gross income of monks, canons, nuns and hospitallers as totalling some £165,000; in view of the omission of the friars' possessions and some undervaluation, £200,000 has been suggested as a more accurate figure. It is unfortunately not yet possible to assess what proportion of the national wealth this represents, nor will economic historians commit themselves as to the equivalent of this sum in modern money. Two-thirds of the income came from land and its produce, and spiritual income accounted for another quarter. A sixth of the income was recognised as tax free, probably an ungenerous figure.

The survey brings out very vividly the inequality of monastic incomes to which we have so often drawn attention, as the following table shows.

Income	Proportion of Houses
Under £20	9%
£20-£100	35%
£100-£300	35%
£300-£1000	16%
Over £1000	4%

Twenty-eight houses were in the last category of which no less than twenty-three were Benedictine, three of the rest being Augustinian, one Cistercian and one

Cluniac. A detailed survey of the contents of the *Valor Ecclesiasticus* was made some years ago by a Russian scholar. This showed, amongst other things, that some 3 per cent of the total income recorded went to charitable purposes. Stated in this way the figure does not appear impressive. But it represented a considerable total sum and the grants it made possible, like the modern old-age pensions, though small probably provided for not a few the vital bridge between living above and below subsistence level. There are certain indications not yet systematically explored, that there were various charitable gifts made especially in kind which were not recorded in the Survey as they were not made by legal necessity but by custom. Glastonbury had the greatest net income (£3311), Westminster being second and having the largest gross income (£3912).

Inevitably this extensive survey betokened no good to the Church, and, aided by fearsome rumours, some monasteries began to expect the worst—lands were leased out, stock sold and probably plate concealed. Meanwhile Cromwell took further action. By the middle of 1535 several trusted royal officials were dispatched to investigate the state of the monasteries by personal visitation. It is not established that either the king or Cromwell was bent on total or partial suppression of the monasteries at this stage, and it is possible that only some drastic overhaul was envisaged. The visitors were civil servants carrying out their master's demands unquestioningly, 'often sagacious, moderate and good-natured in their personal dealings when neither career nor cash was at stake' but 'grasping, worldly, and without a trace of spiritual feeling' says Professor Knowles. They were provided with an extensive questionnaire framed on traditional lines and a set of injunctions. Many of the latter were also quite traditional but some had novel features. They opened with reminders of the oaths to the crown and against the pope already taken under the Acts of Succession and Supremacy and included two provisions that were to cause trouble, though not perhaps originally planned so to do. One of them forbade a monk 'by any means to go forth of the precincts (of his monastery)'; the other evidently excluded from a monastery members of the opposite sex. As general rules these were both sound enough, and had been long accepted. But common sense demanded the acceptance of certain legitimate exceptions—e.g. absence from the monastery to carry out its temporal or spiritual affairs or to attend a conference or preach, and the permission of women related to monks to see them at intervals. Such legitimate relaxations were now forbidden.

The visitation now carried out contrasted violently with those of ancient days. The new visitors were laymen with little sympathy for the monastic life or understanding of it, not as of old, ecclesiastical officials accustomed to the problems it raised. The lumbering but scrupulously fair procedure hitherto usual was now dropped. Old standards demanded separate and lengthy examination of each member of the monastery, often long sifting of the mass of evidence thus obtained and finally, some time after, the issue of injunctions which aimed at remedying any defects thus revealed. Cromwell's visitors acted with a haste which was certainly indecent. There is no evidence that they made more than the briefest examination of the brethren and their injunctions were issued on the spot. What they sought was not a general picture with a view to reform but only matters useful for the process of suppression, the state of the finances of the house, evidence of alleged sexual offences and 'superstitious practices' which might be useful for propaganda purposes.

The visitation was certainly unsatisfactory in other respects. Thus several counties, including Lincolnshire, which had a large number of monasteries, do not seem to have been visited at all. The whole affair was marked by a remarkable brevity, being concluded in the space of half a year (August 1535–February 1536), about the same amount of time which it took the bishop of Norwich under the old dispensation to visit the monasteries of his diocese. Some years ago J. R. Tanner, a constitutional historian with no axe to grind, wrote of these visitors as 'men of doubtful character' and commented that 'the rapidity of the visitation deprived it of all claim to be regarded as a judicial proceeding'. It is difficult for those fully briefed in the case to dissent from his verdict.

Before the visitation was anywhere near completion, or its findings digested, Cromwell had decided on wide-scale suppression. Like Hitler he knew how to use the thin end of the wedge and his first move was to prepare a Bill to suppress only monasteries which had an income of less than £200 a year and less than twelve members. The preface to the Bill painted a wildly inaccurate picture of the monastic situation, referring to the little monasteries as very bad, and big monasteries as very good—'manifest sin, vicious, carnal and abominable living is daily used and committed amongst the little and small abbeys, priories and other religious houses . . . divers great and solemn monasteries of this realm wherein thanks be to God, religion is right well kept and observed'. There is nothing to show that the monasteries were intensely unpopular with any major section of society, however much a good grumble about them was enjoyed. But by the time this Bill came up, the Commons were well used to being employed as a rubber stamp for royal proceedings, and propaganda now vilified the monastic name. At the same time hints were quickly circulating that royal yes-men might well get a share of the spoil. It is also possible that Henry put on special pressure to ensure that there was no opposition. In March 1536 the Bill passed and it was clear that no small section of English monastic property was coming on the market.

The resulting surge to climb on to the band waggon stares in the face any reader of the official correspondence of the time, and illustrates very vividly the latent power of human greed. High and low of every kind bombarded the government for monastic property, for which they had real or imagined claim, at times accompanying their letters with bribes or promises thereof. Cold-bloodedly, Cromwell went ahead organising the greatest land-sale in English history. Charge of the confiscated monastic property was vested in a new body created for the purpose, the Court of Augmentations, and in April steps were taken for commissioners in each county to take over the monasteries affected, rendering strict account of their stewardship. The revenue of each house was to be newly assessed and details sent in of the numbers of religious and their servants and dependants, and of the value of the chattels of the house, notably plate, bells and lead (used for roofing and then a valuable commodity). But the considerable number of monasteries affected could not be effectively dealt with straight away, partly because of the severe practical problem of transferring to other monasteries those monks and nuns who wished to persevere in their calling, a concession embodied in the Act of Suppression. As a result about seventy or eighty houses, almost a quarter of those involved, bought permission to continue, mostly paying through the nose for the privilege, some pathetically pawning their goods to help to provide the necessary cash. In the process Cromwell seems to have feathered his nest very comfortably. Otherwise the community was dismissed, its estates taken over, its plate and jewels seized, its livestock and movables sold. Most of the buildings, as well as their contents, were sold for what they would fetch, but an insufficiently noted provision of the Act of Dissolution ordered the retention of 'an honest, continual house and household in the . . . site or precinct' of suppressed houses; this was clearly done to increase the market value of the estate by providing it with a 'desirable residence'. In practice, as we shall see, this often meant maintaining the abbot's or prior's apartments with adjourning domestic buildings, these being clearly the most suitable part to retain as a house (see page 139).

A curious incident in this scene of widespread collapse was the foundation of two new monasteries by Henry VIII, a further sign of his religious conservatism when self-interest did not get in the way. An abbot and fourteen Benedictine monks were installed in the dissolved Augustinian priory of Bisham and very adequately endowed with properties from Chertsey abbey and elsewhere (1537). The previous year the Lincolnshire house of Stixwould was re-founded for Benedictine nuns from Stainfield, but these were replaced the following year by Premonstratensian canonesses. Both houses were to pray especially for the king and queen Jane (Seymour). But their lives were brief, Bisham was dissolved in 1538 and Stixwould a year later.

By the time these houses were established a popular revolt suddenly flared up which took royal officials unawares and got them badly rattled. This was the so-called 'Pilgrimage of Grace' which broke out in the autumn of 1536 and at one time or another engulfed almost all northern England and Lincolnshire. As with various so-called religious movements of the sixteenth century, ecclesiastical factors were inextricably tangled with social and economic factors, and it would be foolish to attempt to assess the relative potency of the various causes. But there is no doubt that resentment at the religious changes recently introduced in England was a powerful element in the revolt. With feeling against change in doctrine and worship we have no direct concern, but it is important to note the considerable body of feeling among the rebels that insisted that the dissolved monasteries should be set up again. The revolt was not planned by monks but by faithful laity, who, unhappily, were mostly naïve and badly led. Some sought to involve the monastic personnel in active participation with the revolt but with very little success.

The leader of the movement, one Robert Aske, wrote feelingly of the value of monastic life: 'the abbeys in the north parts gave great alms to men and laudably served God . . . by occasion of the said suppression the divine service almighty of God is much minished, great numbers of masses unsaid . . . to the distress of faith and spiritual comfort to man's soul . . . none hospitality now in those places kept. . . . Also divers and many of the said abbeys were in the mountains and desert places, where the people be rude of conditions and not well taught the law of God. And when the said abbeys stood, the said people had not only worldly refreshing in their bodies but also spiritual refuge both by ghostly living of them and also by spiritual information and preaching . . . for none was in these parts denied, either horsemeat nor mansmeat, so that the people were greatly refreshed by the said abbeys, where they now have no such succour. . . . Also the abbeys were one of the beauties of this realm to all men and strangers passing through the same; also all gentlemen were much succoured in their needs with money, their young sons there succoured and in nunneries their daughters brought up in virtue; and also their evidences and money left to the uses of infants in abbeys' hands, always sure there; and such abbeys as were near the danger of seabanks were great maintainers of sea walls and dykes maintainers and builders of bridges and highways and other such things for the commonwealth.'

From the first there was an unfortunate lack of coordination amongst the rebels and a marked absence of an able leader. York was made their centre and from there a motley host moved southward to Doncaster where they met the Royal Commissioners. The latter were not in a position to make any major concessions, so fobbed off the rebels with hazy words. Naïvely these were believed. The rebels drifted away and once the military danger was over the government acted vigorously and ruthlessly. Henry sent the duke of Norfolk to stamp out all opposition, ordering him to 'cause dreadful execution upon a good number of the inhabitants hanging them on trees, quartering them, and selling their heads and quarters in every town'; 'all monks and canons that be in any wise faulty' were to be hung 'without further delay or ceremony, to the terrible example of others'. A number of religious accordingly suffered and various laity including Robert Aske, whose utter self-sacrifice to the truth as he saw it stands out brilliantly in an age dark with weakness and greed. One or two movements of a similar nature were planned elsewhere, including one projected by a small group of laymen at Walsingham, one of whom noted: 'You see how these abbeys go down and our living goeth away with them; for within a while Bynham shall be put down and also Walsingham and all other abbeys in that country'. But news of this conspiracy leaked out at an early stage and on government orders its few members were executed 'without sparing'.

By this time the position of those monasteries that had not fallen under the axe of the Act of 1536 was becoming intolerable. The visitors of 1535–6 had ejected all professed brethren under the age of twenty-four and, by a harsh interpretation of their terms of reference, had forbidden the rest to leave their houses on any circumstances whatever. Following a flood of understandable protests Cromwell gradually relaxed this, further feathering his nest in the process. At the same time dissension was spreading in some communities, owing partly to the spread of Reforming ideas, partly to a government regulation encouraging brethren to act as tale-bearers. Everywhere thunderstorms of unrest broke out, shattering the calm of the cloistered life.

Already a few of the greater houses had surrendered, including Lewes and Castle Acre, mostly ones in some sort of trouble already. Quickly a new phase opened, which made it clear that the government were determined to bring the Dissolution to an abrupt end, instead of allowing the monasteries to die out gradually as had happened in Scandinavia and was to happen in Scotland.

By the beginning of 1538 Cromwell had dispatched his visitors on a new series of visitations which aimed at getting individual houses to sign their own death warrants by handing over all their property to the crown. To do this, bullying and cajolery was much used, but the major factor in effecting surrender must have been the obvious hopelessness of continuing the fight against a determined and pitiless government. 'The abbeys go down as fast as they may' wrote a government agent in February 1538. Great care was taken to give the surrenders a superficially voluntary appearance, and every legal technicality employed to give them an authenticity which would attract buyers. To slow down alienations of lands and chattels by monasteries that sensed the end was near, Cromwell disseminated entirely false assurances that no such thing was in the government's mind. Pressure was considerable, no respite feasible, and house after house surrendered to the commissioners as 1538 and 1539 wore on. To make the legal position completely unassailable, in May 1539 an Act of Parliament was passed vesting in the crown all monastic possessions surrendered or to be surrendered since the Act of 1536. In March 1540 Waltham abbey surrendered, the great foundation king Harold had set up as a secular college and king Henry II converted into a house of Austin canons; with it the last important spark of organised monastic life in England went out.

Whilst all this had been going on, one or two smaller operations were carried out which were pendants to it. When the visitations were resumed, Cromwell sent off commissioners to pillage some of the wealthiest shrines. Here fresh propaganda was not so valuable as in the case of the attack on monasticism, for it was not so necessary. For a good two centuries the practice of pilgrimages and cult of relics, or, as some would put it, abuses in connection with them which were allowed to go so largely unchecked, had inspired vigorous words of criticism from faithful churchmen. This criticism was now taken over and put to anti-Catholic use by Cromwell. Various of the wealthiest pilgrimage centres were plundered. The famous shrine of St.

10

Thomas at Canterbury provided several waggon-loads of jewels and precious metals and at Walsingham in July 1538 the chapel of Our Lady was looted of 'all suche golde and syllver with such other thynges as weare there'. The famous statue of Our Lady there with that of Our Lady of Ipswich and 'all the jewelles that hunge about them' were sent to London and apparently there destroyed. At the shrine of St. Edmund at Bury 5000 marks of gold and silver, as well as many precious stones, were acquired. What was the total wealth thus acquired is not known. It was clearly a smallish item in the grand total of monastic property, but not a negligible one.

Meanwhile, in 1538, the suppression of the friars was undertaken and effected with a cohesion not seen in the case of the other orders. As we have seen, the friars had next to nothing in the way of property and only modest treasure, so were no very rich prize for a greedy government; being of old exempt from episcopal jurisdiction they had not been affected by the Act of 1536. The visitors sent round to their houses found much austerity and some dilapidation; and a good deal of local pillaging went on. By the spring of 1539 the friaries of England were stamped out and their property confiscated.

CHAPTER TEN

THE AFTERMATH

WHAT happened to the immense monastic possessions now seized by the king, and what happened to the men and women so suddenly ejected from the cloisters they had expected to inhabit till their life's end? Both these questions have attracted much attention in recent times and the general outline of the answers to them is clear.

In the early days of the campaign to suppress the monasteries, the government had declared the intention of devoting some of it to social betterment. The Act of 1536 after alleging that the wealth of the monasteries concerned was being 'spent, spoiled and wasted for increase and maintenance of sin' promised that it should be 'used and converted to better uses'. If by this was meant direct social, educational or religious improvement, the undertaking must rank high amongst the unfulfilled promises of politicians, for only a minute part of monastic wealth went directly to charitable causes.

It is true that, for one reason or another, Henry VIII and his servants were very careful not to interfere extensively in the non-monastic side of Church property. As we have seen, they respected the rights of parishioners who had an altar in monastic churches, and, in the same way, they respected the cathedrals that had been so long established in monastic precincts. These last numbered eight—Canterbury, Rochester, Winchester, Ely, Norwich, Worcester and Durham which were Benedictine, and Carlisle which was Augustinian. In place of the monks, a secular organisation of clergy was now established headed by a dean and canons, as had long been the case with the non-monastic cathedrals. For their support part of the endowments of the old monastery was set aside. This was only a fraction of the total sum but was at any rate something saved from the wreckage.

More laudable was the allocation of some old monastic revenues to the establishment of new bishoprics. In Mediterranean lands, dioceses had long been two a penny, as they still are in modern Italy. But in outlying areas of the West, like England and the Low Countries, the opposite was the case, their number being far too few to be efficient. This was an evil that had been long admitted and long tolerated. In 1534 an admirable plan was mooted to create no less than twenty-six new English dioceses. But the secular figures dominant at court were unwilling to foot the bill for this, and in 1539 another scheme reduced the number to eighteen. In the end, only six were set up, all being monasteries now converted into secular cathedrals—Westminster, Gloucester, Peterborough, Chester, Oseney (later St. Frideswide's Oxford) and Bristol. However, the bishopric of Westminster only lasted a few years, as did the two collegiate churches now established at the ex-Benedictine abbey of Burton and ex-Augustinian abbey of Thornton.

As the suppression of the monasteries gathered momentum, a few houses had tried to save themselves by pleas to be converted into secular establishments. The prior of the great house of Our Lady of Walsingham strove to have his house made into a house of secular canons, Evesham asked to continue as an educational establishment and it was suggested that Coventry might be made into a college of learned men for preaching. But in no case were such petitions successful, and it is noteworthy that education came away empty handed from the whole proceeding.

It is thus apparent that the dissolution of the monasteries under Henry VIII differed flagrantly from all previous dissolutions not only in its unlimited scope, and in the violent manner of its execution, but also in its almost complete disregard of the antique rule that suppressed monastic wealth should not be used for secular purposes.

It is conceivable that a more avaricious and cold-blooded king than Henry VIII— his father Henry VII for example—would have sold off only the bare minimum of monastic property necessary to balance a parsimonious government expenditure. Such a course might have had immensely important repercussions on English history. If it had sufficed to provide the means for the establishment of a despotic monarchy on the Continental model, it might have diverted the flood of English constitutional development from that highly original and influential course it was to carve out for itself haphazardly during the sixteenth and seventeenth centuries.

Be this as it may, the likelihood of Henry VIII and Cromwell pursuing such a cheese-paring course was always remote. Monastic wealth quickly poured into the pockets of hundreds of gentry and non-gentry, creating a vested interest that was, under the conditions of the day, the most effective guarantee that the work of the Dissolution would not be undone and could not be undone. These beleaguered high officials and the Court of Augmentations, as we have seen, had been set up to sell and administer the confiscated monastic property. The latter worked with great efficiency, thanks to careful organisation and a competent and well-paid staff of officials. A few gifts there were, for Henry himself had, at least in certain moods, the improvident generosity of a naval rating. To Sir Thomas Curwen, a prize Cumberland archer who had shot with the king, Henry asked, 'Curwen why doth thee begg none of thes Abbeys? I wold gratifie thee someway.' Curwen contented himself with a twenty-year lease of Furness abbey, though the king bade him take it for ever. But such cases were few. It is notable that only a very small proportion of monastic property (perhaps about $2\frac{1}{2}$ per cent) was given away, and even this was liable to certain obligations. A select few acquired largish estates at cut rates, but the great majority of the new owners are now known to have bought their property at the old rate of twenty years' purchase for landed estate and ten or twelve for urban property. At first much of the old monastic property was let out on lease, but long before the death of Henry VIII extensive sales of it were taking place.

The total net annual income of the English monasteries in 1535 is thought to have been about £149,000 and this was roughly the income of the Court of Augmentations in its first ten years. In effect this rather more than doubled the royal income. But very soon less than half of this revenue of the Court was income from capital, the rest being produced by sales. Although there was a steady rise in prices at this time, this was very much more than offset by the drop in income due to the steady alienation of ex-monastic property. The biggest item was the sale of lands, which reached a maximum in 1544 and 1545 and then declined markedly. The sale of monastic goods and movables (on which see pages 134 ff.) reached its height in 1541-3 and thereafter sank even more rapidly to minor importance. Henry's successors were faced with grave economic problems and had weaker weapons with which to fight them, so after his death in 1547 this alienation of monastic property went steadily on, and by the time the new century opened only a minute fraction of it was feeding the royal exchequer.

The disposal of monastic goods as distinct from monastic lands was a smallish item in the general balance sheet, but of immense cultural importance. It was only to be expected that the chattels of a monastery would be put up for sale at an early date, since there was no special point in delaying their sale and their custody was not an easy problem. Accordingly, soon after a monastery had been suppressed normally steps were taken to record its contents with a view to sale. Certain things such as plate and lead might be reserved for government use and sent to London. Everything else was sold off at an auction on the premises; occasionally, as is so usual throughout history, after those in charge had had first pick. The surveys made at this time are often scrupulously detailed, giving a complete inventory of the then contents of various parts of the monastery. Unhappily they only survive for a small fraction of the monasteries, whilst a number of those that do exist were made at a late stage in proceedings, so give nothing like a full picture.

There can be no doubt that the monastic goods were sold off with immense haste and immense waste. The literary losses suffered constituted one of the greatest catastrophes in the history of English learning. The artistic losses were equally severe and have only since been rivalled by the piecemeal architectural demolitions of recent years.

An account of the selling up of the Cistercian abbey of Roche has survived and does not seem to be exaggerated. 'Every person had everything good cheap. . . . It would have pitied any heart to see what tearing up of lead there was, and plucking up of boards, and throwing down of the sparres . . . the lead was torn off (the roof) and cast down into the church, and the tombs in the church all broken . . . and all things of price either spoiled, carped away or defaced to the uttermost. The persons that cast the lead into fodders plucked up all the seats in the choir, wherein the monks sat when they said service, which were like the seats in minsters and burned them and melted the lead withall, although there was wood plenty within a flight shot of them . . . every person bent himself to filch and spoil what he could.' As one of those concerned later admitted, his view was, 'Might I not as well as others have some profit of the spoil of the abbey? for I did see all would away; and therefore I did as others did'. As we shall see, the literary carnage was equally appalling (see pages 135-7).

Amongst the most valuable commodities was the lead from the roof, which was often melted down on the premises, as at Fountains and Monk Bretton, where traces of the fires used for the purpose have been found. In some cases stained-glass windows were broken up so as to obtain the trifling amount of lead that held their glass together. The lead seems to have been melted down into pigs marked with the royal seal. By some odd twist of fortune four of these pigs were left behind at Rievaulx and discovered there in 1920. Three of them were given to the re-leading of the glass of York minster and one preserved on the site where it can be seen, marked with the Tudor crown. Two other pigs of lead of similar origin were long preserved at Ixworth priory, but have recently found permanent homes in the museums of Bury St. Edmunds and Ipswich. Most of the lead from roofs and gutters seems to have been melted down for government use as were the bells, except a few which were sold locally. Almost all the magnificent woodwork in English monasteries was left to rot, or used for firewood. In a few cases bits of it seem to have been bought for use elsewhere like the magnificent stalls in Lancaster priory church, thought to have been acquired in this way from the near-by abbey of Cockersand, and the equally interesting stalls in Whalley parish church, from the abbey down the road. But the total destruction here must have been appalling, including not only hundreds of the magnificent timber roofs and screens in the production of which medieval England so excelled, but also a host of lesser things and an enormous amount of the panelling which, as the *Rites of Durham* show us, was extensively used in the church and various of the domestic buildings.

Equally heavy must have been the casualties in the stained glass windows. Most parish churches had all of these they wanted and such things could not be much utilised in private houses. Occasionally some monastic glass found its way into a local church, like that from Dale abbey in Dale church, and that from Cartmel priory at Bowness-on-Windermere. But the total amount to survive in this way was insignificant.

Even more serious were the casualties amongst pictures. It is necessary to visit some region like Italy to have any conception of the mass of pictures which medieval churches accumulated in the later Middle Ages, for the total number of surviving pictures from English medieval monasteries scarcely reaches double figures. The remarkable portrait of Richard II in Westminster abbey and fine retable from a Dominican house in East Anglia now in the church of Thornham Parva (Suffolk) [Pls. 31a, 31b] are two of the rare reminders of the store of this sort of beauty that once existed and of the high standard already attained. Less lovely but probably more typical is the painted retable of Bishop Despenser in Norwich cathedral. Mural paintings are slightly more numerous, being less easy to remove, but the total number surviving in ex-monastic churches is minute. As we have noted, there are important examples in Westminster abbey and some in most ex-monastic cathedrals (see page 53).

Government officials obviously made a bee-line for plate and jewels. Some of this was secreted at the time and may possibly yet await discovery, and some more had been pledged or sold before the officials arrived. But the great mass was secured and sent for royal use. The amount of this must have been enormous. A rich house like Fountains abbey had plate valued at the time at over £900, the equivalent of many thousands of pounds in modern money. The total of chalices in use in English monasteries at the time of the Dissolution (all of precious metal) must have numbered not a few thousands, yet not one of them is known to have survived.* The same is true of the patens which accompanied them. Even objects of lesser metals disappeared equally, only a handful surviving through some special chance. The censer from Ramsey [Pl. 30b] survived through being thrown into a near-by bog, perhaps to preserve it at the time of the Dissolution. The same sort of action saved the lectern and candlesticks found in a pond at Newstead in Sherwood and now in Southwell cathedral. The fine candlestick given to Gloucester abbey in 1110 [Pl. 30a] has been preserved, through its having wisely migrated to the cathedral at Le Mans before the Reformation.

The famous English embroideries and the less common tapestries equally have left few relics out of the thousands that once existed in monasteries of the day. St. John's College Oxford has some interesting vestments from the Cistercian college whose site it acquired, and a set of tapestries made for Christ Church Canterbury found their way to the cathedral of Aix-en-Provence.

Somewhat less devastating and less important was the effect on the Dissolution of such other furnishings of English monastic churches as the rather mass-produced alabaster panels and statues, which are said to have been exported by the shipload. Tiles—which defy all but the toughest treatment—have survived more often; though it is rare to find any considerable area still *in situ*, odd ones often with interesting designs have been found on a number of monastic sites.

What of the monastic libraries? Their fate after the Dissolution has been effectively studied and the answer is quite clear. A census of surviving English medieval manuscripts that can safely be attributed to monasteries of the period shows a pathetically small total (about 3600). Even if we make some extra allowance for surviving manuscripts whose provenance is uncertain there cannot be the slightest doubt that those which have survived certainly represent a very small fraction of the whole. The size of this fraction cannot be exactly determined as we have very little information about the size of all but a few of English monastic libraries of the Middle Ages. Some large monastic libraries had about two thousand manuscripts and many houses must have had several hundred. Hence it does not seem rash

* The attribution to St. Albans of the fine early sixteenth-century chalice at Trinity College Oxford is not now accepted.

to estimate the total books in the 900 English monasteries existing in the opening of the sixteenth century as several hundred thousand. If this were so the surviving element cannot represent more than a very minute percentage—perhaps 5 per cent would over-estimate it.

This immense holocaust of manuscripts—easily the greatest single disaster in English literary history—is understandable enough if we consider the circumstances which attended their dispersal. The most unfortunate factor was the almost complete absence in England of any literate class of non-ecclesiastical society which might be interested in preserving such things. Even at this late date the number of laity literate in any effective sense of the word was extremely small, and many of these were too intoxicated by the immature wine of Renaissance ideas to show much interest in medieval learning. Secondly, there was little government action to save the manuscripts, such as was not ineffective when the French monasteries were dissolved at the Revolution, or the Italian ones rather later. It is true that some slight efforts were made to save choice manuscripts for Henry VIII, various items from monastic libraries being sent up to London to be preserved in the royal library. But the number involved was very small. The third important factor was the highly unfavourable conditions that marked the monastic sales. Notice was brief, publicity bad and the very limited market for such things as manuscripts fantastically swamped. As a result the scholarship of centuries was sold for a song. As a Protestant scholar wrote in 1549: 'to destroye all [monastic] libraries without consyderacyon, is and wyll be unto England for ever a most horryble infamy amonge the grave senyours of other nacyons. A great number of them whych purchased those superstycous mansyons reserved of those librarye bokes, some to serve their cakes, some to scoure their candelstyckes and some to rubbe their bootes. Some they sold to grossers and sopesellers, and some they sent oversee to the bokebynders, not in small nombre bat at tymes whole shyppes full, to the wonderynge of the foren nations. . . . What maye bring our realme to more shame and rebuke, than to have it noysed abroade that we are despysers of lernynge.'

Only at the end of the century, when the storms of the Reformation had abated somewhat, did a few enlightened men seek to preserve what was being lost. Such were Matthew Parker, archbishop of Canterbury, who assembled a magnificent library of manuscripts (including the Canterbury Gospels [Pl. 27a*]) which he left to Corpus Christi College Cambridge and the citizen of Ipswich who gave a large collection of manuscripts from the lordly abbey of Bury St. Edmunds to Pembroke College Cambridge. But by this time the damage had been done. One or two of the old Benedictine cathedrals preserved many of their old books, notably Durham and Worcester cathedrals and here much of the original libraries are to be seen to this day. But for the rest the great mass had been destroyed, though odd ones long lay around in curious places, like the manuscript from Glastonbury discovered by an

* This is a sixth-century Italian manuscript which way well have been brought to England in the time of Augustine.

Oxford antiquary in 1722 through some tobacco being sent to him in a leaf of it. Admittedly some of the thousands of lost manuscripts had texts known to us from others that survived either here or on the Continent so that, for example, many of the lost liturgical manuscripts or texts of the fathers would give us little fresh information. But it is equally certain that the massive proportion of medieval libraries now so wantonly scattered contained much of first-rate interest to students of art, literature, history and theology.

From the historical angle almost equally regrettable was the very heavy destruction of monastic archives. In a very few cases these survive largely intact, but these are principally archives of small houses suppressed before the Reformation (like Selborne priory) or large houses which continued after the Reformation in another guise (like Westminster abbey and Ely cathedral). Several million documents of one kind or another perished, specially heavy being the casualties amongst those which had no possible legal importance such as account rolls.

What was the fate of the buildings that sheltered all these things now scattered and destroyed wholesale? Part of the answer has already been given. So far as the monastic churches were concerned, the only places normally spared were such parts of the conventual church as were already given over to the use of parishioners, normally in effect all or most of the western limb. Portions of a handful of churches not having parochial status were spared for worship as at Bolton and Holm Cultram, probably because they were the only available places of worship in a few remote areas. If the parishioners or some local dignitary were prepared to buy a non-parochial church or part of a church they could do so, but they had to act quickly and would saddle themselves with considerable upkeep in the future. Not surprisingly this was a comparatively rare event, occurring in only a score of major cases, such as Tewkesbury, Christchurch (Hants.), Sherborne, Dorchester and Cartmel, though several dozen small monastic churches are intact.

As we have noted, almost without exception in cases where the conventual church or part of it was spared, the main cloister buildings have almost completely disappeared, as at Christchurch (Hants.), Cartmel, Malton, Dunstable and Waltham. It may very well be that this was a deliberate act to prevent the possibility of the dispossessed brethren returning when the commissioners' backs were turned. The documents of the time make it quite clear that the government was well aware of this danger and took vigorous measures to stop it.

If there were no parochial rights to save part of the church, either because the place was non-parochial in origin (like the houses of the Cistercians and the friars) or because the parish altar had been moved to a separate church (like the larger Augustinian and Benedictine houses) the church was likely to be largely or completely demolished. There were, however, one or two exceptions to this. In a handful of cases, in one way or another the parishioners acquired the eastern part of an ex-monastic church as their place of worship. This occurred before the

Reformation at Chetwode, and after it at Pershore, Boxgrove, Milton and Abbey Dore. Very small churches largely without aisles could be easily converted into dwelling-houses. This occurred, for example, at Stavordale and Worspring, both in Somerset, as can still be seen, and was also the case in the now vanished house at Calwich, where the first lay owner 'made a parlour of the chancel, a hall of the church and a kitchen of the steeple'. Cases of a cruciform church being adapted as a residence as at Buckland are very rare, for such adaptation was far from easy. We have a perhaps unique pre-Reformation adaptation of this type made by the Franciscan nuns of Denny, who, when they took over a small cruciform church, much enlarged the eastern limb as their chapel, but turned much of the rest of the church into something suspiciously like a small block of flats. In most cases the church was left roofless, but considerable amounts of it and the attendant buildings might survive if conditions were favourable.

The availability or unavailability of building stone in the area and the presence or absence of a large population likely to want building material were immensely important in deciding whether such a ruined monastery was largely destroyed or not. Thus in southern and eastern England, notably in East Anglia, there was a large population and a considerable scarcity of building stone, with the result that comparatively few monasteries in this area have left imposing remains and many have left nothing beyond unattractive lumps of rubble. In the extreme north and west, the contrary tended to be the case. Population was scanty and good building-stone prolific, with the result that a very high proportion of the best preserved ruins in England are to be found in this area. Everything dictated much destruction of houses of friars (which stood in thriving centres of population) and comparatively little destruction of Cistercian houses (which had been deliberately founded 'in places removed from the habitation of men'). And in the case of the latter, demolition and transport were likely to be arduous and the need for it not great.

Another factor governing the extent to which monastic buildings were wrecked, was government policy at the time of the Dissolution. This had two main aims. The most obvious was to prevent the brethren returning to the nest, once the royal officials' backs were turned. Demolition was costly, then as now, and normally no complete destruction of the site was thought of, but attempts were made to render it uninhabitable by a community. Official instructions of 1539 which may well mirror earlier practice, order the destruction 'to the ground' of 'all the walls of the churches', steeples, cloisters, refectories, dormitories, chapter houses and the rest. The buildings specified are of course the chief ones necessary for the life of a resident convent and were principally in the eastern and southern ranges. Archaeological evidence suggests that this order was often at least partially carried out, for buildings in these areas very seldom remain intact. As has already been pointed out, chapter houses and dormitories very seldom survive as do cloister-arcades (though some of their bases and capitals can often be found lurking in local rockeries).

The second government intention, at least in the case of a large number of the houses, was to preserve on the old monastic site buildings which could be offered as a 'desirable residence' for the new lay occupant. This 'honest continual house' was specifically ordered in the small houses affected by the Act of 1536 (see page 127) and was often retained in other houses. Houses of friars, however, from their nature were unsuited to this sort of thing, and seem largely to have been sold for civic or trading purposes, like the chancel of the Chichester Franciscans [Pl. 24b] which was used as a Guildhall.

As we have noted, the part of the monastery retained for residential purposes varied. In some of the large houses the great gatehouse with its guest chambers was kept as at Pentney, Butley, St. Osyth and Thornton. But very much more obvious and more common was the retention of the lodgings of the superior, be he abbot or prior; there was sometimes thrown in for good measure the cellar under the refectory (as at Herringfleet and probably Hickling) or even the refectory itself as at Walsingham (Augustinian) and the kitchen. Specially common was the retention of the prior's lodging when it occupied the end of the western range, and had the kitchen and refectory adjoining. Michelham is a good example of this as is Shulbrede and probably also Bricett and the lost building of Bradenstoke (in the last two cases the kitchen perhaps disappeared at a later stage). At Walsingham and Ixworth the prior's lodging was at the south end of the eastern range and was preserved, along with the refectory.

As already noted, apart from the gatehouse which might be utilised as a porter's lodge or an entrance gate, few of the buildings of the outer courts were of enough utility to be preserved, with the exception of barns, though the latter were often a good deal larger than the new owner needed them to be.

What of the inmates of the monasteries suppressed by Henry VIII? This was for long a subject of controversy, but modern research has given, if not the whole picture, at least all the main features of the treatment accorded to them.

The Act of 1536 dismissed from their monasteries all professed members under the age of twenty, and allowed any of the rest who wished to be dispensed from their vows and (if they were men) to be made eligible to receive some non-monastic ecclesiastical post, such as a benefice or a chaplaincy. This privilege does not seem to have been extensively utilised at this stage, and it seems unlikely that much hardship was caused, since all the more constant monks and nuns had the right to be transferred to existing monasteries.

With houses exempt from the Act of 1536 a different policy was inevitable. With certain exceptions which we shall note later, in general ex-monks and ex-nuns might expect to receive a small lump sum together with a small pension and (if priests) legal privileges to take a benefice or chaplaincy. No fixed amounts were laid down, but the average pension seems to have been about £5:10s. a year for men, young members sometimes getting slightly less and older members slightly more. The payment varied somewhat according to the wealth of the house concerned, and it is probably this factor which explains why the pensions paid to nuns was much lower (about £3), for, as we have seen, their houses were nearly all of small resources. From these sums certain deductions were made, and they were soon to suffer a serious loss in purchasing power, owing to the steady rise in prices that marked the second half of the sixteenth century. It would seem that for some years at least ex-inmates of houses of men were probably in much the same position as a modern old-age pensioners—able to manage so long as they lived very quietly and were not faced with the need of any heavy expenditure. On the whole the pensions were regularly paid and in one respect their holders were better off than old-age pensioners, for there was no means test; all in priest's order could augment their income by taking an ecclesiastical post, if they could get one. Their way to this was made easier by many of the English bishops who for fifteen or twenty years after the Dissolution held few ordinations, presumably so as to avoid flooding an already overladen market.

It is unfortunate that evidence as we know it at present, does not enable us to see what proportion of religious received pensions in the way just noted, or what proportion were later able to secure some sort of ecclesiastical post, though it is clear that the latter varied considerably from house to house and district to district. Professor Knowles, in the most recent survey of the evidence, concludes: 'with those who held clerical preferment, those who had from the beginning adopted secular employment, those who had died within the first few years, and finally, the faithful few who had gone into exile, at least two-thirds of the pension-worthy religious can be accounted for, at least in broad categories'.

Some fared notably better and some notably worse than the great majority. To the modern mind, few things are more remarkable in this context than the very handsome compensation paid to ex-heads of monasteries, both male and female. Very often this was 'ten or twenty times as great as that of their subjects, together in many cases, with a house and land and stock'. Here Henry VIII, like many of his predecessors, saved himself money by using ecclesiastical posts as a form of payment. Nearly all the bishops and deans of the new cathedrals were ex-monastic and a couple of dozen abbots or priors acquired bishoprics within a few years of the Dissolution. These pensions also varied to some degree according to the resources of the house. The ex-abbot of Bury St. Edmunds drew the princely sum of £330 a year, the abbot of Fountains £100, but heads of lesser fry had only a few dozen pounds. Of the rest, the nuns came off badly because of their low pensions and the impossibility of augmenting these by ecclesiastical posts. The friars seem also to have done badly over pensions, owing to the smallness of their houses' revenue, though they may have been fairly successful in obtaining benefices. Inevitably those found guilty of treason through participation in the Pilgrimage of Grace or similar acts of protest, had no right to a pension and the same was the case with the unknown number of inmates of religious houses who fled abroad or 'went underground'. But, in general, in this respect at least, the picture now revealed is one favourable to the government. 'It would not be easy to point to any revolution of the sixteenth century, or indeed to any comparable secularization of modern times, in which compensation on such a scale and with such security was offered' (Knowles).

A challenging feature of the Dissolution was the ease with which it was effected. In 1534 the Oath of Supremacy, rejecting the ancient recognition of the pope, was taken by both the monasteries and the outside world without any vigorous opposition save that of a very small minority, who were punished for their refusal in a singularly barbarous manner. It is, of course, arguable that some part of the thousands of religious who accepted this were not acting from cowardice. Some would be convinced on theological grounds that the Roman supremacy of their day was an improper growth in history, others might feel it permissible in the general interest to bow to the present storm and hope that the tempest would soon spend itself.

Neither of these reasons can apply to the marked refusal of hundreds of monks and nuns to fight for the life to which they had so solemnly vowed themselves before the high altars of their churches. Whether it would have been proper or not for them to have used force against the force used against them is a contentious question. One might indubitably have hoped for some silent witness to the paramount claims of their triple vow. Instead there was at best, a great deal of bowing to the storm, at worst much real spiritual treachery. This latter is very visible in the way in which so many heads of houses accepted very comfortable pensions and, apparently contentedly, spent their last years as members of the local gentry. Visible also in the readiness with which the great majority of their flocks accepted the new dispensations. There is little sign of attempts to maintain the common life to which they were pledged. Even the celibacy on which it was based was not preserved by at least a substantial minority. Exact figures are lacking, but in Lincolnshire two local surveys show a good quarter of the nuns whose careers were traceable to have married after the Dissolution and it seems likely that the figure for ex-monks was substantially higher. It is the last illustration of a clearly evident fact—that the monasteries of these latter days, faced with the trying choice of maintaining quantity or maintaining quality in their recruits, had taken the easy but ultimately pernicious course of preferring the latter.

This is not quite the end of the story. In 1552 Henry's son, Edward VI, was succeeded by Mary Tudor, a passionate and most conservative Roman Catholic. She at once restored the connection between England and the papacy which her father had broken, and strove to do something to restore the monastic life that he had abolished. By now the obstacles in the way of any extensive reclamation of monastic lands were quite insuperable. Even if the new queen could afford to give back such monastic lands as were still crown property, it was unthinkable that she should attempt to dislodge the hundreds of owners of the rest. Their titles were completely valid in English law and had been bought with good English cash. The pope appreciated the position and in 1555 officially recognised the legal fact of the Dissolution without in any way thereby implying approval of it.

The financial obstacle alone made any rapid resurgence of English monastic life quite out of the question. All that the queen could do was to sow a little seed which might in the course of time produce a mighty harvest. Westminster had become a house of secular canons. In 1556 it was made a Benedictine abbey once more, and within three years had assembled forty brethren; the body of Edward the Confessor, hidden of late years, was returned to a rebuilt shrine. Hopes of restoring Benedictinism at Glastonbury and St. Albans came to nothing, but in 1555 Observant Franciscans were re-established at Greenwich and about the same time Dominicans installed at St. Bartholomew's Smithfield. The Carthusian order which, under Henry VIII, had borne heroically a persecution as vile as that Mary was now inflicting on innocent Protestants, was given a house at Sheen. Bridgettine nuns went to Syon and Dominican nuns to Dartford once more. By 1557 four houses of men and two of women were thus in existence; they had about 100 inmates.

But the following year Mary died. Elizabeth does not seem to have had any animus against the monastic life as such, but her requirement that her subjects should reject the papal supremacy could not commend itself to the newly established communities. The great majority quickly departed to the Continent, their houses were dissolved and the last spark of medieval monastic life in England went out.

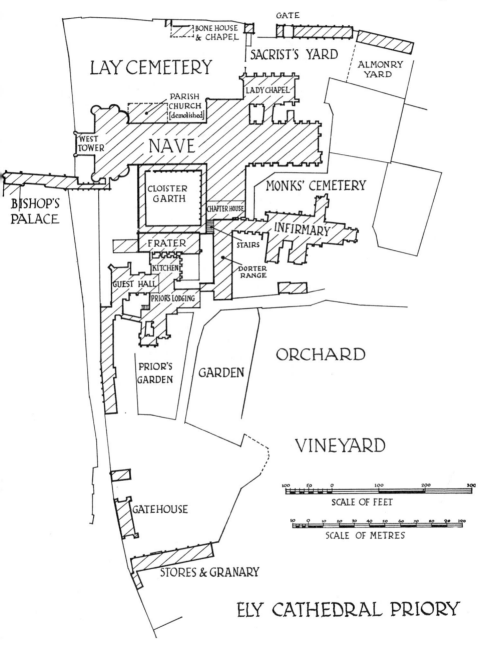

BONE HOUSE & CHAPEL

GATE

SACRIST'S YARD

ALMONRY YARD

LAY CEMETERY

PARISH CHURCH [demolished]

LADY CHAPEL

WEST TOWER

NAVE

CLOISTER GARTH

CHAPTER HOUSE

MONKS' CEMETERY

BISHOP'S PALACE

FRATER

STAIRS

INFIRMARY

KITCHEN

DORTER RANGE

GUEST HALL

PRIORS LODGING

ORCHARD

PRIOR'S GARDEN

GARDEN

VINEYARD

100 50 0 100 200 300
SCALE OF FEET

10 0 10 20 30 40 50 60 70 80 90 100
SCALE OF METRES

GATEHOUSE

STORES & GRANARY

ELY CATHEDRAL PRIORY

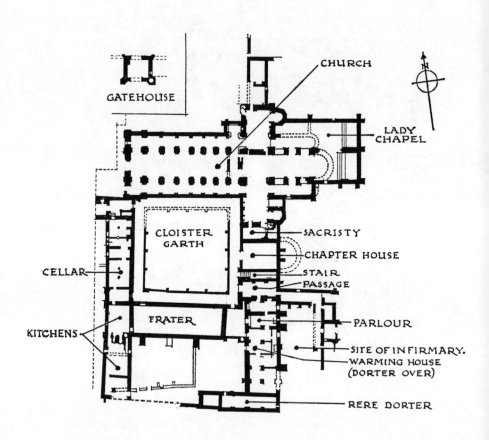

GATEHOUSE

CHURCH

LADY CHAPEL

CLOISTER GARTH

SACRISTY

CHAPTER HOUSE

STAIR

PASSAGE

CELLAR

PARLOUR

FRATER

KITCHENS

SITE OF INFIRMARY.

WARMING HOUSE (DORTER OVER)

RERE DORTER

SCALE OF FEET.

SCALE OF METRES.

THETFORD PRIORY

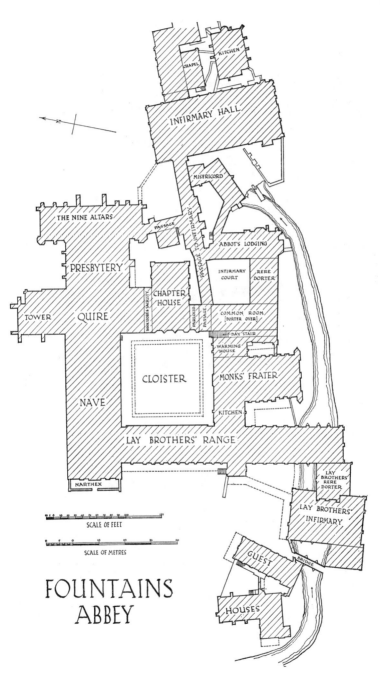

FOUNTAINS
ABBEY

SCALE OF FEET

SCALE OF METRES

146

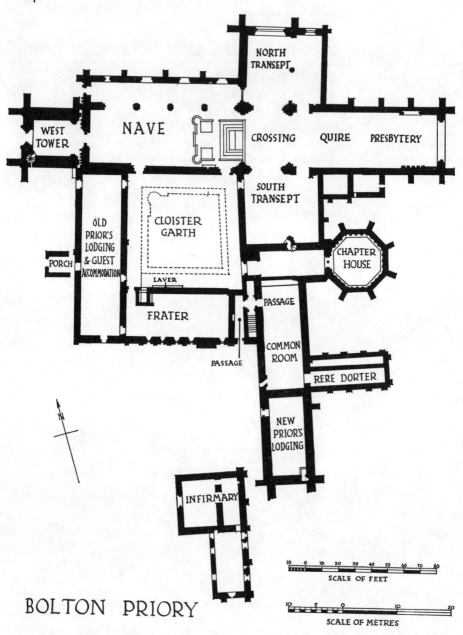

WEST TOWER

NAVE

NORTH TRANSEPT

CROSSING   QUIRE   PRESBYTERY

SOUTH TRANSEPT

OLD PRIOR'S LODGING & GUEST ACCOMMODATION

PORCH

CLOISTER GARTH

CHAPTER HOUSE

LAVER

FRATER

PASSAGE

PASSAGE

COMMON ROOM

RERE DORTER

NEW PRIOR'S LODGING

N

INFIRMARY

SCALE OF FEET
10 0 10 20 30 40 50 60 70 80

SCALE OF METRES
10 5 0 10 20

BOLTON PRIORY

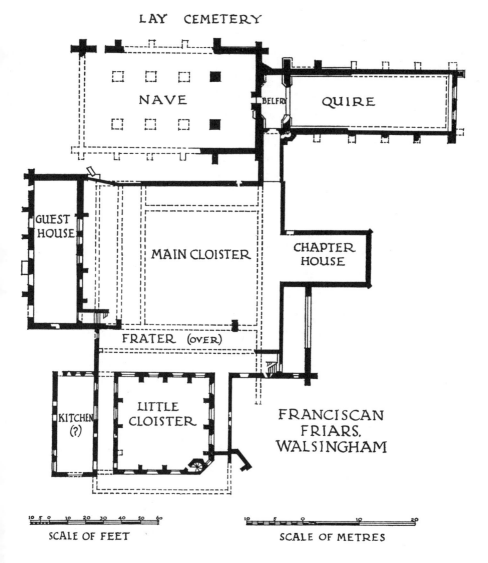

LAY CEMETERY

NAVE

BELFR

QUIRE

GUEST
HOUSE

MAIN CLOISTER

CHAPTER
HOUSE

FRATER (over)

KITCHEN
(?)

LITTLE
CLOISTER

FRANCISCAN
FRIARS,
WALSINGHAM

SCALE OF FEET

SCALE OF METRES

ILLUSTRATIONS

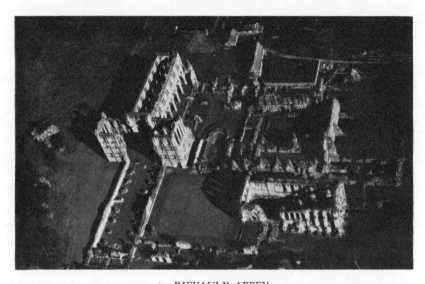

2a. RIEVAULX ABBEY

Left: Church. *Centre:* Chapter House and Cloister. *Right:* Infirmary Court and Refectory

2b. HAUGHMOND ABBEY

Left: Church. *Centre:* Chapter House and Cloister. *Right:* Infirmary Court, Hall and Abbot's Apartment

3a. COGGESHALL ABBEY. GATEHOUSE CHAPEL

3b. FOUNTAINS ABBEY. GUEST-HOUSES AND CHURCH

4b. HAUGHMOND ABBEY. WELL-HOUSE

4a. IXWORTH PRIORY. UNDERCROFT OF EASTERN RANGE

5a. ELY CATHEDRAL. MAIN GATEHOUSE

5b. ST. OSYTH'S ABBEY. MAIN GATEHOUSE

6b. CASTLE ACRE PRIORY. WEST FRONT

6a. NEWSTEAD PRIORY (NOTTS.). WEST FRONT

7. CROWLAND ABBEY. NAVE LOOKING EAST

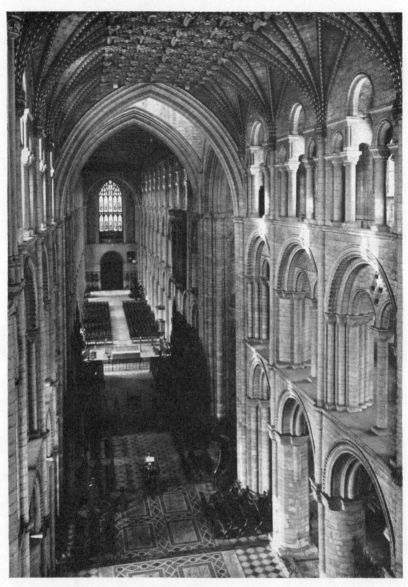

8. PETERBOROUGH CATHEDRAL. INTERIOR, LOOKING WEST

9a. ROCHE ABBEY. THE TRANSEPTS

9b. JERVAULX ABBEY. A TRANSEPT CHAPEL

12

10a. HEXHAM PRIORY. PULPITUM

10b. KIRKHAM PRIORY. SLYPE IN WESTERN RANGE

11a. HEXHAM PRIORY. THE NIGHT STAIR

11b. FOUNTAINS ABBEY. REFECTORY DOOR AND LAVER

12b. RIEVAULX ABBEY. 'EAST' END OF THE CHURCH

12a. WYMONDHAM PRIORY. NAVE, SHOWING MODERN ROOD

13a. BOLTON PRIORY. CLOISTER FROM S.W

13b. LILLESHALL ABBEY. N.E. CORNER OF THE CLOISTER, SHOWING
BOOK-CUPBOARD

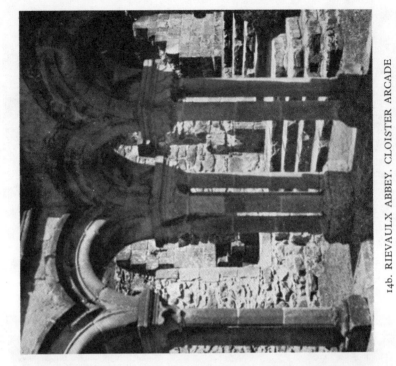

14b. RIEVAULX ABBEY. CLOISTER ARCADE

14a. CHESTER CATHEDRAL. REFECTORY PULPIT

15. GLOUCESTER CATHEDRAL. CLOISTER ALLEY,
SHOWING SITE OF CARRELS

16. NORWICH CATHEDRAL. NORTHERN CLOISTER ALLEY

17b. RIEVAULX ABBEY. ENTRANCE TO THE REFECTORY

17a. NORWICH CATHEDRAL. CLOISTER DOOR

13

18a. FURNESS ABBEY. CHAPTER HOUSE

18b. FOUNTAINS ABBEY. EASTERN SIDE OF CLOISTER COURT,
showing recess for book-cupboard and triple entrance to the Chapter House

19a. FOUNTAINS ABBEY. S.E. ANGLE OF THE CLOISTER
Centre: Undercroft of Eastern Range. *Right:* Chapter House

19b. CLEEVE ABBEY. THE DORMITORY

20a. CARTMEL PRIORY CHURCH, FROM N.W.

20b. LANERCOST PRIORY. REFECTORY UNDERCROFT

21. FOUNTAINS ABBEY. THE CELLARS

22a. BRADENSTOKE PRIORY. WESTERN RANGE (demolished)
Left: Kitchens and Slype. *Centre:* Hall. *Right:* Prior's Lodging

22b. GLASTONBURY. ABBOT'S KITCHEN

23a. NORWICH (DOMINICAN). THE CHURCH, NOW ST. ANDREW'S HALL
The tower no longer survives

23b. NORWICH (DOMINICAN). THE NAVE

24a. BURNHAM NORTON (CARMELITE). THE GATEHOUSE

24b. CHICHESTER (FRANCISCAN). THE CHANCEL

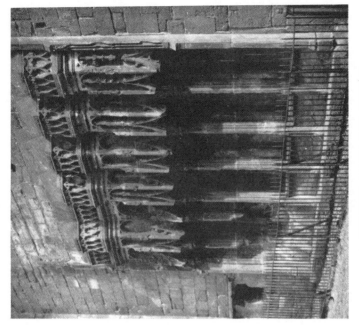

25b. FURNESS ABBEY. THE SEDILIA

25a. MOUNT GRACE PRIORY (CARTHUSIAN).
A CELL DOOR

14

26b. CANTERBURY CATHEDRAL. 'ST. AUGUSTINE'S CHAIR'
(the Archbishop's chair)

26a. ST. ALBANS. REMAINS OF THE SHRINE OF ST. ALBAN

27b. CHERTSEY ABBEY. Tiles showing a queen (32¼" × 9"), now in the British Museum

27a. THE CANTERBURY GOSPELS
A 6th century manuscript from Italy, now in Corpus Christi College, Cambridge

(a)   (b)

28. CRESSETS (a) Blackmore Priory (12″ × 7″)
(b) Furness Abbey (8⅞″ × 4½″), now in Barrow-in-Furness Museum

28c. WESTMINSTER ABBEY. REFECTORY GONG
(diameter 12″)

29. DUNSTER PRIORY. DETAIL OF SCREEN

(30a)

30a. CANDLESTICK, made for GLOUCESTER CATHEDRAL about 1110 and now in the
Victoria and Albert Museum (bell-metal richly gilt, height below pricket 19⅞″)

30b. CENSER, FROM RAMSEY ABBEY. Silver gilt with silver chains, 14th century
(height 10⅘″, diameter 5³⁄₁₀″) now in the Victoria and Albert Museum

31a.

31b. RETABLE from a Dominican house in East Anglia *c.* 1320 (now in Thornham Parva Church)

32. ST. ALBANS. NAVE ARCADE

GLOSSARY

ALB a long white linen garment with tight sleeves, worn with a girdle.

ALTAR the table of wood or stone at which the Eucharist or Mass is celebrated.

AMBULATORY the passage round the east end of larger churches between the presbytery or choir and the side chapels.

AMICE a piece of linen worn round the neck, like a collar, along with an alb.

APSE the semi-circular or polygonal end of a church or chapel.

ARCADE a series of arches carried on columns or piers.

AUMBRY a cupboard in the wall of a church or sacristy where sacred vessels, books etc. were kept.

BOSS a projecting ornament (generally circular) covering the intersection of ribs in a vault, ceiling or roof.

CARREL a small alcove in the monastic cloister containing a desk, and used as a place of study.

CATHEDRAL the chief church of a diocese, containing the bishop's throne or *cathedra*.

CELL (1) a monastic establishment (generally of small size) legally dependent on its mother house; (2) the private apartment of a monk or nun.

CELLAR a vaulted chamber beneath a monastic refectory or other similar building, often principally used for storage purposes.

CENSER a metal vessel suspended on chains used for the ceremonial burning of incense.

CHANCEL the part of a church east of the nave, crossing and transepts.

CHAPTER HOUSE a building primarily used for meetings of a medieval monastic or collegiate community.

CHASUBLE an almost circular vestment worn by the celebrant at Mass.

CHOIR the part of the eastern end of a church which contains the seats of the clergy.

CLERESTOREY a range of windows along the central walls of a church.

CLOISTER a space (generally square or rectangular) enclosed by covered alleys which generally had arcades on their inner side.

CLOISTER GARTH the open area between the cloister alleys.

COPE a semi-circular vestment worn like a cloak and fastened across the chest by a brooch or band.

CROSSING the area (generally square in plan, with a lantern tower overhead) between the chancel, transepts and nave of a cruciform church.

CRUCIFORM having the shape of a cross.

CRYPT a cellar or vault below all or part of certain monastic buildings, sometimes termed an undercroft.

DALMATIC a loose tunic slit at the sides worn at mass by the deacon.

DAY STAIR the staircase leading from the monastic cloister to the dormitory.

DORTER a dormitory.

15

FRATER   a refectory or dining-room.

GATEHOUSE   the building containing the major entrance to a monastery or castle.

GROINED VAULT   a vault whose intersecting edges have no ribs.

LADY CHAPEL   a chapel dedicated to Our Lady.

LANTERN   the open space at the bottom of the tower over the crossing.

LECTERN   a stand or desk on which a service book is placed.

MARTYROLOGY   a calendar of the saints, daily commemorated by the Church.

MISERICORD   (1) a bracket on the underside of the hinged seat of a choir stall. (2) a small hall where, for special reasons, better food than the ordinary was supplied.

NARTHEX   an ante-chamber to the nave of a church.

NAVE   the western limb of a church.

NIGHT STAIR   the staircase in a transept leading from the monastic dormitory to the conventual church.

PARLOUR   a small room off the cloister, where conversation was permissible.

PISCINA   a basin with a drain, used for washing the sacred vessels, near altar and generally set in a wall.

PRESBYTERY   the part of the church east of the choir containing the main altar.

PULPITUM   a massive screen between the rood-screen and choir stalls.

REREDORTER   the building containing the monastic latrines.

REREDOS   a decorated screen or hanging behind an altar.

RETRO-CHOIR   the area behind the choir stalls.

ROOD   a cross or crucifix generally having accompanying figures of Our Lady and St. John. The main rood was set on a beam over the rood-screen.

ROOD-SCREEN   a screen separating all or most of the nave from the rest of the church.

SACRISTY   a room where vestments and vessels used in the services of the church were kept.

SEDILIA   a series of seats to the south of the altar used by the clergy during a sung or high Mass.

SLYPE   a narrow passage across a cloister range.

SPANDREL   the triangular-shaped space above the side of an arch.

TREASURY   an apartment where title deeds, money and treasures were kept.

TRIFORIUM   a gallery between the main arcade and clerestorey of certain large churches.

TUNICLE   a vestment similar to the *Dalmatic* worn by the Sub-deacon at High Mass.

UNDERCROFT   *see* CRYPT.

WARMING-HOUSE   an apartment where a fire or fires were maintained for the use of a monastic community during the colder parts of the year.

SELECT BIBLIOGRAPHY

THE monastic history of medieval England inspired an enormous number of books and articles, the latter mostly in the publications of local archaeological societies and other such periodicals as *The Archaeological Journal*, *The Antiquaries Journal* and *The Journal of the British Archaeological Association*; details of some important record publications can be found in E. L. C. Mullins, *Texts and Calendars* (1958).

Unfortunately there is no general bibliography of this material in print, the slip index of the Library of the Society of Antiquaries of London being the best available. Most of the historical studies noted below contain bibliographies which partially fill the gap, and the libraries of local archaeological societies and local authorities have generally got useful topographical collections covering the monasteries on their areas.

W. Dugdale, *Monasticon Anglicanum* (revised J. Caley, H. Ellis and W. Bandinell, 6 vols. in 8, 1817–30) remains an invaluable work of reference; it contains an enormous mass of medieval documents and adds illustrations and miscellaneous introductory information. The latter is sometimes in need of revision, particularly over the dates of foundations of English monasteries. For this and other useful details reference should be made to D. M. Knowles and R. N. Hadcock, *Medieval Religious houses of England* (1954); this digests, *inter alia*, the information regarding the English monastic population contained in J. Cox Russell, 'The Clerical Population in Medieval England' in *Traditio* (1944). On other matters N. P. Ker, *The Medieval Libraries of Great Britain* (1941) and J. Harvey, *English Medieval Architects* (1954) are valuable.

I. ARCHITECTURE AND ART

There is no extensive general survey of English monastic architecture. The following cover particular orders: J. Bilson, 'Architecture of the Cistercians' in *Archaeological Journal*, lxvi (1909), 185-280; A. R. Martin, *Franciscan architecture in England* (Manchester, 1937); W. A. Hinnebusch, *The early English friars preachers* (Rome 1951); A. W. Clapham, 'The architecture of the Premonstratensians with special reference to their buildings in England' in *Archaeologia*, lxxiii (1924); W. H. Godfrey, *The English Almshouse* (1955). *The Cathedrals of England and Wales* (*The Builder* series), London, 1894, with its magnificent plans, and J. Harvey, *English Cathedrals* (1950) cover the monastic cathedrals.

The volumes of the county surveys of the Royal Commission on Historical Monuments give plans and brief reports of existing monastic remains but, through smallness of staff, proceeds at what it would be unrealistic to call snail's pace. The *Victoria County Histories of England* (also incomplete) includes some account of monastic sites; these vary in quality and recently have not always included plans. For areas untouched by these surveys the appropriate county volumes of N.

Pevsner, *The Buildings of England* and *The Little Guides* (Methuen) give brief but often useful details. A high proportion of English monastic ruins are in the charge of H.M. Office of Works which has issued cheap booklets with plans for most of them, details of which are given in Stationery Office Sectional list No. 27. Much major excavation of monastic sites was carried out by W. St. John Hope, details of which may be found in the Bibliography of his writings (privately published, 1929).

D. M. Knowles and J. K. S. St. Joseph, *Monastic Sites from the Air*, gives air photographs of many English monastic sites with brief notes and bibliography. The Office of Works and the Department of Air Photography at Cambridge University have major collections of air photographs.

It is impossible to mention the numerous monographs on particular religious houses, but a few are of special importance. T. D. Atkinson's massive *Monastic Buildings of Ely*, W. St. John Hope, *Kirkstall Abbey* (Thoresby Society, xvi, 1917) and A. Hamilton Thompson, *Bolton Priory* (Thoresby Society, xxx, 1924) survey the sites in question in considerable detail, and incidentally illuminate the general architectural history of the orders to which these houses belonged. C. Hodges, *Hexham Abbey* (1888) and E. A. Webb, *Records of St. Bartholomew's*, Smithfield (2 vols., Oxford, 1921) are particularly well illustrated. *The Historical Monuments* volume on Westminster Abbey (1924) is fundamental.

For English medieval art the appropriate volumes of *The Oxford History of Art*, though not impeccable in matters of detail, should be consulted, and have useful bibliographies. A. W. Clapham, *Romanesque architecture in England* (2 vols., Oxford, 1930, 1934), covers the early development of English architecture. For Gothic architecture G. Webb, *Architecture in Britain: the Middle Ages* (1956), may be consulted, and F. Bond, *Gothic Architecture in England* (1906) is still valuable. For particular aspects the following are valuable: A. Gardner, *English Medieval Sculpture* (Cambridge, 1951); A. Gardner, *Alabaster Tombs* (1940); E. S. Prior and A. Gardner, *Medieval Figure Sculpture in England* (1923); F. Bond, *Misericords* (1910); G. H. Cook, *Medieval Chantries and Chantry Chapels* (1947); J. D. Le Couteur, *English medieval painted glass* (1932); G. McN. Rushforth, *Medieval Christian Imagery as illustrated by the painted windows of Great Malvern Priory Church* (Oxford, 1936); C. J. P. Cave, *Roof Bosses in Medieval Churches* (Cambridge, 1948); A. Vallance, *Greater English Church Screens* (1947); F. Bligh Bond and B. Camm, *Rood Screens and Roodlofts*, 2 vols. (1909); A. G. J. Christie, *English Medieval Embroidery* (1938); C. C. Oman, *English Church Plate, 597–1830*, (Oxford, 1957); E.W. Tristram, *English medieval wall-painting*; (i) The twelfth century (1944); (ii) The thirteenth century, 2 vols. (1950); (iii) The fourteenth century (1955).

II. HISTORY

Indispensable are Professor D. M. Knowles' volumes, *The Monastic Order in England* (c. 943–1216), and *The Religious Orders in England*, 3 vols., 1949–59. No detailed study of the early period is available but it is discussed in M. Deanesly, *The Pre-Conquest Church in England*. Bede, *Ecclesiastical History of the English people* (available in a number of translations) is the classic early source. J. A. Duke, *The Columban church* and L. Gougaud, *Celtic Christianity* (1932), A. Hamilton Thompson (ed.), *Bede, his life, times and writings* (Oxford, 1939) are also useful. For post-Conquest orders see E. M. Thompson, *The Carthusian Order in England* (1930), R. M. Clay, *The Medieval Hospitals of England* (1909), J. C. Dickinson, *The Origins of the Austin canons* . . . (1950), H. M. Colvin, *The White Canons in England* (Oxford, 1951), R. Graham, *St. Gilbert of Sempringham* (1903), Hinnebusch *op. cit.*, the volumes of the British Society of Franciscan Studies, and E. Power, *Medieval English Nunneries* (Cambridge, 1922). *The Chronicle of Jocelin of Brakeland* (ed. H. E. Butler, 1947) and Walter Daniel, *Life of Ailred . . . of Rievaulx* (ed. F. M. Powicke, 1950), give vivid pictures of some aspects of monastic life; both have translations. *The Rites of Durham* (Surtees Society) is an invaluable account of the buildings and life at Durham Cathedral on the eve of the Dissolution. R. V. H. Burne, *Chester Cathedral; the middle ages* (in the press) is a useful modern study dealing with a monastic cathedral. D. M. Knowles and W. F. Grimes, *Charterhouse*, London, 1954, and J. C. Dickinson, *The shrine of Our Lady of Walsingham* (1955) discuss important sites.

The *Victoria County Histories of England* includes articles on the history of individual monasteries. The earlier ones vary in quality but they generally provide at least a valuable starting point and sometimes much more.

Of the monastic observances, prescribing the detail of the monastic life, the following are good specimens and are provided with English translations. T. Symons, *The Regularis Concordia* (1950), D. M. Knowles, *The Monastic Constitutions of Lanfranc* (1951), J. W. Clark, *The Observances in use at the Augustinian priory . . . at Barnwell* (Cambridge, 1897). For details of worship A. A. King, *Liturgies of the Religious Orders* (1955) and various volumes of the *Henry Bradshaw Society* are useful. Episcopal visitations of medieval monasteries are numerous; A. Hamilton Thompson, *Visitations of Religious Houses in the Diocese of Lincoln, 1420–49* (3 vols., 1914–29) are typical episcopal visitations and are printed with a translation. A. Savine, *The English Monasteries on the Eve of the Dissolution* (1909) analyses English monastic finance in the light of the *Valor Ecclesiasticus* of 1535. T. Wright, *Three chapters of letters relating to the suppression of the monasteries* (1843) and M. E. C. Walcott, 'Inventories and valuations of religious houses' in *Archaeologia*, xliii (1871), 201-49, illustrate the process of suppression. *Map of Monastic Britain* (H.M. Ordnance Survey) is an invaluable aid to study.

INDEX